Stay Put? Make a Move?

Stay Put? Make a Move?

From Lake Waccabuc to Omotesando

Thomas Nevins

Matador
9 Priory Business Park,
Wistow Road, Kibworth Beauchamp,
Leicestershire. LE8 0RX
Tel: 0116 279 2299
Email: books@troubador.co.uk
Web: www.troubador.co.uk/matador
Twitter: @matadorbooks

ISBN 978 1785890 871

British Library Cataloguing in Publication Data.
A catalogue record for this book is available from the British Library.

Typeset in 11pt Aldine401 BT by Troubador Publishing Ltd, Leicester, UK

Matador is an imprint of Troubador Publishing Ltd

Dedication and Acknowledgments.

To Alice H. Cook, Professor Emerita of the Cornell University School of Industrial and Labor Relations. Dr. Cook established and became the first University Ombudsman. Alice Cook House at Cornell is named after Professor Cook. Thirty seconds with Professor Alice Cook after class in the Ives Hall hallway, and events that followed, totally changed my life.

To our mini dachshund, "Sausage" who also runs by the names of Luna, Luna-Tuna, Lu, Lu-chan, Huna, Hu, Hu-chan, Pu, Chibi (runt), Chib, Honey-Bunny etc. German bald-eagle like vision to gradual blindness from age 3. Into a dark, pitch-black world from 5 or 6 years old. Her genki/cheerful, and indomitable spirit, and hardness of skull are a constant inspiration—yet never a murmur or yelp. When about 5 years old, a painful hernia led to a full-length, top of the spine operation which the Vet said "may leave her paralyzed—often does, sorry." First day home Lu-chan stood up once and fell down—otherwise dragged herself with her front feet most of the day. Second day, took 5 steps once and fell; third day about 15 steps during the day. Within 3 weeks Lu-chan was running after her bell-attached pink ball. This little doggie has love, loyalty, feels loneliness, guilt, protects and has a soul. Pope John Paul II said animals have souls, and "are as near to God as men are". Now Pope Francis makes a lot of us feel good, because "paradise is open to all God's creatures". (But I'm no Vegan. Will eat just about anything on 2 legs, 4 legs, or fins. Maybe that's wrong. The only thing that makes humans special is the ability to talk, teach and organize better—exponentially building upon one breakthrough after another. And that's only because some apes "made a move" out of the comfortable, verdant and fertile jungles, to the dry, open savannahs, and then up north. They learned to stand up and run between trees. They needed arms free to carry things, throw rocks, and 1 or 2,000,000 years later, spears. Wanderlust-types like me or refugees of bullies learned to cope with cold, harsh and barren Northern climates.

To Rocky, Rambo, Bill Murray, Ken Takakura and Bunta Sugawara (both deceased in November, 2014), Rekha, Chow Yun-fat, Susanne Barth, Takeshi Kitano, Arnold Schwarzenegger, Sean Connery, Chieko and Mitsuko Baisho, Gerard Depardieu, Tatsuya Nakadai, Omar Sharif, Morgan Freeman, Sayuri Yoshinaga, Michael Caine, Christopher Walken, Toshiyuki Nishida, Jean Reno, Clint Eastwood, Shinichi/Sonny Chiba, Giancarlo Gianni, Harrison Ford, Kin'ya Kitaoji, Sophia Loren, Alain Delon, Togo Igawa, Steven Seagal (my son Johnny and I shook his hand thanks to Bill Ireton), Mel Gibson, Anthony Hopkins, Antonio Fagundes, Meryl Streep, Albert Filozov, Bruce Willis and Michael Douglas (both sometimes in Bedford Village—my H.S. movie date spot), Fanny Ardent, Richard Geer (who runs an inn and restaurant also in nearby Bedford Village), Nikita Mikhalkov, Paul McCartney, Aharon Ipale, Jackie Chan, Mick Jagger and his buddies—Keith Richards (in Waccabuc), Amitabh Bachchan, Rutger Hauer, Anthony Sher, and Sting—all old enough to kick back a notch or two. They are rich, and they don't have to keep trying and working but they do. During these 43 years, I missed all the USA etc. TV shows, but caught pretty much all the movies (not dubbed in Japanese but subtitled) in the Tokyo movie houses. I hope many of us will want to keep working to keep contributing to the social security programs for the younger generations. So good jobs to the youngest and oldest people too!

Thanks and acknowledgement to the many others who will appear in this book. And to so many more friends, supporters and teammates. I don't usually name drop. But we all can identify with the more well-known people, those stories, that history. This book is meant to be a surprise, and hopefully a gift to them. So they don't know it is coming. I didn't talk with them about the stories, or confirm the facts with them. The responsibility lies solely with me. I can only thank my publisher for tolerating this zany and quirky format, and sometimes bizarre content. This book has no single focus. It hops topics faster than the Easter Bunny on a bad speed trip. I want it to appeal to many people with different interests. And I don't want to rant on about the same subject too long without providing a break. It is primarily aimed at my two totally different cultures and worlds—Japan and New York. But the rest of the world too. I'm fortunate, because so many people have touched base, or at least know something about both Tokyo, and the NYC area.

This book is written toward multiple purposes, including getting us to look back to our roots; consider a move or change; increase Japan's sinking population; encourage inbound tourism and investment in real estate and business everywhere (instead of corporations sitting on their cash!); but also, hopefully particularly in my home grounds, the Tokyo and the NYC area, as an aid to encourage foreign language learning; and to make a bigger difference in Japan and other countries by passing on my human resource and labor consulting know- how. Working with strong parties we hope to combine better human resource management with helping corporations with their M & A, or start-ups. We also want to make it easier for foreign corporations to purchase industrial, or commercial property in Japan. And to make it easy for wealthy non-Japanese-speaking foreigners to be able to understand, and seamlessly purchase luxury residential homes, or very upscale condominium properties in Tokyo and Japan.

I hope there are others like me who don't like to spend much time on the same topic! Leonard da Vinci, Benjamin Franklin, Thomas Edison, and Dr. Yoshiro Nakamatsu "Dr. NakaMatsu" who holds over 4,000 patents) also lacked a single focus. After finishing the book, I felt it fair to George Bush Jr., to look into what lead up to the USA wars in Iraq and Afghanistan. What I discovered was shocking and sickening. I think sometimes we must lead, rather than trust and follow our leaders.

Any scholarship within this book is half-baked, and combined with a spice of raw intelligence. I did not want to overcook this feast with footnotes. I have almost never looked at a footnote. Instead of footnotes in the back that no one sees, I sometimes tried to give credit right where the credit was due. Other than that…

Special thanks to public open sources, and to Jimmy Wales, his colleagues at Wikipedia and the some 300,000 Wiki contributors and 30,000 more consistent contributors. I also want to thank Mr. Bill Gates and his crew for Windows, Marc Andreessen, the Google Founders and Team, Vincent Cerf, Robert Kahn, Tim Berners Lee, and of course Vice President Al Gore for inventing the internet. If this book sells well, and I can sell this five-storey Omotesando building at a good price, I want to do more for Wikipedia, and other causes that help us so much. Microsoft's Surface Pro 2 tablet, with a large, useable, lifelike, removable keyboard, also did a good job on the 10 Japanese and English YouTube "Tom Nevins Omotesando 5flrs gokai/5th" videos of the building available on YouTube. I don't hold stocks in any of these companies.

And of course most of all, I am forever indebted to my family, and to my many wives (two marriages) for all their help, and for moulding me into my many shapes.

Despite the uncanny, remarkable resemblance, and shared swashbuckling lives, my mother's recurring stories and ample evidence that I am related to Clark Gable did not appear in this text.

Thank you to Mike Bastin for creating the illustration
on the front cover of this book!

To check out more of his work, visit:
http://www.mikebastincreative.com

Also a special thank you to Annie Gullen, two years older than me at my John Jay High School. She 'stayed put' in my hometown. Before marrying big brother Jack Gullen, Ann Longridge Hayden was Secretary of her class freshman and junior year, and Secretary of the Student Council senior year. Also a Campus Queen candidate and cheerleader, and much more!

Annie's many pictures of Waccabuc, our hometown schools, Lewisboro and John Jay, and the Fifth Division Market, are on the book's website at www.thomasnevins.co.uk, and on the book's 1' 30" video/trailer on YouTube. Please take the visual tour!

Lucky Settings, Unlucky Settings: People, Places, and Events that are the Atoms of Our Lives and Our World

1. Roger Stone (The Stone Zone), the most powerful strategist and 'self-admitted hitman' usually for the GOP/Republican Party, was my high school Student Council President election Campaign Manager. Roger went on to topple NYS Governor Eliot Spitzer in an escort scandal. Mr. Stone also stopped the Florida vote recount, probably resulting in Vice President Al Gore losing the presidential election to Bush Jr. Changed history.

2. Were we hoodwinked by Bush Jr. and Dick Cheney's predetermined decision to invade Iraq, leading to ISIL/ISIS, the Islamic State? Watch and listen to them on YouTube. Read their words and study the facts. You be the judge. Unfortunately Tony Blair, with his Oxford English, sounded intelligent, and gave cover and credibility to this continuing human and economic tragedy.

3. Like me, if the USA Senators and Congressman drove from Earls Court, London to Katmandu as part of a 7-month trip around the world, and saw the hippy's head on a stake in Afghanistan, I hope they would not have voted to send an army even into Afghanistan. Didn't Russia get bloodied and beaten there? Remember how much the colonials appreciated British boots in Boston?

4. If Bush Jr. comes to town, should Mayor Boris Johnson follow through on his words, and have a couple of London Bobbies arrest Bush Jr. as a war criminal? Hah-hah-hah?

5. President Reagan had class and intelligence. He turned the other cheek, and cut our losses after 241 marines were killed in the Beirut barracks bombing. Reagan got out of the Middle East. Did not go recklessly diving in.

6. Change of pace. Where are the tallest mountains and largest lakes in the world? How many peaks are taller than Japan's Mount Fuji? Which lake has 20% of the world's fresh water? More of it than all the water in all 5 of North America's Great Lakes combined. Which lake, and its shores, have about 1,150 species of plants and animals found nowhere else?

7. What inland body of water has no outflow, is 27 meters/92 feet below sea level, has one-third the salinity of the ocean (1.2%), and 3.5 times the water volume of all 5 of North America's Great Lakes? What is the longest river that drains 20% of greater Europe? What is the highest 'mountain' in my Westchester County above NYC?

8. Bobby Reich, 'the genius', famous author, President Bill Clinton's Secretary of Labor, got his Senior High and my Junior High Student Councils together once a month. Mr. Reich was a great student leader, with a big heart, in a rather short body (1.49 meters/4.88845 feet).

9. Like me and my brother Art, Donald Trump made his boys chop down trees, mow the lawns, and shovel the snow. His estate overlooking nearby Byram Lake was 57.5 times larger than our Lake Waccabuc home of 4 acres/4,900 tsubo/16,170 square meters/177,870 square feet. "No drugs, no cigarettes, and no alcohol!!" And probably not much talking back to The Donald. It worked! So Mr. Trump's kids can run his business while he runs for President. Manhattan, and other NYC residents drink Byram Lake, and Lake Waccabuc water—after a little purification treatment.

10. Also in my hood, a Beach Boy, a Rolling Stone, Sean Combs/Puff Daddy/P. Diddy, Gwyneth Paltrow, some of my movie heroes like Bruce Willis, Michael Douglas and Richard Gere. Mr. Gere owns an Inn in Bedford— one of my high school movie date spots. He played the Professor in the *Hachi* (dog Hachiko) movie. Mr. Gere also plays Tora-san on Japanese TV. There were 48 full-length Atsumi Kiyoshi Tora-san movie house films from 1969 to 1995. Richard Gere has the hat, but is missing the trademark Haramaki/belly wrap or band. I sang the Otoko wa Tsurai Yo/'It's Tough Being a Man' song to Atsumi Kiyoshi/Tora–san in front of my parents. It was at Haneda Airport, before there was a Narita Airport. Hen na gaijin/ strange foreigner!

11. My gymnastics senpai/trainer and mentor in so many ways, Barefoot Richie—descendant of leading Judge John Hathorne at the Salem Witch Trials (1692-93) where twenty people, including 13 girls were put to death. Richie's later born ancestor, Nathaniel Hawthorne (author of *The Scarlet Letter* etc.), added the 'w' to his last name to get out of the dark and gloomy shadow of the Judge. The Hawthorne Brothers 'Tree Service' has been dominant in the greater NYC area for tens of years. One-year-older big bro John was also a star gymnast on our team.

12. Second house down from us on the shore of Lake Waccabuc, were our good friends and high school stand-outs Jack and George Gullen. Their mother and father are both 90 years old and still going strong. Look about age 50! Father still puts out fires from the town fire truck! The Gullen family came in from Scotland and put the Waccabuc Country Club Golf Course on the map. Also, ran the Fifth Division Market. For years, the only food and liquor store within miles.

13. Our next-door neighbor in Omotesando, Hasegawa, Kozo founded and runs www.global-dining.com, about 80 iconic restaurant chains and standalone properties. They include Gonpachi (setting for *Kill Bill* sword fight). President Bill Clinton and Bush Jr. dined there. Global Dining also operates La Boheme, Monsoon Café, Zest, LB, Tableaux, Stellato, Legato etc. We're lucky. Hasegawa-san's inner courtyard garden can also be enjoyed by us. The tree tops come up to our open fourth-floor bath. No tree climbing please!

14. Why does Bill O'Reilly on Fox News seem to be the only one on mainstream media that has the male genitalia to beat up on the likes of The Dick Cheney, and Donald Rumsfeld? Mr. Rumsfeld worked for Nixon at the White House. He was really cool and impressive when he was 39 and I was a 20-year-old White House summer intern.

15. Did you know the first non-native New Yorker wasn't Dutch, and was a man of color born in the older new world? Had the beaver all to himself, until the Dutch closed him down. Then the British came in with four gunships. They didn't have to fire. New York was born!

16. Preparing to film *Bus Stop*, Marilyn Monroe stopped by Waccabuc and married Arthur Miller there on Sunday, June 29th, 1956. I was on the Lake and was thinking of crashing. No 6-year-olds allowed in.

17. Inside story, probably: out of the apartment we recently left, adjacent to the British Embassy, and facing the Imperial Palace, the condo unit was used by the Aum Cult (Sarin Gas Subway Slaughter) to sarin gas the Emperor. Luckily the plot was discovered and foiled.

18. The boys who captured Major Andre, took off from Lake Waccabuc. This led to the discovery of the spying plot to turn the West Point Fort, and control of the Hudson River and northern colonies, to the British. The bigger spy, born in Connecticut, the battle-winning General Benedict Arnold, was saved and picked up by the British. He continued fighting as a British General against the Colonials. He kept winning battles for the British, went to live in England, and was given a State Funeral in the U.K.

19. Twelve years after WWII ended, I gallantly harassed the cows and bulls of President Roosevelt's wartime Vice President. Henry Wallace was the USA's number two WWII leader. Years later, chased by his grudge-bearing bulls, I ended up across the Pacific!

20. My high school (later Harvard PhD) honey's granddaddy, an industrialist in China, flew his own planes to fight the Japanese for Chiang Kai-shek. Then he fought with Chiang against Mao Tse-tung/Mao Zedong. He was a founder of the John Birch Society, and much more. Helped launch Senator Joe McCarthy's fight against commies in the USA film industry etc. Grandpa also helped young Richard Nixon get going.

21. Twelve years later my Beauty Queen girlfriend with a Stanford PhD., had us go to a Las Vegas show with a couple from her Las Vegas high school. Bob Miller was the longest serving Governor in Nevada's history. Like Bill Clinton, now living in nearby Chappaqua, N.Y., Mr. Miller was Chairman, of the National Governors Association.

22. A lucky encounter after the huge New Year's Eve show at the Manila Hotel, led us to making homemade sushi in Tokyo for Mr. Gary Valenciano. He was 21. Gary has continued to be the top star—"the Michael Jackson of the

Philippines". Great song writing, singing, dancing, and more recently film screen star. A great and humble man, also famous for his charity, and being the first UNICEF Philippines National Ambassador.

23. Princes William and Harry, your mother, Princess Diana, returned my wink, shook my hand, and answered my question. Your father, Prince Charles, was also with us. I kept my hand in a plastic bag when showering. Only stopped last year.

24. I was assigned to my straight desk job, the morning 'the Blacks' took over Willard Straight Hall at Cornell University (the first dedicated student union building in the USA). It was the first time there were students with guns on a USA college campus.

25. What do you do to escape a charging, attacking, hungry, and greatly displeased grizzly bear in Alaska? Or anywhere I guess.

26. Nearby Yoyogi Park was Japan's first airstrip. A Tokugawa (Shogun's family) was the first pilot. Then the park became an 827-house suburban neighborhood for the USA military. After that it became the 1964 Tokyo Olympic Athletes' residential village.

27. The most famous Ninja, Hattori Hanzo, was given, and ruled over Harajuku, Jingumae, Aoyama, and Omotesando environs. Reward for saving the life of the General who became the first of 15 Tokugawa Shoguns. Did you know that the river under Cat Street, flows under the Tokyu Department store at Shibuya station? How many people walk across Shibuya's scrambled intersection, the busiest one in the world? With each light change? Per day? How many use the station's 8 train lines each day?

28. The Tom Cruise and Watanabe Ken *Last Samurai* movie pretty much followed history. Find out who the real players were. Except Tom Cruise's role was puffed up, and pretty much non-existent. He was great in the movie, though… Okubo, Toshimichi, and Saigo Takamori were the real deal: childhood, and school playmates.

29. Admiral Heihachiro Togo was educated at Cambridge, Portsmouth, and the Royal Naval College at Greenwich. Apprenticed with the British navy, it's not surprising why he shocked the world by sinking the Russian navy. It was U.S. President Teddy Roosevelt's supervised Treaty of Portsmouth (New Hampshire) peace negotiation that basically handed over control of Southern Manchuria and Korea to the Japanese. Admiral Togo, later on, tutored Emperor Hirohito at a house on the grounds of today's magnificent and stunning Tokyo American Club (TAC). Only about one-third of the members are USA-types.

30. There are some Russian stories in this book because of a lucky encounter with a well-placed lady. I dined on bear meat, and met the owner/host of the Saint Petersburg big log cabin where President Vladimir Putin celebrates his birthday most years. Stood on the balcony where Lenin announced the Russian Revolution—very cool!

31. Why Microsoft's Bill Gates and Oracle's Larry Ellison decided it a good hedge of safety, and a lot of fun, to have huge homes in Japan. I hope other foreigners/gaijin will follow. This book nudges people, even those with no Japanese, to see why, particularly Tokyo, is a great place to live, or operate from.

32. Where are the 82 Konyoku, naked, mixed bathing onsen/ hot springs not too far from Tokyo? I wish I had learned more about this earlier. Pretty busy now, and happily

married these days. How to use Japan's some 40,000 garish and glittering Love Hotels as an integral part of your sightseeing trips around the country, even when not making love? Much cheaper, larger, and more luxurious rooms than most hotels.

33. When I was age 20, I met Ohta Kaoru. He ran for mayor of Tokyo, founded Sohyo (the largest labor union federation in Japan), and invented Shunto/The Spring Wage Offensive. Mr. Ohta helped me distribute thousands of copies of my research survey. It was written with my Professor, Alice H. Cook, from the Cornell School of Industrial and Labor Relations. I was headed for being a 'Supergrade', most elite bureaucrat, at the USA Department of Labor in Washington DC. But punted it to follow through and return to Japan. Maybe a dumb move?

34. A few years later I worked part-time at Zendentsu, primarily the NTT telecommunications company union. It was one of the many labor unions where I worked in my early years in Japan. Yamagishi, Akira was #2 Shokicho/General Secretary of Zendentsu when I knew him. He went on to be the power broker uniting almost the entire Japanese trade union movement into RENGO. Mr. Yamagishi was said to be the kingmaker of the first Socialist Party Prime Minister, Mr. Maruyama. The Aum Cult sarin gas subway attack, and the great Kobe earthquake killing 6,000 people, were on Mr. Maruyama's watch. There were 77 Prime Ministers since 1885. Seven were repeaters; several coming back 3 or 4 times.

35. How was I overcharged by my landlord 63,000,000 yen/$630,000 on my TMT electricity bill? It was over a 25-year period, renting on average about 5 stories of that building. A good reason to buy your own 5-storey building

in Omotesando, and get directly billed by the utility. Our building was built by a construction firm with over 100 years of operating history. They are famous for also building temples and shrines built to take the earthquakes, and last a few hundred years. Just finishing a temple a stone's throw away.

Introduction to the Unholy Bible and its Unusual Format

'The New Testament' is written to hopefully be a decent read for Japanese people, and particularly interesting for New Yorkers, at least Waccabucians, John Jayers, and Cornellians, and people all over the world. It is newer. I wrote it after the 'Old Testament'—after I realized that it was time to pass on my/TMT's human resource and labor consulting know-how with the aim of doing greater good. I deliberately put in peripheral stories and facts related to personal experiences. Who really just wants to read about me, just Lake Waccabuc, or only Omotesando? I realize some of the English humor, wisecracks, and stupid, inane comments will not translate easily or well into Japanese and other languages.

As an afterthought, when I finished the book, I wanted to check and see if I had been too tough on President George Bush Jr., and V.P. Dick Cheney and crew. What I discovered made me angry and sick to my stomach. Since they won't admit error, and won't apologize, as a fellow USA American, I will apologize for them and our country for the horror and terrorism that will more and more cause suffering in more and more places in the world. And ISIS, or Islamic State in Iraq and Syria, or ISIL, the Islamic State of Iraq and Levant, started in Iraq. Iraq is in both names. We wouldn't have ISIL if some USA Americans in leadership positions had not ignored worldwide opposition, and if they/we had not invaded Iraq.

I am hopeful that we come out with full editions in both English and Japanese. Perhaps beyond that in other languages. Just for me or a publisher to check the translation becomes much faster and easier with this unusual approach of numbering and alphabetizing sections in detailed intervals. It also helps the translator make sure he/she does not lose her/his place. And readers with memories twice as good as mine won't need book markers! The New Testament is even more finely calibrated with each paragraph numbered. I hope we can keep it in that numbered format. Unusual as it is! This will make it easier for Japanese people to read and compare the English with the Japanese, and more easily understand the English. It also works effectively with digital applications.

And believe it or not, now there are millions, not many millions, but probably millions of non-Japanese foreigners around the world who can read Japanese pretty well. The key here is to read the paragraph in your native, or stronger language first. Then it is easier to breeze through the weaker language's corresponding text without using a dictionary. Suddenly people have a new faith and confidence that they are strong enough to be able to read that second, third, forth, or in the case of Mr. Alex Shoumatoff, sixteenth language.

With my *Know Your Own Bone* book, only the introduction, and the 3 points at the end of each chapter are presented in both languages. Hundreds of Japanese read the intro first in Japanese, then in English, then the main chapter content which is only available in English. For some of them, it allowed them to feel as they read, and finished an English book for the first time in their life. I hope some foreigners working on their Japanese or in other languages will make this same progress.

You will see that 'The New Testament' is not divided up into traditional numbered chapters. Instead I went for a page numbering on all those many subtitles that break up the text. I believe this will make it much easier to decide what you have time to read, or what you want to read. It will also help you go back and find some of the facts that I impregnated this text with. I always liked facts and information more than: "It was a murky, cool and moonless night, with the palm leaves rustling from the first breezes of autumn. Even the seasoned, rugged nudists at the colony, who should have been used to the chilly air, remained indoors, or would only venture out in the tacky and shapeless clothes available from the dusty, but overpriced gift shop."

Who Will Find Something of Interest in this Unholy Bible?

The New Testament

Nudists, student leaders, political tricksters, exiled Cubans, exotic escorts, well diggers, neo-conservatives, adventurers, Alden Terrace Elementary School Valley Stream Long Island New York graduates, hippies, Koreans, AFS American Field Service graduates, blind dogs, George Bush Jr. and Sr. Dick Cheney Donald Rumsfeld and others, Japanese expats in New York area, Boy Scout Scoutmasters, Eagle Scouts, mountain climbers, New Hampshire's daughters and sons, Bruce Lee fans, USA Senators Congressman Supreme Court Justices, teenagers or anyone realizing that to 'make a move' somewhere or at something can get life more exciting and fulfilling, Takarazuka actresses, Hill Billie's, Taiwanese, Tokugawa family members, cranky or drunken Samurai, paddle tennis players, members of TAC Tokyo American Club, high-school sports coaches, Con Ed Sports Award of the Week winners, world leaders and citizens, beltless high school hoods and bullies, messed up football players, cool American style soccer players, girl witches, West coast South Americans, Nepalese, Pakistanis, Indians, who love their huge mountains, Swiss with a rifle under the bed, tree skinners, Bostonians, high school and college cheerleaders, The Brothers Four, Phi Gamma Delta Brothers, canoeists, brave patriotic altruistic self-sacrificing USA military serving returned or wounded in Iraq and Afghanistan, high school Principals, horsemen missing their heads, Long Islanders, Quentin Tarantino, Beefsteak and Burgundy members, Ukrainians, USA citizens and voters, gymnasts, senior investment bank and leaders of financial institutions, Georgian Italian Swiss French Africans Indonesians with nice mountains, Transcendentalists, people in a rut, cave dwellers, smart bats, bluegrass band jammers, Castle Rock jumpers, Vietnam Veterans, Lewisboro Elementary School graduates, warplane dog fighters, graduates of John Jay High School, Taiwanese and Mainland Chinese, residents of Maine, Americans carrying concealed weapons, native American bakers, former Ambassadors to Japan, The ghost of the Christmas Soldier, Gonpachi and Tableaux staff and customers, parents told that their kids need glasses, cult leaders, Hayden Planetarium lovers, Germans and Australians who wish they had nice mountains, State District Attorneys and Governors, gamblers, spies and traitors, spy catchers, lake and river dwellers, maître d's, rock bands, USA mainstream media, Filipinos, Waccabuc Country Club members, German and Irish immigrants to the USA, native Americans, residents and lovers of Las Vegas and Nevada, history buffs, people who go in the buff, members of Manhattan's Cornell Harvard University of Pennsylvania Yale Brown Princeton and Columbia Alumni Clubs, free rope rock climbers, golfers,

Revolutionary War veterans, residents of Westchester NY and Fairfield Connecticut Counties especially Lewisboro Katonah Bedford Village and Ridgefield, members of the Mead family Waccabuc, N.Y.C. Waterworks people, Apple product fans, stubby fat horses, Jones Beach lovers, wearers of Tuxedos, West Point graduates and cadets, not Free Masons but old slave driver masons, James Fenimore Copper Leatherstocking novel fans, guys that lose their bone, Nishimachi School Tokyo graduates, residents of Manhattan Bronx and Brooklyn, peeping Toms, Pepsi Cola employees, horse riders, State Troopers, Japanese restaurateurs, 'Super-grade' Federal bureaucrats especially at Department of Labor, Cornell Willard Straight Hall Deskmen/women alumni, American Legion Boy's State winners, inbred feral horses, Members of the NLRB National Labor Relations Board, Alaskan antlered Moose fighting over women, tourists to New York City and Westchester County, Alaskans, tourists planning on attending the 2020 Tokyo Olympics, Harajuku lovers, SMAP and other Johnny's Jimusho Boy Bands, Yoyogi Park lovers, Ninjas, Ninja lovers and wanna bee's, city underground river lovers, Meiji Shrine Hatsumode'ers, descendants of Satsuma Samurai, Hachiko's illegitimate offspring, residents of Woonsocket Rhode Island, Trader Vic's bar devotees, hissing monkeys, the interred at Aoyama Cemetery, haunted taxi drivers, subway and train workers, the naked Waccabuc abominable snow-faced axe man, Shibuya and Omotesando station passengers, members of the Foreign Correspondents Club of Japan, the taxi riding lady ghost at Aoyama Cemetery, doggie doo doo pick-up people, couples who married someone they met in front of Hachiko, Japanese sailors and air force pilots, Russian Chinese Korean Taiwanese and other tourists to Omotesando and Harajuku, Apple store staff and customers, Kua Aina Hamburger staff and customers, residents of Saint Petersburg Russia, Russian bear-meat lovers,

Aeroflot airline staff, lake-lovers, Aoyama and Shibuya family descendants, Shibuya IT entrepreneurs, Russian and Alaskan bears, Jewish people fleeing Europe looking for a safe haven, members of Tokyo Jewish Community Center, anybody from anywhere looking for a safe heaven, weird isolated endemic animal and plant species, people from anywhere itching for something new fun and safe, older guys wanting to get rejuvenated mostly with younger girls, people from anywhere wanting to live part time in the exotic orient but with enough support and a live-in property caretaker, people fearing water shortage and climate change, dealmakers wanting a beautiful discreet live-in business base in Asia, people who want easy chances to meet famous people, dam lovers, famous faces that want privacy and a paparazzi-free lifestyle, gluttons that want to dine at 160,000 Tokyo restaurants, people who never want their place flooded again, expats and their families wanting to escape pollution personal danger and instability, Google satellite picture fans, yachtsmen and women who want to sail north and love sashimi.

The Old Testament

Cornell ILR School graduates, Minami-Asagaya residents, JETRO staff, Tora-san fans, Japanese expats working anywhere abroad, Japanese expats or any business executives having to face executing a staff reduction, Japanese or any other owner controlled companies, leaders of foreign capital companies in Japan or anywhere wanting better results, Japanese managers needing to be careful about age and sex discrimination in foreign countries, Japanese companies considering bringing business back to Japan, Japanese Unions and opposition political parties with policies that are counterproductive, Japanese leaders or foreign expats in Japan interested in fixing irrational personnel policies, people needing to decide whether to rent or buy real estate, people about to sign real estate rental agreements, people who suspect their electricity bill is inflated, Japanese and foreigners who want to better understand and communicate with each other, people facing potential natural calamities, Disneyland staff and guests, Portuguese Italian Iranian Chile Chinese Washington DC New York State Alaska California and residents everywhere experiencing earthquakes, Thai, U.K. Pakistan, India etc. flood victims, survivors of the December 26 2004 great Indian Ocean earthquake and tsunami, Tohoku and all Japanese people experiencing and surviving the March 11 2011 magnitude 9 earthquake and tsunami, hotels, universities, concert halls, Tokyo City Hall etc. that helped stranded people so much through Japan's March 11 2011 tragedy, crashing chimney survivors around the world, Lady Gaga, Chinese and Korean luxury-good-buying tourists, members of the many foreign Chambers of Commerce in Japan, people in developed nations who want to keep manufacturing jobs there and stay strong and prosperous, businesses that want a safe and secure environment without fear that technology and intellectual property will be stolen, the USA military personnel who helped in Tohoku with project "tomodachi", people who want tips on communicating better for bigger success, Canadians, noodle slupers, British UK Australian New Zealand people, those with clammy and sticky hands, retail clerk light-touch hand touchers, handkerchief nose blowers, double cheek greeters, Philippine department store ladies, Chinese girls, ladies first, Morning Musume AKB48 Kara Wonder Girls etc., Lions, Moose, Freemasons.

CONTENTS

The New Testament

Acknowledgements of Thanks to those Who Helped Make me in those Early Formative Years on Lake Waccabuc, Lewisboro Elementary School, John Jay H.S. in Cross River, N.Y., and at Cornell. Along with a Presentation of How I Got to Here, and Concluding with Where I Want to Go in the Human Resources Consulting Area. With Good, Strong Partners We Need to Contribute More, and Win Much Bigger and Better Results. (After finishing the book, I felt it fair to President Bush Jr. and crew to revisit 9/11, and the Afghanistan and Iraq Wars. I discovered too much.)

Governments Prove they Can't Do It. The Need is for Leading Global Firms in the Private Sector to Cooperate Together and Create a Synergistic Coalition More Effective at Restructuring, Building Stronger Firms, Carrying out More Effective Mergers & Acquisitions, Creating Flexibility in the Labor Market, Recruiting Top Talent, and More Effectively Utilizing available Manpower, and Womanpower.

Making My Move Closer to Japan. Tremendous   160
Opportunities and Adventures in Alaska. They are
still there in Alaska, Japan, or Anywhere. Just 'Make a
Move' and discover them.

My Job at the Straight Desk at Willard Straight Hall   163
was a Huge Part of My Life at Cornell. I was on Duty
the April 18, 1969 Day Leading to Cornell Making the
Cover of Newsweek and Myriad Newspapers when
Some Gun Toting Black Students Took Over the
Straight Building on Parents Weekend.

Doing Something on the Path Less Traveled. Anyway,   166
Stepping Out and Doing Something Exciting for You
Can Lead to Good Things, such as a Cornell White
House Summer Internship for Me. I suppose the
Wrong Path could also Screw Someone up Big Time.
Donald Rumsfeld Really Impressed Us.

Action is the Key. One Good Thing Can Lead to Another.   168
I Lined up an Internship at the Department of Labor for
the summer before I Came to Japan—a Great and Lucky
Start with Fine and Powerful Friends There. Should I have
'Stayed Put' as a 'Supergrade' at the Department of Labor?

Moving on to Omotesando, and Leaving My old Mostly   171
New York and Stateside Friends Where They are.
Underground Rivers, 827 American Houses in U.S.
Washington Heights Military Base becomes Yoyogi
Park. Johnny Kitagawa of Johnny's Jimusho (Talent
Agency—SMAP, Arashi etc.) gets Inspired, Discovers,
and Recruits his First Boy Band in Our Hood.

No Story about Tokyo and Japan Can be Complete 185 without Mention of the Incredible Train, Subway, and their Station Infrastructure. We have Three Iconic Train and Subway Stations in Our Neighborhood. The 3 lines of Omotesando Subway Station is Close by, and then Shibuya, and Harajuku Stations are about the Same 15-minute Walking Distance.

Omotesando is Particularly Flooded with Foreigners 189 during Christmas and New Year's Holidays, when it is Easier for many around the World to take some Time off. Apple's Only-In-Japan, Fukubukuro/Lucky Bag Sale.

Kua'aina Hawaiian Hamburger Shop—another 192 Success Story in Japan. So Many More Stores in Japan than in Any Other Country. This Chain is founded by a Caucasian Guy in Hawaii, and is now operated by Four Seasons Corporation (not the Hotel Chain).

The Craziest Thing about Camping-Out All Night on 195 the Hard Omotesando Stone Tile Sidewalk in Below Freezing Weather is that it was Not Necessary! Everyone had a Numbered Tag with a Lucky Bag Waiting for Their Morning Pick-up. Japanese People Love these Omatsuri/ Festival Events. Anyway, Make the Scene! Apple would not have Been Responsible for the Frozen Bodies.

Especially After the Economic Sanctions on Russia, Since 196 the Ukraine Crisis, it is Particularly Uncomfortable to Meet Russian Tourists up Close and Personal on Omotesando Avenue. They, like Us, Have nothing to do With the Crisis. They Just Want to Live the Best and Happiest They Can be.

Vote for Yourself, or Risk Losing—Thank You, Daddy!

1. After living until age 6 or 7 in Valley Stream, Long Island, New York State, from second grade until high school graduation, I grew up with a house on the less crowded shore of Lake Waccabuc. We were already there for the summers, from the time I was 3 or 4 years old. Moved from tent life to a summer cottage, then a big addition to the cottage. The Wikipedia listing for Waccabuc indicates there are just over 500 people. Among them, Keith Richards of the Rolling Stones, and Sean Combs/P. Diddy/Puff Daddy apparently have a home there. I suppose they live there some of the time. I was lucky to have great parents. My mother was a New York City public school (the Bronx) art teacher and artist. She had a Master's degree and went to Parsons New School for Design and NYU. Her posters at school leadership election time probably helped me win every election I was ever in. My father had an undergraduate degree, and master's degree from Fordham University. Maybe he also helped me win all the class and student council elections. He always told us to vote for ourselves, because he said he lost an election by just one vote. I believe it was Senior Class President at Fordham. That was his own vote, as he voted for the other candidate through some strange sense of good sportsmanship or chivalry. I have often been dumb like that too. Sure

enough, I won the Junior High School Student Council election against Tommy Huppuch by as I recall just 1 vote.

2. Thank you, Daddy! Tommy H. was a cool guy, successful corporate attorney with DEC/Digital Equipment Corp. and other companies. His big sister, Kathy, two years older and class of '66 was class treasurer, Junior prom queen, and a campus queen candidate. Tommy wasn't a bad looking dude either. Kathy told me in the school library I was going to lose the election. "You're a good guy, but my little brother will win." I figured she should know. A little depressing. Kathy's little bro Tommy has been to Japan many times. Of course he didn't know I was here. But in 2008 we got back in touch and sent each other some long emails. Just after he lost the election, Tom H. went off to boarding school at Vermont Academy. Way too many of my best friends from my public school, in this wealthy area above New York City, went off to boarding school.

Roger Stone Helped get me Elected, but Helped Sink Vice President Al Gore and New York State Governor Eliot Spitzer. Like Father like Son—Both True Professionals at Digging up Dirt.

3. The two years younger Roger Stone, the Republican political consultant and strategist, asked to be my campaign manager for President of the Senior High Student Council. Author of books such as *The Man Who Killed Kennedy* and *Nixon's Secrets* (both Skyhorse). His very interesting Wikipedia entry states that in 2008 *The Daily Beast* describes Roger as a "self-admitted hit man for the GOP". In the June 2, 2008 issue of the *New Yorker* magazine, their staff

writer, and well known senior legal analyst for CNN, Mr. Jeffrey Toobin writes a very interesting article about Roger Stone. The title of the article is "The Dirty Trickster: Campaign tips form the man who has done it all." Millions of Japanese can also get CNN here, and most shows are even simultaneously translated into Japanese. So these millions of Japanese who have cable, or SkyPerfect TV/ Sukapa TV, will immediately recognize Jeffrey Toobin. His bestselling books include *The Oath* (Anchor, 2013), *A Vast Conspiracy* (Random House, 2012), *The Nine* (Anchor, 2008), and *Too Close to Call* (Random House, 2002).

4. On the opposite side of today's political spectrum was Bobby Reich. (Robert Reich, famous author—such as best sellers *Beyond Outrage* (Vintage, 2012), *Aftershock: The Next Economy and America's Future* (Knopf, 2010), *The Work of Nations* (Knopf, 1991), political economist, professor, TV commentator, President Clinton's Secretary of Labor and so much more.) Mr. Reich has authored 15 books between 1982 and 2012. *Time* magazine named him one of the 10 most effective cabinet secretaries in the last century. Bobby, the not very tall (1.49 meters) 'genius', was 4 years older (in my big sister Kathy's class). When 'the genius' was president of our Senior High Student Council, for the first time he made sure my other Junior High Student Council Officers met once a month with his officers. A very nice guy, and a great teenage leader back then.

5. My H. S. honey Laura (later) gave me permission to only take Bobby's beautiful little sister Ellen Reich, one year younger than me class of '67 to the junior class summer dance party. And I mean gorgeous. Just like Laura. The smartest and best of her class. A lot taller than her big brother Bobby. I was junior class president so I needed a date. Laura and Ellen had been cheerleaders together, and

both were leaders of their respective classes. And guess where the dance party was? Waccabuc Country Club beach house, docks, floats and lake shore facility. But we couldn't use the boats. But some kids swam out to the island to get inside the Indian Ovens, or claim the smooth top of the oven rock (later). Several times throughout the whole evening the live band played The Doors' all time best #1 hit "Light my Fire". It was #1 on the charts all summer. It was released just two months before in April, 1967. So this local band were quick learners. Also sounded a lot like Jim Morrison and his boys. The reason for not being able to go to my junior class dance party with Laura? Laura had to take a plane to Belgium a few days before the party (later).

6. Back to Roger Stone, the political campaign man. Roger was in Washington D.C. when the Watergate break-in took place. (As was I–more on that later.) The break-in was June 17, 1972. I was only 22, so my kohai/junior Roger was only 20. Yet, according to the *New Yorker* article "Stone's Watergate high jinks were revealed during congressional hearings in 1973, and the news cost Stone his job on the staff of Senator Robert Dole." Roger probably started his love for politics with my campaign. I assure you we were clean as a whistle back at John Jay H.S. Roger also had a very large role in getting the Florida recount canceled. This may have led to Mr. George Bush Jr. getting elected President instead of Mr. Bill Clinton's' vice president Al Gore. To make the long *New Yorker* magazine story short, Roger used his Spanish-speaking wife and their time spent and connections in Miami with Cuban exiled leaders and activists, to use radio programs and rallies to get several thousand people in front of the vote recount building, the Clark Center. There they screamed, 'Stop the recount!!' (Stone and Bush Jr. were lucky because this vote recount

"came soon after the Elian Gonzalez affair, in which the Clinton-Gore Administration enraged many Miami Cubans by agreeing to return Elian, who was six years old, to his father in Cuba"—Mr. Toobin's article.)

7. Mr. Stone also used his walkie-talkie at his nearby command center trailer, to mobilize one group to rush up the stairs, and another to interfere with "two vote counting Commissioners" who were allegedly "removing 200 or 300 ballots from the voting ballot recount room". So stair and elevator access were blocked by the Roger Stone's mobilized groups—the shouting GOP/Republican activists. According to the *New Yorker* article, "In fact, the Gore official in the elevator, Joe Geller, was carrying a single sample ballot. The dual scenes of chaos—both inside and outside the building—prompted the recount officials to stop their work. The recount in Miami was never restarted, depriving (Vice President) Gore of his best chance to catch up in the over-all state tally".

8. Jeffrey Toobin, of the *New Yorker* and CNN also wrote, "According to Stone, James A. Baker III, the former Secretary of State, who was leading the Bush forces, told his aide Margaret Tutwiler to recruit Stone. (Baker and Tutwiler say that they don't remember this, but that it is possible)". Presumably Jeffrey Toobin, or an assistant, fact-checked this with Mr. Baker and Ms. Tutwiler. I think such smart people, or even way less sharp people, would not forget something like this at one of the pinnacle rubber-hits-the-road points in both their careers. But I truly respect their decency in saying they "don't remember". They could have flatly denied the instruction to pull Roger into the fray. But probably not, because Roger can be pretty scary ☺. I do know in the only phone conversation I ever had with Roger about 15 or 20 years ago, he told me James Baker was his

mentor, and the person he really respects. 'He taught me everything I know (not meaning the dirty trick part)', Roger told me. In the *New Yorker* article Mr. Stone raves more about his relationship and respect for Nixon even than for Reagan. I don't have the John Jay High School yearbooks for Mr. Stone's last two years there, but I can tell you he was elected class president while I was at John Jay. So he could also manage his own campaigns.

9. According to Mr. Toobin's New Yorker article, the FBI approached Stone about the then governor of New York State, Eliot Spitzer. Spitzer had been a hard-hitting New York Attorney General and was governor of New York State from January 1, 2007 until March 17, 2008. That is the day he had to resign due to a prostitution scandal: "…On November 19, 2007, Stone's attorney wrote to (the FBI) agents and recounted the story that the woman had told him (Stone) at Miami Velvet (a club), including the part about (having sex with) the socks (on)… Four months later, Spitzer resigned, after it was revealed that he was a client of the Emperors Club V.I.P., a prostitution ring". Eliot Spitzer was talked up to be a strong Democratic presidential contender. Mr. Spitzer used his own money for these romps. He was a gentleman. In many countries stepping down from his New York State Governorship would not be necessary. The *New Yorker* article said Roger told Mr. Toobin, the writer of the article, that his Dad dug wells. Since a Mr. Stone dug our Waccabuc well in about 1955, when Roger was 3, I'll bet Roger tagged along and watched once in a while. I don't remember seeing him, but the well-digging work would have been done during the weekdays when we were back in Valley stream, Long Island. I guess Roger Stone could also be good at digging up dirt.

Do you have any Personal Friends from Your Hometown, Schools, Workplaces, or Neighborhoods that may have altered the Course of History? Maybe in Better or Smaller Ways than Wasting Trillions of Dollars, and Tens of Thousands of Lives?

10. History is interesting. To what extent did, Roger, an old friend and ally of mine, possibly affect two presidencies? The New York State Governor Roger helped dethrone, Eliot Spitzer, was still more of a long shot. But the seated Vice President Al Gore, had the majority votes of the direct vote of the people nationwide. But because of the halting of the Florida recount, Gore did not win the popular direct balloting in Florida. Thus he lost the all-important Electoral College votes assigned to Florida. (For some of our Japanese and other foreign readers, and maybe some Americans too, ALL the Electoral College votes of a given state go to the candidate who had the majority in the direct popular vote. Even if the majority candidate wins by 1 vote! To the Japanese and many readers from other countries and the USA as well, maybe a silly, irrational system...) Is there someone who has altered history from your hometown, high school, university, or former company colleague?

11. Surely if Mr. Al Gore had been elected, instead of Mr. Bush Jr., the history books would write up the last 15 years, and the future from now, very differently. There will be continuing repercussions of increased instability and turmoil in the Mideast and around the world. And unfortunately to my beloved native country's reputation, global standing, and fiscal health. The wars cost trillions of dollars. (Iraq/Afghan war costs to top $4 trillion, *Washington*

Post, Ernesto Londoho, March 28, 2013; Financial cost of the Iraq War, Wikipedia entry; *Reuters*, Daniel Trotta, March 14, 2013 etc.) There is not even as much written on these costs the last couple years—old news. But let us not forget! Our precious earned money we had to pay as taxes was needed for reducing taxes; repairing or building our roads, bridges, transportation facilities and infrastructure; shoring up our coastal cities to protect them from rising seas and intensifying storms; building huge desalination plants and more dams and reservoirs for California, coastal cities, and other areas suffering from droughts that will surely intensify (even if that means some tiny, spiny, purple cactus plants, small fry or larger mammals, swamp fish, green and blue stripped frogs with that distinct yellow ring around the female's anus, and endangered green and pink polka-dotted butterflies take a hit). We could have better used the treasury of trillions for education, research and development; the space program (now my USA is a country without a space shuttle and we depend on Russian rockets, and rocket engines to launch a satellite or other large pay loads!); the subsidies for training and for local manufacturing that other countries give; more advanced weapons programs, improving a defensive military not an offensive one that wastes lives, equipment, hardware, cripples our soldiers, dishes out collateral damage, pisses off the natives in their homeland, and pushes people to terrorism; defending our borders from unwanted immigration with fences, cameras and personnel—any number of more sensible and pressing needs. From any and all more meritorious agendas that can bring tangible results and value.

12. Bush Jr. needed to prove he was just not Bush Jr. He was recklessly driven to do something bigger and better than

his dad. And without the influence of Vice President Dick Cheney, and neoconservatives such as my seven-year-older Cornell Senpai Paul Wolfowitz, surely the USA would not have ventured into Iraq. And then making Mr. Wolfowitz, the head of his tiny neo-con world, the head of the World Bank... Cheeky move. Thumb your nose at the rest of the world. "If you're not with us, you're against us"/"otherwise you're with the enemy"—puffed up cocky, scary George Jr. (20-second video clip YouTube 'With Us or Against Us' TV speech). So except for the 4 or 5 countries who supported the Iraq War, all the rest of us were Jr.'s enemies—very smooth George, and very presidential. We missed your father's class, breeding and intelligence.

13. No wonder all countries are joining the new Chinese initiated AIIB 'Asian Infrastructure Development Bank' (Wikipedia), including the UK. Although the US strongly asked the UK and our other friendly nations not to support the China initiated AIIB. So as of mid-April, 2015, we sit alone outside the AIIB with Japan, North Korea, and Columbia. Columbia is asking for a name change to something more global than the 'Asian' in the name of the bank. Joining AIIB would seem to be right up Mr. Obama's ally. Although we hear the Congress would never vote on agreeing to join. Not a good thing. China is not our enemy, unless we push it that way. We, the USA, should have welcomed AIIB, embraced it, and contributed to it from the start. Japan indicated it may join. Instead of Japan taking pressure from the USA not to join, I hope Japan coaches the US that it would be better for the States to join ('U.S. grills Japan on report saying it will join AIIB', *Japan Times/Kyodo*, April 12, 2015).

*"If you're not With Us you're Against Us—Otherwise
You're With the Enemy".
Come on… Words and Actions do Count. The World is
Listening, and Watching. If We Lose the World's Respect
and Friendship it's Our Fault. It's Our Great Loss.*

14. First we hit the stunned and incredulous world with the Iraq invasion, our largely US-originated subprime mortgage crises, our Lehman shock, then we create our own rules and fine the foreign banks for not following them. Now we are warming-up to Cuba and Iran. Actually dialogue and cooperation with Iran was recommended in the 2006 Iraq Study Group report, co-chaired by Republican kingmaker James Baker (above) and Lee Hamilton. Should we give back some of the 9.5-billion-dollar US government fine to the French BNP Pariba/Banque Nationale de Paris Bank? (The fines were for disobeying and evading primarily-US initiated and imposed sanctions on Iran, Cuba, and Sudan.)

15. The Mayor of London, Boris Johnson, who may be Britain's next prime minister, wrote an article in the conservative *Daily Telegraph* newspaper. It advised George W. Bush Jr., not to bring his book tour to the U.K. because he could face arrest as a war criminal (YouTube, 6:06 Mayor Of London Warns George Bush He might Face Arrest as a War Criminal'). In his book George Bush Jr. is boastful, proud, and unrepentant about dishing out torture. There was a December 21, 2014 New York Times Editorial Board article entitled 'Prosecute Torturers and Their Bosses'. Pretty heavy stuff. All reflections of the US loss of moral authority, and why the U.K. is thumbing its nose at the US and joining the China initiated AIIB bank against the USA's wishes. London Mayor Boris may also have his

blondish, whitish, shaggy hair in a tussle over the USA making him pay capital gains tax on the London house he sold. It was the first London house he lived in for many years. He didn't even have to pay tax to the U.K. on that sale. Mayor Boris Johnson happened to be born in New York City, because his parents were stationed in the States until he was five years old. (YouTube 2: 30 "Boris Johnson 'intends to renounce US citizenship': World News Now". If you hit 'Show more' the transcript is also there.)

16. Only two countries, the USA and tiny Eritrea in northeast Africa facing the Red Sea, require their citizens living and paying taxes in foreign countries, to also file forms with themselves. (A bit like the United States being virtually the only country not on the metric system—later.) The day after I wrote this, a friend sent me an April 24, 2015 *Bloomberg View* short article by Bloomberg's board of editors. It's titled 'End the American Expat Tax' (wasteful, costly, time consuming, IRS filing requirement that leads to no tax revenue!) And now with the new FATCA law, most banks in foreign countries won't even let US citizens keep their old bank accounts, let alone newly open a bank account. I think at least, long-term, legitimate USA residents living and working in foreign countries should not be included in FATCA reporting requirements. FATCA represents USA coerced extraterritoriality, and 30% fines on USA assets of the non-complying world's financial institutions. Reporting requirements on the world's financial institutions will cost each of them billions of dollars. The world's banks and governments hate the USA for these strong-armed imperialist tactics. The world's financial institutions will take their assets out of the USA, and stop underwriting the USA debt. USA treasury notes will be dumped, and USA financial markets

and the dollar will weaken. It will no longer be the world's reserve currency. This is already starting.

17. It will cost even our own IRS billions, in pursuit of an estimated $800,000,000 in additional tax revenues. That amount runs our government for 2 hours! (Please see the Wikipedia entry on 'Foreign Account Tax Compliance Act (FATCA)'. This is another dumb law driven this time by mostly ignorant Democratic law makers, in a huff about the American tax dodger's accounts with UBS Bank in Switzerland a few years back. A little like our shooting from the hip with the exit tax/penalties because Eduardo Saverin from Facebook, renounced US citizenship and moved to Singapore. Saverin was born in 1983, and raised in Brazil. He did not move to the States until he was 11 years old in 1993. Finally he became a US citizen in 1998. Maybe he didn't even particularly like the US of A, compared to Brazil and Singapore. Such angry, reckless, and impetuous decisions by our political leaders are leading to the suffering of 7,800,000 USA expats living abroad—virtually none of them live and work that way for tax avoidance purposes.

18. May be better to sniper shoot with FATCA, rather than our recent USA trend to drop cluster bombs with reckless abandon. Yeah, an Osama bin Laden special op, rather than War of the Worlds approach. Sniper shoot the real fat cats who live in the States, or screw around with part-time fake residences. And please leave the rest of us alone. It's too much like the patriotic brain explosion over the Afghan and Iraq wars. These overhasty and misguided calls are extremely expensive, and bring the world's scorn upon us. It's a shame that in the last couple years thousands of Americans living abroad have no choice but to give up their US citizenship. How can you live without a job and

a bank account? US citizens living outside the USA, are too troublesome for even our own USA companies to hire (burdensome paperwork, extra costs, risk of draconian fines from the man). So Americans lose their jobs abroad. Wait and see. When foreign banks and institutions, and the world in general get fed up with our shenanigans of recent years, jobs will be lost at home as well. Yet this loser of a law that no congressman read or understood, got passed as part of the 2010 Hiring Incentive to Restore Employment (HIRE) Act!—hah? Multinationals of other countries had always tended to avoid hiring US expats. That means US expats are not there to steer their companies to purchase from other US companies and suppliers. The little dog who wrote this book could do a better job of running our government, because she wouldn't do anything—some barking, but no bite.

We are seeing that the US Military's, by Far the World's Most Powerful, has Been Helpless, and Powerless in Vietnam, (not in Operation Desert Storm), Afghanistan, Iraq and Peripheral Theaters. So Let's Not, Probably through Ignorance and Omission, Do Things to Weaken the USA's Business and Commercial Power Abroad. Only One Other Country that is in Africa, Eritrea, Does that. President Barack's? FATCA Must Go! Or Sniper Shoot with it. Probably London Mayor Boris Johnson would not have Gotten So Mad at George Bush Jr. ☺

19. We are seeing that projection of US military power abroad has its limitations. No tangible victories or good results from Vietnam, Afghanistan, Iraq, or wherever else those politicians and pundits who don't have to fight, want to

send our weary warriors. Now it is becoming extremely difficult for US citizens to live abroad, proudly wave our flag, and promote our country and global US commercial interests and power. An exceptional and unfortunate predicament, yet easily changeable condition. I always wondered why the American Chamber of Commerce in Washington, The Conference Board, and other business lobbies could not get this curious condition fixed. This freaky and queer law was passed because some rich people escaped abroad to avoid the draft at the time of the Civil War over 150 years ago. It's not as though expats in any country get a free ride on taxes. They have to pay taxes in their country of residence. These taxes are often higher than US tax rates. Even if little or no tax is owed to the US IRS, the time and cost burden of filing with the IRS is very wasteful, and does indeed weary the soul. It also builds bureaucracy and wastes the IRS's time, and money because there is often very little in the way of tax revenues. Whether it is a Republican, Democratic, or Tea Party Congressman or Senator, the Executive Branch, the Supreme Court; whatever happened to the Boston Tea Party and "taxation without representation", excessive and unjust double taxation? And why is it so easy to torture and alienate with irrational bureaucracy, and unnecessary IRS tax filings the millions of stars-and-stripes waving United States ambassadors abroad?

20. We also need as many American citizens living in foreign countries as possible. If we have not had a chance to travel with open eyes, ears, hearts and minds, there may be too many of us Americans in the USA who do not realize the degree of freedom and opportunity there is in many countries all over the world. So many countries have so much going for them—just like the USA. There are many

great places in the world. There are thousands of restaurants and businesses run by even-new entry immigrants in Japan. And the more Americans who experience this and live it, the better off we all are. To learn more about how other people in the world see us is important. Traveling gets you out and about.

21. We met an Iraqi waiter in Amsterdam about two years after Rumsfeld's March, 2003 Shock and Awe bombing campaign. He got out of the country within days. So did an Iraqi taxi driver and a street vendor we have met. They all used to be able to go about their lives, and work in safety with no worries of making it home each night. They are in touch with their families who are in constant fear and danger. You can imagine how angry they become when people like Wolfowitz, Cheney, or Bush say "the Iraqi people are better off today than they were under Saddam". Such ignorance, indifference, or lies for political advantage or the preservation of personal ego are why so many suffering people hate us.

22. I think the US of A is getting a little heavy-handed beyond the point that "American Exceptionalism" should allow. It's ironic. The theory of American Exceptionalism was first expressed by a Frenchman Alexis de Tocqueville in 1831. Tocqueville and this term were complimentary of our nation. I think America was exceptionally good and lucky with the way we were able to expand our territory largely because European nations engaged in costly wars needed money and needed to sell their territory to us. We used to watch these other powers fight. We learned from that, and avoided war like the plaque. President Franklin Roosevelt had to be relieved because finally our Pearl Harbor uproar swayed the US public, and Congress to join the WWII effort. The Marshall Plan after World War II,

originated and named after George Marshall (1880-1959), our top general and Chief of Staff (1939-1945) during the WWII, and then Secretary of Defense (1950-1951) was also exceptionally good. So let's not be exceptionally bad.

23. The Iraq invasion DID directly lead to ISIL/Islamic State of Iraq and Levant. The above 2006 Iraq Study Group co-chaired by James Baker had recommended US troop levels be cut back in Iraq, reallocated to Afghanistan (but won't help there either). Mr. Baker and his colleagues' report also held that more troops in Iraq would not help or change the mess in Iraq. In 2008, just before Bush Jr. left the White House, he signed the SOFA/Status of Forces Agreement with Iraq. 'It established that U.S. combat forces would withdraw from Iraqi cities by June 30, 2009, and all U.S. forces will be completely out of Iraq by December 31, 2011' (Wikipedia, 'U.S.-Iraq Status of Forces Agreement'). So this one came before President Barack. General and Secretary of State, Colin Powell, told President Bush Jr., "It's the Pottery Barn Rule. You break it, you own it." Once Iraq was smashed, and other countries in the region became destabilized, it took time, but ISIL was inevitable. Maybe, wrongly, but probably not, Saddam had always been our ally against some of the extremism in the region. The first President Bush, Jr.'s father, knew all that and had experience and wisdom.

24. All neighboring countries in the Middle East except Israel and Kuwait were opposed to the invasion of Iraq in advance of the invasion. Even neighboring countries told us they felt no threat from Iraq. Only the U.K., Poland, Australia, Japan, and a couple other Asian countries went along with the invasion. The Vatican, and ALL other countries on Earth were opposed. Ireland, Taiwan, and Solomon Islands were neutral. If you read the Wikipedia entry 'Opposition

to the Iraq War', just the brief section on 'Opposition from national security and military personnel', you will see that tens of the most senior and knowledgeable USA top generals, diplomats, and national security experts who know the Middle East region were strongly opposed in advance of the Iraq war. This including former President George Bush Sr., and his top advisors such as Brent Snowcroft, Air Force Lieutenant General and National Security Advisor to Presidents Gerald Ford, and George H. W. Bush, Sr. Mr. Snowcroft and others were sent by Bush Sr. to dissuade the tenaciously bullheaded, cocky, and blindly self-possessed son.

The United Nations, The Vatican, All the Nations of the World except the U.K, Poland, Australia, Japan, and a Couple other Countries in Asia were Strongly Opposed to Invading Iraq before the USA Went In. So were Most of The USA's Experts and Generals. Iraq's Neighbors Saw No Threat from Saddam. They Warned All Hell would Break Loose. The USA's Noble History was One of Avoiding War. Why Did We, and Too Many of Our Politicians Get so Sheepish, Hawkish, Politically Partisan, and Brain Dead? How many would bet their Own Arms and Legs on that Vote?

25. There were 24 out of 100 senators who voted against the Iraq War. They were all Democrats except one independent from Vermont, Jim Jeffores, and one Republican from Rhode Island, Lincoln Chaffee. In the House of Representatives, out of 435 members, 126 Democrats, 6 Republicans and 1 independent voted against the unprovoked use of force against Iraq. Their names can be

seen at 'Iraq War Vote in 2002: 156 Congress Members Who Voted…' www.usliberals.about.com. Bush Jr. and a few advisors had a peevish and amateurish determination, no matter what, to get Saddam and the oil (which ended up going to the Chinese and others!). If that's it, why not just buy the damn oil, buy it elsewhere, or 'drill, baby, drill' for your own. I read a long article in the *Cornell Alumni* magazine a few years back about Paul Wolfowitz, Bush Jr.'s Deputy Secretary of Defense. Everyone said he was a kind, considerate, and generous chap. I'll bet Dick Cheney was too. I'd love to share a cold beer with George Jr.—in Tokyo or Texas.

26. His senior year, George Jr. was the head cheerleader at the elite Phillips Academy in Andover, Massachusetts. George Jr. was also a cheerleader at Yale, as was I at Cornell. So we have that in common. His grandfather, Prescott Sheldon Bush (1895-1972) was also a Yale cheerleader, and was Senator for Connecticut from 1952 to 1963. George Jr. was president of his fraternity, Delta Kappa Epsilon, his senior year at Yale, as was his Dad. Dad was also a cheerleader. Both, good likeable chaps for sure. But unlike George Jr.'s grade point of 77%, the first President Bush graduated Phi Beta Kappa in 2.5 years, and was captain of the Yale baseball team. As a left-handed first-baseman he played in the first two college world series. So quite an act to follow. I think it is never easy on sons who have such exceptional fathers. They can become rebellious against their father's greater wisdom. Jr. wanted to be his own man. I guess I missed cheering on the field together with George Jr., probably by 2 years if Bush Jr. also cheered his senior year at Yale. I cheered and tumbled on the field only my sophomore year at Cornell. Forever the cheerleader, Jr. cheered us on to battle.

27. A man or a woman can become much bigger, if they are less sure of herself or himself, more hesitant, and can apologize and have some regret. It's not a sign of weakness. The longest serving secretary of defense (7 years), Mr. Robert McNamara, former CEO of Ford Motors, was the main architect of the war in Vietnam. He admitted in his 1995 *In Retrospect* memoir, that the Vietnam War was 'wrong, terribly wrong'. In a 2002 Errol Morris documentary, *The Fog of War...* Mr. McNamara said, "None of our allies supported us. Not Japan, not Germany, not Britain or France. If we can't persuade nations of comparable values of the merit of our cause, we better reexamine our reasoning." He apologized. His place in history notched up. Staying quiet and lying low are also worth considering. So many have suffered, and will keep suffering so much.

28. In contrast, several times, and in George Jr.'s speech at the dedication to his Presidential Library, 'the decision maker' said, "I'm comfortable" with my/his decisions and with what happened with the Iraq War ('Exclusive: As his presidential library debuts, George W. Bush prepares to return to public stage on his own terms', by Tom Benning, The Dallas Morning News, April 13, 2013.) I wonder if the legless veterans former-president George W, Bush Jr. invites to play golf with might rather have their own legs, rather than the metal ones. Ever really think about it? Did we forget about movies like *Coming Home* (1978)—won 3 Academy Awards for Best Actor (Jon Voight), Best Actress (Jane Fonda) and Best Original Screenplay? *Coming Home* also got 5 other Academy Award nominations including Best Picture. *Born on the Fourth of July* (1989) was a true story written by and about a paralyzed veteran named Ron Kovic—played by Tom Cruise for his first Best Actor Oscar nomination. The film was nominated for 8

Academy Awards and won two for Best Director and Best Film Editing. It also won 4 Golden Globe Awards and grossed $161,001,698.

29. *Forrest Gump* (1994) grossed $677,000,000 alone at its first theatre run. It was the biggest earning film that year. The 'Internet Movie Database' ranks it the 13th best movie of all time. It won 6 Academy Awards in 1995, and lots of other awards. Out of Bush Jr.'s Texas (Houston), the movie led to the Bubba Gump Shrimp Company chain of restaurants. The first one opened in 1996. Wikipedia says there are 43 locations as of September 2014. This includes 29 in the United States, with the rest scattered around the world including 2 in Tokyo, and 1 in Osaka. The Japanese restaurants are run by my Nishimachi School acquaintance the WDI Group (later). We've dined at Bubbas at Lalaport Mall in Toyosu many times. It's a huge mall with normal-people stores, not luxury brand stores, and worth a visit. Half my body was built on other WDI group restaurants such as Tony Romas, and Capricciosa (later) food when I lived over by the Imperial Palace. Although *Forrest Gump* was also a romantic comedy, Gary Sinise as Lieutenant Dan (Taylor) in his legless, miserable, and bitter state made a big impression on me. Yeah. He got his 'magic legs' (titanium alloy prosthetics), and lucky for him and Tom Hanks' Forrest Gump, they ended up happy and rich. But a lot of the guys and gals coming home from Iraq and Afghanistan are physically and mentally devastated wrecks.

30. I like my legs, arms and hands. The ability to tie our shoes, wear a necktie, unscrew a bottle, button our shirts, pet our dogs and cats, hug our kids and spouses, more easily get dates and lovers, decork a bottle of wine, have our faces in one piece, type on our PCs, drive a car easily and safely, play catch-ball with our kids, run to catch the train... Not

be stared at by kids at the mall, or avoided by the eyes of their parents. How about you? For World War II, when the German nation's war machine swept over and controlled almost all of Europe within a couple months, and Japan did the same thing throughout China and all of South East Asia, yes. For the Korean War, when the North invaded the South with big support from China and the USSR, yes. For the Vietnam War, and the last 15 years, no.

After 241 Marines and Military Personnel were Killed in the 1983 Beirut Lebanon Marine Barracks Bombing, in the Face of Great Criticism, President Reagan Decided to Pull the Troops Out of the Middle East instead of Go to War. That Decision Probably Saved Much, Much More than Mr. Ronald Reagan's Presidency.

31. As I recall, President Ronald Reagan (1911-2004), was the only presidential campaign I ever contributed money to. Two years into his first term, on October 23, 1983, 241 U.S. service personnel, including 220 marines and 21 others were killed by a truck bomb at a Marine compound in Beirut, Lebanon. At the same time, another suicide truck bomber killed 58 French paratroopers on their base also in Lebanon. It was the deadliest one-day attack against U.S. Marines since the battle of Iwo Jima in February 1945. Instead of allowing for a brain explosion, and fighting back with troops on the ground and a major invasion force, President Reagan decided to pull U.S. troops out of the Middle East. (Later on U.S. troops in Saudi Arabia was always Osama bin Laden's biggest beef.) President Reagan went on to be re-elected president, and held the office for 6 more years until 1989.

32. I predict that if President Reagan had immediately started a war in the Middle East, it would have escalated, and would not have succeeded. There would be a tremendous budget deficit, and he would have ended up as a failed and unpopular president. Maybe even lose his second term election. He took great criticism for his decision to turn the other cheek. He did spend money on *Star Wars*, our defense (not offense) spending, and was able to reduce taxes. President Reagan watched the Soviet Union bleed to death in Afghanistan in their war between 1979 and the end of his Presidency in 1989. His wise decision nicely changed history. That is what a real leader does: a leader with class that we can be proud of who leads in a sensible, practical direction, and does not go along with, and further incite patriotic hysteria. President Reagan 'stayed put', and decided to 'make a move' out, rather than rush in and benefit from a short-term boost in his popularity.

33. Without our own family and friends being drafted, most of us didn't know a National Guard Reservist, an unfortunate graduate of West Point, a university ROTC/Reserve Officers Training Corp. program guy or gal, or a brave member of our voluntary army, whose lives ended up on the neocon's hands. Shame on us. There could be more capricious, counter-productive deployments to boost a politician's ego, image and ratings in the polls. George Jr. would do anything to get a second term, unlike one-term Bush Sr. 'My Dad', who should have gotten 'political capital' by continuing on to Baghdad during the 40-day Operation Desert Storm from January 17, to February 28, 1991. Bush Sr. with another 33 nations, and 14 countries sending combat troops, lost only 292 soldiers, about half by non-hostile accidents. There were only 467 soldiers wounded in action during the 5-week Operation Desert Storm deployment. 'Small successful

wars boost your popularity and ratings'. George Jr., bad call. Not 'little war'. Big bloody bankrupting war. It's torn apart the Middle East, with overflowing problems elsewhere. In the future, our vigilance is required. For those of us who did not care enough, google Tomas Young, 'The Last Letter—A Message to George W. Bush and Dick Cheney from a Dying Veteran'. Mr. Young is the one with the guts. He is the true patriot. He believes in the great country we always were and must be. Tomas Young is dead.

34. Perhaps the Taliban and Afghanistan could have also been handled with a little more care, respect, perhaps financial consideration to the Taliban, and adroit diplomatic skill from very senior, or top levels for greater success. I know we didn't need to send in an army, and spend $1,000,000 for every $1 the 'the bad guys' spent. That's a bad bet. That's bad business except for Halliburton. And Mr. Cheney's Halliburton got much business without the normal, legally required government contract bidding requirement! As of April 2015, even the Taliban are opposed to ISIL. The Taliban was never Al Qaeda. The Taliban are more likely to fight foreign Al Qaeda operatives, as they are willing to host their training camps. The contents of the Wikipedia entry for 'Saleh v. Bush', a class-action lawsuit filed against the Bush Jr. administration for the Iraq invasion is a good summary for some, or a real shocker for others. The 6 key, top officials who are the defendants are being represented and defended by the U.S. Department of Justice under President Barack Obama. More than an example of non-partisanship, I can see reasons why it is so. Disagreeing parties can go in and edit Wikipedia. Unusually, there are no contradicting inputs, or claims of inaccuracies in the evidence cited against the defendants in this short 4 or 5-page Wikipedia entry.

35. I never had time; never took the time to study this stuff. Except for email attachments some friends sent me— mostly my businessman buddies on the right. They are usually tough on President Obama and the liberals or left. For example, very professionally produced and credible looking evidence/mini-documentaries that Hillary Clinton and Michelle Obama are men. Yes. Men with peni—one each. Other lies that Barack never graduated, or even attended the schools he went to. Actually I have never seen such bold-faced lies coming from the left about the right. Maybe they exist... Okay, I guess the 9/11 conspiracy theories of no airplanes can be equally off the wall. Some of those videos, actual government memorandums, have probably been contrived and doctored-up too. Bush Jr. 'Swift Boat' campaign TV commercials, lying and shedding doubts that John Kerry was not wounded and did not save the lives of his men in Vietnam did hurt John Kerry when he ran against Bush Jr. for president. John Kerry was the true war hero. I would have split for Sweden or Canada if my draft birthday lottery number had not been around #215. The 'Swift Boat' lies were very professionally created to neutralize Bush Jr.'s draft avoidance military record. He got special treatment/allowed absence from his National Guard commitment ('Swiftboating', Wikipedia).

36. I never even took the time to look at YouTube until about 10 weeks ago. The actual speeches, interviews, talk shows, media coverage etc. on all these and other leaders, and on all these topics, and everything under the sun is there on YouTube. Easy and fast to search for. We forget. If you are like me, and never even looked at YouTube, please check out a 4 minute/4', 41 second/41" segment with 79,751 hits when I looked. It's called 'This Bush Lie Mashup will Make

You Angry All Over Again'. The above hits are nothing compared to hits on the 9/11 conspiracy theory stuff. But there was all the evidence and the knowledge the 9/11 plane attacks would probably come. So they probably came. The Bush administration had the information, but have often pleaded ignorance and surprise. See the Wikipedia entries of the above 'Saleh v. Bush', or 'September 11 attacks advance-knowledge conspiracy theories'. The conspiracy theory that there were no airplanes, the Pentagon was instead hit with a missile, no people in some planes, and no bodies found in Pennsylvania etc., etc. are largely debunked here.

37. With all this advance warning of airplane attacks, and with Dick Cheney taking the unusual step of taking more personal direct control over NORAD three months earlier, could it be the attacks were known to be imminent (A YouTube 6:18 video 'NORAD Ordered to Stand Down on 9/11 by Dick Cheney')? Evidence that the 9/11 attacks were coming was there. Maybe better not to stop the attacks so we can push on to Iraq? I sure as hell hope not. But with all the bold-faced lying, and making fools of the public's memory and intelligence… In the CNN November 29, 2009 Report: 'Bin Laden was withing our grasp', according to Gary Berntsen, the CIA operative who led the pursuit of bin Laden at Tora Bora. Mr. Berntsen's requests at Tora Bora which would have made possible bin Laden's capture were turned down. There are details and evidence on these nightmares but this was supposed to be a fun book. It is best for every voter to do their own individual research, issue by issue—both sides and up the middle. Never again should we allow our emotions to be so mustered, and to be so rallied, railroaded, and steamrolled over.

I, and I Guess all of us, should have Cared More, Studied More, and Thought Things Through. At the End of the Day, It is Informed Individual Citizens that are needed to Save Lives and Money, and Protect Our Democracy, Freedom, and Prosperity.

38. Also maybe check out a 1'06" YouTube CNN segment called 'George Bush Caught LYING Again About 9/11', or 2:31 CBS News 'Afghanistan—losing limbs to stop admitting the war is lost', or a longer 13'19" 'US ACCEPTS LOSING IN AFGHAN'. There was also a CBS News 60Minutes.com segment called 'McChrystal's Frank Talk on Afghanistan', which gives we lucky and blasé civilians going about our peaceful, normal lives, some needed insight. General McChrystal was fired by Barack Obama because of content in that *Rolling Stone* magazine interview, that he and his subordinates had. It's good to see on YouTube two Fox News Bill O'Reilly videos where he gets tough with Dick Cheney and tougher on Donald Rumsfeld—'Fox Bill O'Reilly attacks Rumsfeld over Iraq', and 'Bill O'Reilly Grills Dick Cheney On Iraq'. Mr. Bill O'Reilly is so sharp, it is surprising he could not see in advance that the Iraq war was going to be a big blooming boo-boo.

39. I put this almost finished book on hold, and spent hundreds of hours studying the last 10 weeks. I wanted to see if I was being too harsh on Bush Jr., his kindred spirits, and the rest of us who went along with the deadly and expensive buffoonery. I had ended the critical macro discourse against the neocon wars with paragraph #10, and a much shorter/edited version of Paragraph #11. I learned too much, got shocked, almost puked a few times, and found it difficult to sleep at night. So I had to add

much of the above content. I hated what I learned, and hated every minute of this editing. But this book can't be about this tragedy of foreign and military policy. And it certainly is not my area of professional expertise. Let's just study harder, not believe what we hear from people we are supposed to be able to trust. Let's not be dumb patriots, clueless sheepish followers of shepherds drugged on their cheap Kool-Aid extreme ideology, and wishful, overly optimistic assessments about very serious matters of life and death.

40. And we, the taxpayers end up paying. Let's not let way too much of the media stir us up. I don't get it. The media anchors and correspondents are more informed and experienced than most of us are. The major advertisers are not defense contractors or oil companies. They are consumer brands such as GM, Proctor and Gamble, L'Oreal, AT& T, Toyota… I know we have brilliant Walter Conkrites in the media ranks. Let's please come forward, and speak out more often. Tough to figure why so much of the media tapped their feet to the beat of the neocon war drum. There is a tough and painful question for USA Americans. Did our own overblown fears, shock, desire for vengeance, and furious irrational anger after 9/11 World Trade Center encourage and play to Bush Jr. and his buddies, partially molding their political/gain popularity/get reelected agenda? Or did we get played by George Jr. in his Ground Zero fire chief hat (the debris had long fallen), and his buddies, for their political/reelection/hold on to and gain power and wealth agenda? Maybe way too much of both. And tragedies like this may be in our future. I hope we can be smarter.

41. By the way, I was not a distant, nonchalant, observing critic of the 9/11 World Trade Center tragedy. I have a one year older

brother Art (more later). He is a New York and New Jersey attorney. He passed the bar exams and practices in both States. He was to deliver a deposition, or some such lawyer thing to a New York City court the morning of 9/11. He comes in from New Jersey, and has to take the PATH trains with the station down in the World Trade Center buildings. He got a last-minute phone call of postponement that morning, just before he was leaving his place in New Jersey.

Surprisingly, Japan-Based Tokyo Tommy got Pretty Close to the 9/11 World Trade Center Building's Ground Zero. I almost lost My Big Brother Art in the Basement. The USA ended up reacting exactly How Osama bin Laden Hoped We Would. We Need Cool Rational Heads even if Heads Roll, and Pilots are Burned Alive.

42. Otherwise my big brother Art would have been in the World Trade Center when the buildings collapsed. No more big brother. Even if Artie was killed under the collapsing World Trade Center Building, I know he and I would not have a brain explosion and allow lots of American soldiers and Afghan Taliban and civilians to die over primarily a bunch of Saudi Arabian rich kids with box cutters. I got my white *gaijin* butt on a plane soon after the 9/11/2001 World Trade Center tragedy. His office was in 221 Broadway, near the Woolworth Building, and St. Pauls Chapel. His windows faced and overlooked the World Trade Center Ground Zero. The building landlord would not allow him to use his office for some time. When I visited his New York office, I think the first day he also saw it, some windows were blown out, and dust and papers were everywhere.

43. I knew it was dumb, dumb, and dumber to send a full army into Afghanistan. And if clueless Tokyo Tommy knew that, why so many nutty fruitcakes? It was too early for Thanksgiving. On August 5, 2014, 14 years after we invaded Afghanistan on October 7, 2001, the highest ranking US military officer since 1970 during the Vietnam War, was killed by one of his own local Afghan soldiers within the army base—Major General Harold J. Greene. By the same infiltrated 'ally' and properly uniformed gunman, a German Brigadier General and two Afghan Generals were also wounded in that same incident. According to this August 6, 2014 Associated Press 'Afghan soldier kills US general, wounds about 15' article from the *Daily Mail Online*, 'Insider attacks rose sharply in 2012, with more than 60 coalition troops!—mostly Americans— killed in 40 plus attacks that threaten to shatter the trust between Afghan and allied forces.' Dah… We should not have gone into Afghanistan, and it does no good to stay there.

44. What was killing me right from the beginning after 9/11, was that we did exactly what Osama bin Laden and his boys hoped we would do. Kill, wound ourselves, and bleed our treasury to death (4 to 6 trillion dollars)— tens of thousands of our troops and many times more civilians. A Fox anchorwoman I like—doesn't matter who because the statement could come from many of us, questioned, "Would the beheading of an American woman (by ISIL) get Obama to put American boots on the ground?" Answer from the on-air expert: "I certainly hope so." That is what ISIL wants! I hope Jordan doesn't expire, and bite the dust over the horrible burning alive of their pilot. But, clearly problems within countries are better handled by people of those countries. They share

more in common in terms of religious beliefs, culture, knowledge of local customs and languages. Long periods with occupying foreign soldiers and administrations have a poor record of success.

45. From 1768, with two years of British troop presence, today's Tea Party leaders know how much we hated British boots on the ground in Boston. Recall March 5, 1770: snowballs, insults, and other objects thrown at the British sentries in front of the Old State House in Boston. The building is still there on State Street. This was the seat of British colonial government from 1713 to 1776. In this infamous Boston Massacre, 9 British soldiers were greatly pressured by a mob of 300 or 400. After a first single panicked shot, a couple of the British Redcoats got clubbed by an American patriot. Then the Brits finally fired and killed 5 and wounded 6 Boston colonial Americans. This was a big contributor toward our War of Independence against Britain. Later it was enough to turn us into 'terrorists' in the eyes of the British Redcoat soldiers and Britain's King George III.

46. Careful and measured responses are what we need. And President Jimmy Carter's babblings about human rights always irritated the hell out of me. Bush Jr.'s spreading democracy, and our liberties and free way of life—"they hate us because of our freedoms". Hello? No. They hate us because we have military bases in their region, and, with the best of our intentions, our brave soldiers cluelessly have to stumble around their villages knocking down doors. Our true and straight-as-an-arrow soldiers are assigned to look for a 40-year-old male insurgent with a beard and an ethnic hat named Mohammed. Hello (again)? So 10 middle-aged guys with beards get pulled out of their houses. They hate that we have the air superiority and can bomb or drone

attack them at will. They are powerless to stop that. And now extra hate, rape, violence, murder and plunder is methodically drummed up by ISIL/Islamic State of Iraq and Levant, and its growing international membership and affiliated groups. Wouldn't people hate us because we are primarily the ones who upset that apple cart?

47. How would we feel about foreign soldiers amongst us, or the helplessness of being bombed at will by a foreign power? Human rights, democracy, freedom... Whose standards? In what situation, and with what mind-set, culture, history, religion, historic feuds, levels of violence, and bad blood are we dealing? Clearly strong leaders, even if dictatorial, were needed in these and other countries. They need to work it out themselves, or within their own region. Time for the USA to step back. If we step back, probably Russia and China will relax. What are we so afraid of? It is alright to let other countries like China or Russia lead, and/or get themselves in trouble, if they also overstep. Look what happened to the Soviet Union in Afghanistan from 1979 to 1989—10 long years which helped break up the Soviet Union. We're smarter. We can fight on in Afghanistan for 15 years, and still at it! Time to till our own garden, rather than choke on our own ribs.

We, the USA Boston Tea Partiers, and other Patriotic, Colonial Americans, had Zero Tolerance for Foreign, British Boots on the Ground. Even though We Shared the Same Language, Culture, Prayers, Christmas and Easter Celebrations. Time to Till Our Own Garden, Rather than Choke on Our Own Ribs.

48. One of the perhaps minor, but expressed justifications for taking us all to war in Iraq: "After all, this is the guy (Saddam) who tried to kill my dad," said Mr. George Bush Jr. during a campaign speech in September, 2002 (Jim Lobe, International Press Service, Washington October 18, 2004). Oh, that's just great... So we all went off to war for that? And both Messrs. Cheney and Bush had only daughters. No need for their sons to Rambo-up and go off to volunteer to fight in their daddys' wars. All 3 of us fathers were afraid, and did not want to fight in Vietnam.

49. Very different from U.K.'s Prince Harry who had the guts, the honor, and the sense of duty to be on the frontline in Afghanistan as a forward air controller calling in airstrikes. And he flew attack helicopters there from 2012 to 2013. Now he will support the rehabilitation of wounded service personnel. I believe, a leader of that caliber, who has the valor and braveheart to be there, is less likely to take us there in the future. And such a leader does not need to flex his or her Commander-in-Chief muscle. "Who do you want [in the White House] answering the [red, hotline] phone [in an emergency late at night]?" (This was a stupid Presidential campaign slogan from one of our largely useless, pandering political party's TV campaign advertisements—don't even want to know which one.) Our answer: someone who will not raise hell in other people's countries, fritter away our soldiers, our money, our good-will capital, and our international standing.

50. Instead of young Prince Harry risking his life, we have old, powerful men sending National Guard Reservists into wars of choice. That was not in the army reservists' life plan. I repeat. I guess we need a draft again. So the majority of Americans are touched by the pain and suffering

of wars. According to www.chartsbin.com 'Military Conscription (Draft) Policy by Country', there are 64 countries with conscription or a draft on all continents except Australia. In alphabetical order a few of these countries are Austria, Bermuda, Bolivia, Brazil, Cambodia, Columbia, Cuba, Denmark, Egypt, Finland, Georgia, Greece, Iran, Laos, Mexico, Mongolia, Norway, Paraguay, Russia, Singapore, Switzerland, Taiwan, Thailand, Turkey, Ukraine, Venezuela, Zambia, and many other African, and former Soviet Union break-off countries. With a draft, unnecessary wars of choice or conflicts embarked on for the political or business interests of the few, would be less tolerated by the rest of us. Or we could go back to the way we were and take away the President's, or Executive Branch's power to deploy troops, let alone wage war.

51. These were not wars that had a clear end game. I still can't figure out who drugged Mr. Anthony Charles Lynton Blair. He sounded intelligent. Unfortunately it gave credibility to the whole rollicking caper. Unlike World War II's Hitler and Tojo, there was absolutely no tangible threat to the USA as a nation, perpetrated by powerful nations such as Germany and Japan, with all their economic and military might. So there is no logic, no reason, and no nation to invade. It's been the most deadly form of big government tax spend. In the end it was a special ops, operation that took out Osama bin Laden 10 years too late. CIA, FBI, NSA—police work, not nation destroying, rebuilding, cutting, running, and leaving in ruins. George Jr., 'compassionate conservative'?—my ass. Conservative comes from conserving or conservation of water, resources, or energy. Synonyms are to save, keep, preserve, act in moderation, and cut back. Opposites are to spend, waste, and squander. George Jr. is the most radical,

liberal spending, risk-taking and squandering-on-a dumb-cause-President we have ever had.

52. No Afghans, and no Iraqis among the World Trade Center and Pentagon 9/11/2001 attackers—15 Saudis, 2 UAE, 1 Egyptian and 1 Lebanese. National Guard school teachers, factory engineers, so many had to go off and never come back. And so many people in those countries have suffered so much. It's funny. I was always very impressed with Mr. Dick Cheney—the content and the way he spoke, and the manner in which he handled himself. For example, in a 1994 C-Span interview, he outlined so clearly and cogently why continuing and taking out Saddam Hussein in the first Gulf War would have been disastrous (see YouTube 1:14 '1994 Clip of a C-Span Interview with Dick Cheney'). Mr. Cheney displayed a total grasp of the issues and players in Iraq and the region, and why removing Saddam would lead to civil war, and chaos. I certainly hope his Halliburton gig was not his primary motivator for the change in thinking. I trust not. But he's not senile. A real mystery.

53. As mentioned above, I believe in October 2013, Mr. Bill O'Reilly on his Fox News *O'Reilly Factor* TV show really grilled Mr. Cheney in the context of what a waste of a trillion dollars, and loss of life to US military and their families, not to mention a messed-up region (YouTube 8:12 Bill O'Reilly Grills Dick Cheney on Iraq "What Did We Get Out of it"'). All the statistics of the dead and injured, and the financial costs were up on Mr. O'Reilly's program's board. Mr. O'Reilly's refrain was, paraphrased, "What did we get out of this mess in Afghanistan and Iraq?" Mr. Cheney was definitely more impressive at the 1994 C-Span interview when he believed in his argument against the interviewer confronting Mr. Cheney about why Saddam was left in place. With people like Richard Perle and George Jr., who

didn't know the difference between a Shia and a Sunni (nor did I on 9/11/2001, but Mr. Cheney did), in the mix, maybe smart people can be led to make big mistakes.

54. A December 9 2009 article in *Time* magazine by Vivienne Walt, "U. S. Companies Shut Out as Iraq Auctions its Oil Fields" or a June 2, 2013 article in the the *New York Times* by Tim Arango and Clifford Krauss, "China is Reaping Biggest Benefits of Iraq Oil Boom", well document that it ended up that the USA didn't get the oil. If that was a reason for getting into this quagmire. So no WMD/Weapons of Mass Destruction, no oil: just lies, and changed lies in the above video clips. Later on a brazen admission from George Jr. on TV that there was no connection between Iraq and Al Qaeda. Unavoidable, because the lack of connection had been proven even before 9/11. Changes in story: "We never said there was a connection between Saddam and Al Qaeda".

55. I am convinced The Bush Jr. administration was pretty sure there were no Weapons of Mass Destruction. That is why they rushed the Iraq invasion, although the weapon's inspectors pleaded for only a few more weeks to completely finish their job. So many Bush Jr. statements were fabrications, and could only be based on nothing. In a Cincinnati, Ohio Speech, October 7, 2002, Bush Jr. said, 'We know that the regime has produced thousands of tons of chemical agents, including mustard gas, sarin nerve gas, VX nerve gas.' Bush went on, 'We've also discovered through intelligence that Iraq has a growing fleet of manned and unmanned aerial vehicles that could be used to disperse chemical or biological weapons across broad areas. We're concerned that Iraq is exploring ways of using these UAV's for missions targeting the United States.' Bad, bad, bad, bad. Very bad, Mr. Bush.

56. In the January 28 2003 State of the Union Address Bush Jr. told us, "Our intelligence officials estimate that Saddam Hussein had the materials to produce as much as 500 tons of sarin, mustard and VX nerve agent." Two days before 'Shock and Awe' bombing started, in Jr.'s Address to the Nation on March 17, 2003, the man we elected president twice said, "Intelligence gathered by this and other governments leaves no doubt that the Iraq regime continues to possess and conceal some of the most lethal weapons ever devised." Could these possibly be intelligence failings? Or were we made fools of in a child's childish game?

57. In the Wikipedia entry on the 'Big Lie', there is a passage from Chapter 10 of James Murphy's translation of Hitler's *Mein Kampf*. Hitler coined the term 'big lie' as he dictated this 1925 book to his assistant Rudolf Hess while Hitler was imprisoned. I'm sure Bush Jr. and Cheney never read it, nor did I read any part of Mein Kampf until today. In summary, it is the use of a lie so 'colossal' that no one would believe that someone 'could have the impudence to distort the truth so infamously'.

58. In more detail: '... *All this was inspired by the principle—which is quite true within itself—that in the **big lie** there is always a certain force of credibility; because the broad masses of a nation are always more easily corrupted in the deeper strata of their emotional nature than consciously or voluntarily; and thus in the primitive simplicity of their minds they more readily fall victims to the **big lie** than the small lie, since they themselves often tell small lies in little matters, but would be ashamed to resort to large-scale falsehoods. It would never come into their heads to fabricate colossal untruths, and they would not believe that others could have the impudence to distort the truth so infamously. Even though the facts which prove this to be so may be brought clearly to their minds, they will still doubt and waver and*

will continue to think that there may be some other explanation. For the grossly impudent lie always leaves traces behind it, even after it has been nailed down, a fact which is known to all expert liars in this world and to all who conspire together in the art of lying.'

Adolf Hitler, *Mein Kampf,* vol. 1. ch. X

Fly Infested European Hippie's Head on a Spike.
"Afghan Girl, No!"

59. Mr. Dick Cheney for much of his long career served his country well with honor and distinction. I'm hoping Mr. Cheney leaves this world with a cleaner finish, and can be more favorably remembered by a larger number of American people and people in other nations. Mr. Obama's troop build-up in Afghanistan, also No. Sorry. It will not work. Some things in our lives we can't control, and should not venture to try and control. And President Barack, can we please cool it with the drones? Someday they could be used against us.

60. I took a long, slow drive across Eurasia, from London to Katmandu, and up and down Afghanistan (and Iran, and Turkey, but not Iraq) when I was 20. Roger Bason, a good friend, and living on Twin Lakes Road between Lakes Oscaleta and Rippowam (connected by channels to Lake Waccabuc—later) was the AFS/American Field Service Representative from John Jay High School in my one-year-older brother Art's class. Roger Bason chose or drew the Afghanistan straw for either the summer, or maybe even a full year. He ended up with perennial amebic dysentery. I was luckier. I only got sick once on a 7 or 8-month drive and trip from London to Tokyo. At a British Petroleum

camp in Turkey, I opened a can of Dinty Moore beef stew, and ate it raw from the can without cooking it. I had eaten it cooked about 100 times as a Boy Scout. So it's not Mr. Moore or Mr. George A. Homel's fault.

61. I'm sure Roger Bason knew, and I know I knew (a Rumsfeld 'known known') Afghanistan would never work. When I was walking in a village, I saw a young, decaying, fly-infested European traveler who looked like a guy I met earlier—probably in Turkey. This time his head was on a pike—just for I suppose hitting on a local Afghan girl— John Lennon glasses still on his nose. When I turned a shade of green, a passerby said, "Afghan girl, No". History talks. And seeing that would keep even Playboy Enterprises Hugh Hefner celibate, at least when he traveled. Actually, our 5-storey building would make a pretty good Far East Playboy Mansion with a Playboy Enterprises Japan/Asian Regional office. Marilyn Monroe was Playboy magazine's first cover girl and center fold in Playboy's first October 1, 1953 edition. Two years and 9 months later, Ms. Monroe married Arthur Miller in Waccabuc—later. Actually, I did remain a virtual virgin for the rest of my travels and then some. One of my sons called me from the States on the night of the 9/11/2001 World Trade Center tragedy. He said, "Dad this means war. I sure as hell hope I don't get drafted." He was 20 years old. I laughed, and said, "Johnny, who is there to fight? It wasn't a country." Johnny's answer. "Dad, you've been out of this country too long. We'll find someone to fight."

Dusty Moffman Still Dreaming it Might have Been Mrs. Robinson.

62. On a lighter note, Mr. Roger Stone, the Republican Party self-admitted "hit man", brought me to his house a couple times. Roger talks and writes about his working-class roots. I would say between Rogers's fitness club work outs and clubbing, and strategic political work, he works pretty hard himself. When visiting his house, I remember being introduced to his mom, who I thought must be his big sister. She was in a very skimpy bikini sunning herself next to their pool. And this was no rubber-duck, temporarily erected plastic-lined pool. It was a fine pool indeed. His Mom had the kind of tan that Roger always sported later on in life. I was in my swimsuit, so yeah, it was definitely a nice pool. I'm not sure if Roger was standing with me. If he was, it's probably the day he decided to become a body builder. His mom said, "Tom, you have such a muscular back and strong shoulders." As many of my Swiss clients used to say, that made me feel "not too bad" (an understated Swiss expression for very good). In fact, my hand had to cover my—forget it... this bible is not that unholy.

63. Not that many women have said that to me—like just two other ladies. 'I like big men'. I get that a lot. Unfortunately, they are talking about my muscles. It would be another 10 or 15 years before I would have returned anything except, "Thank you, mam". But I will admit, I have seen a vision not a few times in my REM/Rapid-Eye-Movement sleep, my slow eye movement sleep, or just about any old time at all. Mrs. Stone is Mrs. Robinson. I'm Dustin Hoffman. Except Dustin's on steroids and has not graduated yet. Not even from high school. So the well-digging Mr. Stone was quite well off, and did quite well for himself when he first dug up and took out that (Mrs.) stone.

64. In Jeffrey Toobin's *New Yorker* article it is written that Roger had 4 Jaguars. I have 4 overcoats, including an old

tweed London Fog with a "Made in the USA" label—before Nixon and Kissinger went to China. One of Roger's Jags was driven by a chauffeur that day. Roger took Mr. Toobin somewhere. So Roger can afford to buy a few copies of this book, give it out to his friends and enemies, and have a chuckle. Not that snarl Jeffrey talks about in the last paragraph of his *New Yorker* article. Anything about Mr. Stone involves his amazing wardrobe—"200" double-pleated and cuffed trousers with, of course, a matching suit jacket! I should mention that even in elementary school, he was the only kid in our school district, who wore at least a dress jacket and tie EVERYDAY. Almost always double-breasted jackets. Sometimes full double-breasted business suits when he was 3 feet tall. Working class; my… what rhymes with class? — My donkey's hindquarters.

65. Lake Waccabuc is in the county above the northernmost Bronx borough of New York City. Above the Bronx you had White Plains (where we went once a year to do Christmas shopping—mostly at low-end Alexander's, maybe a little higher end sometimes too), then Mount Kisco, then nearby Katonah, and Bedford Village. Ridgefield, Connecticut was the nearest town, about 5 miles away. There was a movie theatre in Ridgefield and Bedford, not in Katonah. We went to Catholic Church every Sunday in all 3 villages. The Japanese expats who, like my Dad, mostly worked out of Manhattan, are more familiar with the houses or apartments their companies rented for them in Bronxville, Tuckahoe, and Scarsdale etc. For some reason, it was our joshiki/ common sense that there were lots of these Japanese expats across the George Washington Bridge in Fort Lee, New Jersey. At least that was often told to me out here in Japan. Surely not presidential hopeful New Jersey Governor Chris Christie, but an overzealous sub or two messed up these

poor Japanese expat's commute into and out of Manhattan (September 9 to 13, 2014 traffic lane closure 'scandal' as political revenge). For those commuters who were looking at or coming from the George Washington Bridge those days, it took hours. 'So close, yet so far away...' (Elvis Presley)

Spearing Frogs, and Eating Skunk Cabbage to Survive
in the New Hampshire White Mountains.
Before Soaring with the Eagles.

66. My dad made me stay in the Boy Scouts, "instead of hang out at the John Jay H.S. gym at the Friday night basketball games". The Friday night scout meetings were in the Lewisboro Elementary School gym. When my dad was no longer worried about that, I made my own decision to stick at Boy Scouting even through my senior year. The Assistant Scoutmaster, Mr. Dick Attridge, would only be Scoutmaster if I stuck at it: "Tom, if you don't come back this year, all the older guys will quit, and I don't want to be a baby sitter." We agreed to do it together. Just the two of us on Mr. Attridge's back lawn. We shook hands over his backyard barbecue. I went on and got 16 Merit Badges in about 5 months so that I could get the rank of Eagle. (In Japan Kiku or Chrysanthemum scout and then if on to Venture Scouts, "Fuji" scout.) We were the #1 troop that year at the Camporee in our Muscoot district—15 troops. It took discipline and perseverance. It made its own contribution to me and a bunch of the other kids for sure.

67. Maybe 2 or 3 summers before this, 4 scouts, Richard Hawthorne (later) my older brother Art, Roger Miller (who also lived on Twin Lakes Road between Oscaleta

and Lake Rippowam), and I, went on a fairly challenging adventure. I was the youngest. It was a one-week survival hike in the Presidential Range of the White Mountains of New Hampshire. My dad drove us one way. And Mr. Dick Reilly (below), our incredible Scoutmaster drove us the other way. Not sure which was which. The Presidential Mountain Range is in New England in the state of New Hampshire. The same State where the USA Presidential primary election always kicks off. New Hampshire is the 42nd least populated state in the USA. It has 1,326,813 people according to the 2014 census estimate. For Japanese people or any USA person, it might be interesting to know that California has a higher population than the population of the 21 least-populated States combined.

68. But the California situation is not as extreme as the greater Tokyo area with arguably 35,000,000 to 40,000,000 people. According to a February 7, 2015 *Japan Times* article, for the 19th year in a row, the greater Tokyo population increased. In 2014 the inflow over the outflow of population was 109,408 people. So Tokyo is sucking population away from the rest of the country. Let's say that the greater Tokyo area has about the same number as California's 38,802,500 people. Japan's total population is 127,220,000 people. Looks like Japan's population is down 0.7% from 2012 or 2010. So the greater Tokyo area would be 30.5% of Japan's population. Yet the greater New York City metropolitan area would be about 4,000 sq. kilometers /2,500 sq. miles larger than the extended Tokyo area. God, I wish the old US of A would swing over to metric! What on earth are we thinking, or not thinking☺!? It really does make us look a bit strange. Certainly impresses no one. It puts us in the rarified atmosphere with only Liberia and Burma. ALL other countries are on metric!

69. Okay. We are back to survival camping in the Presidential Range of the White Mountains. There are 8 peaks in the Presidential Range. Our goal was to climb the ones that go off in the same direction and are a bit closer together, Mounts Washington, Clay, Jefferson, Adams, and Madison. East of the Mississippi River, there are only 7 mountains higher than Mount Washington. All of them are in the Smoky or Blue Ridge mountains in Tennessee or North Carolina. Mount Washington is the highest mountain in New England at 6,288 feet or 1,917 meters. Mount Fuji is almost twice as high, and gradually comes up from sea level. It is 3,776 meters, 12,388 feet, and stands all by itself. That's why it is such a sight. Fuji-san is the highest mountain in Japan. The next highest is Mount Kita in Yamanashi where the stars were so beautiful at our country house on the Dusk till Dawn New Year's Eve road trip (later). Mount Kita is 3,193 meters/10,476 feet, so it is 583 meters/1,913 feet shorter than Mount Fuji.

70. Japan is a country famous for its mountains, but things are relative. I guess it is a matter of scale, and scales can be so different. In the world there are 472 mountains taller than Mount Fuji, according to Wikipedia and www.scaruffi. com/travel/tallest.html, and after processing and playing around with the data. A lot of us think of the European Alps when mountains come to mind. But starting with Mount Everest at 8,848 meters/29,029 feet, mostly in that region of the world, all of the next 56 highest mountains are in Asia! These tallest 56 are surprisingly mostly in northern Pakistan, and more commonly in our thoughts—Nepal. They are also in northern India, China, Tibet, Tajikistan, and with 1 each in Bhutan, Afghanistan, Kyrgyzstan, 1 straddling China/Kyrgyzstan, and 1 on the border of Bhutan/Tibet.

71. Then South America, with its tallest Aconcagua peak in Argentina dominates mountain rankings along with central continental Asia. These gargantuan South American mountains are on the southern tip and all along the west coast of South America. So located in Argentina, Chile, Peru, and Bolivia with just one very high peak in Ecuador, and some fairly high mountains in Columbia too. But not in the central and east part of South America in countries like Brazil. The highest 104 mountains are all in Asia, and South America. Next Mount McKinley in Alaska comes in at 105th with 6,194 meters/20,322 feet. But then it is Asia and South America again. And actually all but one mountain from #106 up until the rank of #123 are in South America.

Everyone knows that the Central Asian Himalayan Mountains are Monsters. But Between the 76th Highest Mountain and the 182nd Highest Mountain, Only 18 are Not in South America.

72. Except for those monster central Asian Himalayan Mountains, South America totally dominates from the 76th highest mountain at 6,550 meter/21,490 feet to the 182nd highest mountain at 5,215 meters/17,110 feet. Out of that ranked list of 106 (182-76) mountains, between the 76th and the 182nd tallest mountains, only 18 are not in South America. They are in Asia and mostly the same Himalayan region, with 7 peaks in North America, 1 in Africa and 1 in Europe. The African mountain is Kilimanjaro in Tanzania ranked #124 at 5,895 meters/19,341 feet. As everyone knows it looks a bit like Fuji-san, because a big old volcano blew up in the middle of nowhere. Kilimanjaro

is the highest free-standing mountain in the world. If we are going to talk about free-standing mountains, and if we count what is below sea level, Mauna Kea on the 'Big Island' of Hawaii claims the jackpot. It is almost 1 mile taller than Mount Everest. Mauna Kea is 13,796 feet/4,205 meters above sea level, but from the ocean floor this inactive volcano has 19,700 feet 6,000 meters underwater.

73. So as a free-standing mountain Mauna Kea is 33,500 feet/10,120 meters in height. Because it is in the middle of the Pacific, and at night the island residents are kept at a respectful distance, and have to dim their lights or have them aimed toward the ground, there are 13 telescopes from several nations including Japan, on this mountain— even better than our Yamanashi country house to view the stars (later). And you can ski and snowboard around the telescopes during the day (www.livescience.com/32594-which-mountain-is-the-tallest-in-the-world.html)! The tallest European mountain is Elbrus in Russia, ranked #153 at 5,633 meters/18,481 feet. The highest mountain in North America after Mount McKinley in Alaska is Mount Logan in Canada, ranked #125 and just behind Kilimanjaro in Africa. There are 33 South American mountains higher than Mount McKinley. Out of the top 200 highest mountains, all are in Asia, mostly the Himalayans, and in South America, except for 8 in North America, 6 in Africa, and 3 in Europe.

74. To get back to our beloved Mount Fuji, out of the 472 mountains taller than Fuji-san the really tall ones are basically in that central Asian region, or in South America. But at lower altitudes there are 151 mountains in the USA taller than Fuji-san; 53 in Europe; 27 in Canada, mostly in Yukon, with some in British Columbia, and some shared with Alaska (Mount Malaspina in Yukon is exactly the same

height as Fuji-san); 26 in Africa, and 11 in Oceania (mostly Papua New Guinea, Indonesia, Malaysia) and Antarctica. The USA, especially Colorado, has a lot of medium size mountains not too much taller than Mount Fuji. I didn't realize the USA had 5.6 times more mountains over Fuji-san's height than Canada has, even though we also hear a lot about the Canadian Rockies and Banff National Park etc.

75. I'm starting to get as interested in the World's mountains as I am in lakes (later)☺. It's stuff I did not know much about, even though this is the only precious planet I/ we have. To give a little more perspective on a sampling of who's got the mountains of what height… India and Nepal share the #3 mountain, Kangchenjunga at 8,586 meters, India's second tallest is #18 Nanda Devi 7,816 meters, and third highest in India is #23 Kamet 7,756 meters. China's highest mountain shared with Nepal is Xixabangma Feng (Gosainthan) at #14, China's second highest is #25 Muztagh 7,723, and third highest is #27 Muztagh Ata 7,546 meters.

76. I never realized it, but Mexico has some big peaks. Citlaltepetl (el Pico de Orizaba) is #138 at 5,754 meters, second tallest in Mexico is #165 Popocatepetl 5,452 meters, and the third-highest summit is #177 Ixaccihuatl 5,286 meters. Even though I crisscrossed, and upped and downed Iran by slow-moving truck, I forgot Iran had #150 Damavand at 5,671 meters, #212 Alum Kuh 4,840, and Iran's third highest (a close third!) #213 Sabalon Kuh at 4,821 meters. Recall Fuji-san is ranked #472 at 3,776 meters, and the only Japanese peak on this list of the 555 tallest mountains. Then other than the #153 ranked Ibrus in Russian at 5,633 meters, finally Europe enters the scene, but it is not the Swiss yodeling and cow bells yet.

77. It is Georgia—not 150 meters from my desktop PC, Coca Cola (head office under reconstruction) 'Georgia' brand coffee, but the Georgia that used to be part of the Soviet Union. (In Japan, for years the Coke Japan subsidiary always made more money/profit from a 'Georgia Coffee' brand than from their regular and diet Coke brands.) Georgia has the second to fourth highest summits in Europe!—#183 Ruswtaveli at 5,201 meters, #188 Dykh-Tau at 5,198, and #201 Kazbek at 5,047 meters—pretty close together in size. Maybe brothers and sisters ranging from the same family. Then let's take a look at Turkey—a beautiful country I drove across, and visited more recently. Mount Ararat (Buyukagri Dagi) where Noah's Ark crash-landed or docked☺—maybe so. Ranked #191 in the world at 5,165 meters, then moving down to #262 Suphan Dagi 4,434 meters, and number 3 for Turkey, #375 Gelyasm (Resko) 4,136; and still looking down on Fuji-san.

The European Alps, and Canadian Rockies are Comparatively Peanut-Sized Mountains. There are 472 Mountains on the Planet that are higher than Mount Fuji. There are 204 in Central Asia and South America, 151 in the USA, 53 in Europe, Only 27 in Canada, 26 in Africa, and 11 in Oceania.

78. Now to Secretary of Defense, Mr. Donald Rumsfeld's 'Old Europe', France and Italy's Monte Bianco, or Mount Blanc is the tallest at rank #214 and 4,807 meters. Actually Italy straddles or shares the largest number of tallest mountains in Europe. A surprise to me even though I have been there many times. Next in Italy there is #230 Monte Rosa shared with Switzerland at 4,634 meters, than Dom

also shared with Switzerland at 4,545 meters, and another shared mountain between Italy and Switzerland, #551 Cervino (The Matterhorn) at 4,478 meters. Before this at #247 is the Weisshorn which Switzerland has all to itself. Switzerland and Italy also share #283 Dente Blanche 4,357, and #303 Nadelhorn, with a smaller horn than The Matterhorn at 4,327 meters.

79. I knew Italy for pasta, pizza, wine, Naples handmade Christmas mangers, Venetian masks, shoes, leather fashion, all kinds of fashion, and for the gentle purr of my Ferrari, Lamborghini, and Maserati parked down in my garage—not. And the mountains are also amazing. Italy and Swiss also share #314 Grand Combin 4,314, #323 Lenspitze 4,294, and Italy has a chunk of Jorasses ranked #366 and 4,208. France has #383 Pic Lori 4,102 meters, #424 La Meije 3,983, and #455 La Grande Casse located only on French territory. But these mountains are getting less La Grande, but still a bit higher than our bewitching 6 or 7 month snow-capped Mount Fuji. Austria's tallest two summits are shorter than Fuji-san—#473 Wildspitze; I hope it's not the way it sounds, spitting wildly into the wind up there. Again Italy shares with Austrian #489 Weisskugel 3,739 meters. But Austria has to itself #508 Grossvenediger 3,674 meters, probably meaning something less gross and more beautiful in High German.

80. Taiwan is another big surprise to me, even though I thoroughly hitchhiked it in 1970. There is a mountain higher that Fuji-san, Yu Shan (Jade Mountain) coming in at #433, with 3,952 meters of jade. With Taiwan and the China-sphere's love for jade, and great economic success, this mountain is probably getting whittled down shorter every year. May not show up on a Google satellite by the

time the Tokyo Olympics are underway in 2020. Taiwan also has #488 Lam Whoa Shan 3,740 meters, and #498 Jong Yong Gien Shan at 3,703 meters. I think I was served a slice of that in Yokohama Chinatown last month. For a change of scene there is #477 Mount Cook in New Zealand 3,764, and just 12 meters shorter than Mount Fuji. I once had lamb at a restaurant kind of like on the side of that snow capped mountain. Not as tasty as Chinese, but it was a good-sized rack of lamb.

81. Canary Islands' Teide at #494 and 3,718 meters impressively pops up out of the ocean. And let's mention Denmark, but must be in Greenland Gunnbjorn Fjeld at #501 and 3,694 meters. Did you notice among these highest 555 mountains there are none from countries like Germany, Spain (except for Teide in the Canary Islands), Portugal, Korea, Iceland, Sweden, Norway, Finland, Hungry, Czech Republic, Romania (even with its Transylvanian vampires and werewolves), and the countries that were part of the old Yugoslavia I drove through when I was 20 years old. Anyway, a bit surprising to me. But then again Japan has many beautiful snow-capped mountains, but only Fuji-san makes this list of the top 555 mountains all over 3,500 meters/11,483 feet.

82. Compared to these mountains, the White Mountain, Presidential Range, is big stuff east of the USA Rocky Mountains, but they are hills to the world mountain climbers and adventurers. Coincidently, the highest peak in Australia is almost exactly the same height as Mount Washington— again, the highest mountain in New Hampshire—on the east coast up in New England. Bimberi Peak in Australia is 1,913 meters/6,276 feet— just 4 meters shorter than Mount Washington. In New England by ranking in terms of altitude, next come Adams, Jefferson, Monroe, and Madison—all

over 5,000 feet (1,524 meters). Mt. Washington long held the record for the highest wind speed recorded on the surface of the Earth. This was 231 miles per hour, or 372 km/h. This is about 50 kilometers per hour faster than the top speed of today's Japanese Shinkansen/bullet train. Back to the Boy Scouts…

83. Our challenge on this trip was to drink and eat off the land. Never stay in any lodges or cabins, and not buy any food. All we brought with us was some homemade 'trail mix' of nuts, dried fruit and some chocolate. All broken up and mixed together. But we were not to eat it. We also had some bags of horrible dry food. Add water, and voila!—total yucky-ness. We didn't eat that crap either. So mostly thanks to Richard Hawthorne, who was Mr. Stanley Grierson, our school and local naturalist protégé, we lost some weight. But we had a ball. Richard was the enforcer. None of those goodies we brought could be eaten. Richard knew which snakes, frogs, mushrooms, plants, and berries we could eat. The ones that were not poisonous! In the low-lying, swampy areas between the mountain peaks, there was lots of skunk cabbage. Smelly. But not like getting targeted and sprayed in the face by a skunk's butt about a meter away. We also brought salt and pepper. We didn't know about 'Jane's Krazy Salt' in those days. I wonder if Richie knew his great, great, great grandfather Nathaniel Hawthorne died in Plymouth, New Hampshire, while climbing and touring these same White Mountains (more on that later).

Don't think! Feeeel!…It's Like a Finger Pointing the Way to the Moon…" Bruce Lee.

84. We didn't bring bows and arrows; Too bulky and there were local hunting and hiking ordinances. But we were all good at making spears for fishing, frogging, and crawfishing in the shallow crystal clear brooks, swamps, and ponds. I had sometimes brought down birds in flight with rocks, even when I was much younger. Felt really bad the first time when I was about 7 years old, because I was about to go home to a nice dinner. That little birdie should have been able to fly home too. Actually, I didn't think I would hit it. Didn't want to hit it. Although, I blurted out to my big brother with great bravado, "See that bird?" as I let fly my stone. We went out to look for the poor little bird. But the grass was high. The sun had set, along with the darkness. The key: 'emotional content, not anger... don't think! Feeeeel!! It's like a finger pointing the way to the moon. Don't concentrate on the finger, or you will miss all that heavenly glory'—Bruce Lee.

85. I know this because it's one of my wife's lines when I think too much. Chika is from Kobe. Her step-mom was part of one of those famous Takarazuka all female acting and dancing troups. I'm not sure if her Mom was male or female—specialized in male or female roles. The Takarazuka troupe was founded in Kobe. So was my wife, Chika. But also in Tokyo, there are hundreds of girls and ladies lined-up outside and not far from the side entrance of the Imperial Hotel in the Hibiya/Ginza area. They wait there before and after the shows hoping to catch a glimpse of the Takarazuka stars going in and out of the theater. It's a weird Japan thing. More than an LGBT thing.

86. Back to Bruce Lee. I think this 'feeeel' thing applies to golfers, baseball pitchers, football quarterbacks, gymnasts, figure skaters, basketball, soccer and ice hockey penalty shooters—all such activities. I wish Tiger Woods would

look at some of the Dragon's YouTube clips. Tiger needs to get himself up and over his own psychological barriers, says the Gaijin Omotesando shrink. We have always been good with our Wham-o sling shots. Just like with a gun, it is a 'feeeel' thing. You don't have to line up the target with the weapon sight. There's usually no time. Shooting from the hip can work better. So the poor squirrels, rabbits, some birds were also on the menu. We did not bring matches, lighter fluid, and of course no charcoal. We were all good with our flints and steel. We would boil water, or use the Halazone water purification tablets we brought with us. We were all skilled with our compasses. From the top of the peak we were on, we simply took a bearing on the next nearest tall peak we had to climb. We climbed all our peaks. We got back on time to the pre-appointed rendezvous gasoline stand in the pre-appointed town— Probably Plymouth where *The Scarlett Letter* author died. Nathanial Hawthorne and Richard are dead ringers if you look at the elder's old daguerreotype photos. And we ate almost none of the trashy, cheesy rations we had brought along just in case of emergency.

87. One more not so quick Boy Scout story. We were once shot at by Hillbillie's. No they were not trying to hit us. Unless they were really drunk. So it was no *Deliverance* film situation, as in that Burt Reynolds and John Voight (Angelina Jolie's father) film that got 3 Oscar Academy Award Nominations, and 5 Golden Globe nominations. At our fraternity house we figured it was the most talked about and best film in 1972 when I graduated from Cornell. Mr. Reilly, our tough as nails, almost as strong as Arnold Schwarzenegger, unbelievably dedicated and energetic scoutmaster, picked out a handful of the tough scouts to go down to the Cacapon River in West Virginia,

some of the best whitewater canoeing or kayaking in the East. Depending on the water depth it gets pretty hairy. (I'll have to check the Japanese translation here☺.) In those days nobody wore helmets. Everybody knew you didn't sue each other. I'm not sure we even had life jackets. We all grew up swimming with the fish. There were a few howls, hoots, and a lot of buck shot hitting the tree limbs above us. The aluminum canoes enhanced the sound of the buck shot rainstorm. We figured the best thing to do was keep one hand on the paddle. A big smile. A big, "Howdy." Gave a big wave with the other hand. And then it was a 'Don't think! Feeeel' our way for the fast-pass water shoots, to get the hell out of there.

'Howdy', and Roadside Eye Contact Differed in Japan. To Keep Your Head, You kept it Safely Placed in the Dirt.

88. For our primarily Japanese and non-Japanese readers, I always understood that a commoner's eyes looking up at a Samurai could result in the commoner's death. And little recourse to the commoner, unless a drunken, psychotic Samurai pulled out his sword too often. Then Mito Komon, a true historical figure might come, or get someone to come to the rescue. Mito Komon was a kind and just vice shogun, and member of the ruling Tokugawa family during the Edo period (1603-1868). His full name was Mitsukuni Tokugawa (1628-1701). There were 15 Tokugawa shoguns and about half of them are buried at Kaneiji near Ueno station. We used to make money. My first wife had made, and then erected two huge 3-meter/10-foot tall cemetery grave stone monuments, one each for my two boys at Kaneiji—when they were maybe 11 and 8!—you figure. Their names have

already been carved in the huge grave monuments for over 25 years. Kaneiji Shrine is where the Shogun's forces held out after the Tokugawa Shogun had already surrendered Edo Castle. On July 4th, (USA Independence Day!) 1868 this last resistance in Tokyo fell to the Imperial forces led by Saigo Takamori, who at this point was fighting for the Emperor. There is a statue of Saigo with his dog in Ueno Park. A lot of people meet up there, before cherry blossom or museum viewing. (This doggie isn't related to Hachiko (later), but Japanese people like to meet in front of dogs and bells.)

89. Kaneiji temple, and about 1,000 houses in Ueno and Nezu burned down from the fire of 13 cannons from Hongo, which later would be the center of the University of Tokyo campus. Nine years later, on September 24, 1877 Saigo Takamori would fight against Imperial forces along with Tom Cruise as in the 2003 *Last Samurai* movie with Ken Watanabe modeled after Saigo Takamori (later). In 1629 the above Mito Komon had a house and garden built just behind Korakuen where there is the Tokyo Dome Stadium. I went to a Michael Jackson and Backstreet Boys concert there. Korakuen amusement park, and the Tokyo Dome Hotel are also located there. You can visit the Mito Komon property. It is called Koishikawa Korakuen Garden. It is a 5 to 10-minute walk from Iidabashi station which has 5 different train and subway lines. Very much in the center of town. The *Mito Komon* TV series went from 1969 to 2011. A slimmer, white goateed *Perry Mason* (USA TV drama 1957 to 1966) with a sword.

90. Bad or cranky Samurai—that's why commoners often went down on their knees with their heads down touching the soil. Especially if the swordsman had been in his sake. And, of course, commoners could not carry swords. In

contrast, in the States, Australia—Canada, I guess just about anywhere—let's say you are traveling on a road all by yourself in the middle of nowhere with no one around. If you got down on your knees, you'd be shot anyway, mistaken for having rabies, or maybe an Indian, with his ear to the ground listening for horses coming. So he gets shot too. So instead, from a long distance away, we give a big wave, a big smile, and a big, "howdy," to show we mean no harm. We're not going to steal your gold, your land claim, your wife, your shot gun, your beans, or... Not the Japanese style.

91. Now more on our amazing and stalwart scoutmaster. Mr. Dick Attridge's predecessor as our scoutmaster was this amazing Dartmouth football star graduate, Dick Reilly. Mr. Reilly was a house builder at first. He got me and my older brother off our own waterfront's dock and float on Lake Waccabuc to gladly start illegal work at 14 and 15, maybe even 13 and 14. Dad wondered why we gave up water skiing, sailing, snorkeling, rowing, canoeing, rod and spear fishing, motor boat tennis ball fights, and Castle Rock (check out the idiots jumping off the rock on YouTube) to sweat it out doing the grunge and site clean-up work at Dick Reilly's construction sites. Mr. Dick Reilly went on and pioneered paddle tennis court construction. He was inducted into the Hall of Fame at the Platform Tennis Museum. He helped spread paddle tennis across the world. He also invented and built the first aluminum paddle tennis court. Probably including those at the Waccabuc Country Club.

"Your Mother and I are going to Travel and Enjoy Our Life. You Screw-up, You're on Your Own."

92. My parents wanted us to enjoy the beautiful Lake Waccabuc, and not start working so young. They were the same parents who just a couple years later made it clear to us that if we blew it at Cornell, and Syracuse U. for my big sister (she graduated and Uncle Walt—Walter Cronkite—was the convocation speaker), it would be community college, and on our own for all of us. Even though we all had our own individual bedroom, with two more bedrooms to spare. It was also made clear that after college we were out of the nest, and would have to make it on our own. We could not live at home. "Your mother and I are going to travel and enjoy our life." That also had to be good for us. Kids having to, or wanting to work, or at least do a lot of chores at home from a very young age seems to determine so much later on in life. I think there is a big difference here in Japan, and in many families in Asia, most certainly so in Japan. Asian parents often do the push-ups, and pull-ups for their kids. They too often tolerate too much frivolous pursuit, and too much ne'er-do-well, feckless behavior. They do too much for their kids. They set their kids up for life with homes, or with living at home. So there are too many young "parasite singles"—already an old-fashioned term by now. Also because of the extra intensive cram schools/juku, and other reasons, fewer kids start at a young age in the workforce.

93. Much of my "Formative Years in the States" was added to my LinkedIn profile as of a few months ago. One thing that triggered it was a guy out here in Japan who I respect. He had Eagle Scout on his LinkedIn profile. Then I noticed one of the smartest kids and best athletes who went through my John Jay H.S., but a year younger, Kim Schappert, writes on LinkedIn about how he got two varsity letters at Harvard in baseball and football. He writes he was also a College World Series participant. One day I

recognized his picture on the front page of the *Japan Times* newspaper, the oldest newspaper in Japan and the paper that usually goes under the door of your hotel room here. The *Japan Times* published two of my books. At that time Kim was president and CEO of JP Morgan Investment Management. Later on, Kim was vice chairman and regional head of the American Asset Management of Credit Suisse. So I figured, yeah, maybe talking about formative years is okay.

94. So I also would like to thank my John Jay H.S. athletics coaches. The head of athletics, Mr. Marty Todd; my soccer coaches, Mr. Boissy, and Mr. Burcroff and Mr. Dave Cutler, the gymnastics coach. At that time, in my high school's history, by one or maybe two years, I was the youngest and only kid who made the "Gold Group" as a freshman. The names were prominently displayed over the entrance door to the gym. It was Head Coach's Marty Todd project. We had to go through all kinds of physical exercise tests. The one that challenged me was having to run the mile in I think 5 minutes and 20 seconds. Well, Coach Todd either helped me out, or I actually ran the mile in 5 minutes, and 19 (I think) seconds. And Mr. Todd was pushing me the whole way with the backwinds of his spirit. My senior year, Mr. Todd, and I guess our truly exceptional school principal, Mr. Robert Williams, put my name and bio in to Consolidated Edison (the monopolistic regional power company). I won their "Westchester Sports Award of the Week" for sporting and academic excellence. In, I think, 2007 I showed one of my sons my H.S. He was 26. It was summer. They let us roam around after checking me out in the '68 Yearbook. In the gym, I heard, "Dad, why the huck is your name here on the wall?" Thanks to Coach Todd, Coach Cutler, Principal Williams, and Con Ed there

were about 12 of us on the wall during the history of John Jay H.S. (opened 1956). The award was started in 1951. Kim Schappert must have been up there too.

95. I was walking with my family in Ward Pound Ridge Reservation one fateful day when I was in 5th grade, so 10 or 11 years old. This is the largest public park in Westchester County. One of the Leatherman's (later) favorite caves was here long before it became a public park in 1938. There was a number on a building. I think it was 57, but not sure. I could not read it. So off I was taken down to Sterling Optical in White Plains to get glasses. With each upgraded version of stronger lenses in my glasses, I could see the ripples on Lake Waccabuc from our dining room bay window, maybe 120 meters away as the bats fly (later). I could see the detailed texture of the bark on the Hemlock trees. But gradually not. Within a week certainly not. So what was happening? Immediately one's vision gets weaker instead of getting trained and strengthened. A hands down no-brainer. We all end up with Coke-bottle lenses. Over the years I would say that to our two-door-down lake-shore neighbors, the older Gullen brothers (later), to my parents, to my teachers, and to the optometrist. "No. It's because you're growing." Bull meadow muffins!

96. But I was always the misguided foolish boy. We all ended up with Coke-bottle eyes. Getting contacts sometime during my sophomore year slowed down the horrible, degrading, abasement of my poor eye balls, and the brain behind them. I did not want my boys to get glasses. Better to ask to sit upfront in the classroom. Even though they were told by the pros that they were needed. One of them firmly held the line. His eyes are still fine. Tommy, the older one, ended up being captain of a high school sports team at his boarding school. He was strong at soccer and

basketball. Chosen as the most athletic senior. Still no glasses for one boy to this day. Think about it: as my wife said the other day, "In the old days—middle ages, and much later—how many people had glasses and contact lenses?" Getting contact lenses instead of glasses as soon as possible helps stop the progression to stronger prescriptions. I've found placing very weak reading glasses over contact lenses also allows very old contact lens prescriptions to keep you seeing distances clearly for years. Wearing weak readers when reading even for younger older people who can still read okay without readers, is also probably helpful in preserving better eyesight—forever the consultant☺.

Junior High School Hoods should wear Belts on the Days They Get Water Boarded—Just Helping out 'Mighty Mouse'.

97. But I became a 'MA glasses', a 'four eyes'. Back in 5th grade a friend, Peter Crone said, "You won't be the same, old Nevins." And I was only 10 years old! Okay. Enter John Jay Jr. H.S. down the slope from the H.S. on the same huge lot. You're in 7th grade, still 12 or 13 years old. You are new to this campus. The boss of the hoods, with the taps on their heels and the slicked-up hair, calls you 'four eyes' just for having to take a pee. He trips you, knocking you down as you walk into the boy's room. All his friends from Katonah Elementary School, not our Lewisboro Elementary school, laugh loudly. A couple kids who knew me cleared their throats and stayed quiet. They are all puffing away on their cigarettes. The boss was from Katonah Elementary School—we just merged into one in the junior high school. What do you do? You have to think fast, or the bell for the next class will ring, and save the big

hood's tush. Before water boarding was invented by Mr. Cheney, I grabbed him (not Cheney) by the shirt collar and pants (no belt) and I brought him over to the toilet stall. I stuck his head in the toilet water.

98. Made him drink some, *eau d' toilet*, and promise never to smoke in the restroom again. Because he was too cool for a belt, his trousers ripped off—torn button and zipper. I don't know how the blazes that loser got around school that day. So hoods should wear their belts. This was a big help to Mr. Martin, the short math teacher, but the only teacher who had the male genitalia to go into the men's room and come pretty close to co-inventing water boarding. So you can see I'm not a liberal after all. I think a campaign contribution to President Reagan was the only one I ever made. I don't know what the jumble I am. As I also have to tame labor unions, and professionally have always been called in to smoke out 'the losers', underperformers, or whatever they may, at that particular point in their career, be deemed to be, or give them their skates—depending on the season. Richard Hawthorne, the above White Mountain survivalist, gave Mr. Martin the nickname 'Mighty Mouse'. I don't know if Corinne Martin knew this. Mr. Martin's beautiful daughter Corinne was also smarter than me, and was the star of our girls' gymnastics team. My Laura was her teammate along with both of Head Coach Todd's knock-out daughters. And some other very in-shape young beauties. It was hard to be Corinne's boyfriend with such a scary daddy.

99. Alright. As long as I'm at it, a couple more enforcer stories. If you love your school, hate bullies, and you took the Boy Scout Oath and honored The Scout Law (Google them!), you have no choice. Rick Walker, a good guy, but maybe he never fully understood how cool I was ☺. He was an

all-league football star, and co-captain of the football team our senior year along with Doug Owen (later). But Doug was also All Westchester County football with a tight end, senior class president, and campus king. Then there was my good buddy, fat ass Rick Walker. Muttonheaded (American style) football players used to make fun of (American-style) soccer players—even more in those days. The truth is our Dad would not let me and my brother play American football, which is a shame as we would have been stars. No one can get evidence to the contrary—luckily. No football for us because one of my dad's brothers, Uncle Joe, broke his neck. The other, Uncle Bill, broke his back. They still can't sit up straight—laid out in coffins as they are. Practice is over. The football players and the soccer players actually always have to run back to the lockers. Remember? I don't know why the coaches don't let us walk. Anyway, Wayne Vlachos, a soccer player, who is two years younger than me, is in front of fat ass Rick Walker. Rick gives him a big push that sends little Wayne flying through the air, hitting the pavement. He gets scrapped up.

100. Wayne Vlachos lives in Waccabuc. I took the school bus with Wayne, his big brother Wendell, and with their beautiful big sister Janet my whole life. Wayne is one of my boy scouts. Senior year Janet is campus queen, and my Laura, and Cathie Gordon who helped me count the money at the Lovin' Spoonful Tri-School Concert (later) were two of the four run-up candidates for campus queen. So what does a guy HAVE to do? Again think fast! Your buddy Rick is in full football shoulder, hip, thigh pads, and elbow and knee pads. He probably has one of those souped-up plastic cup jock straps. Not that he needed it. But it's required. So an unbreakable cup is in place to protect his peanuts. Rick is always blocking for

Kim Schappert (above), the quarterback. That way Doug Owen and Billy Fitzgerald (hairy like an ape from age 12, but Fitzy a great guy) can catch Kim's balls. Every game Rick Walker dishes out a bone-crunching defense. So the dude is in full armor. Even without the armor, Rick weighs 250, maybe 300 pounds. Luckily I saw everything from behind them when Wayne got pushed. Because coaches made us run like cretins into the locker room, I already had momentum.

101. I floored it, and gave Rick a flying Jean Claude Van Damme style double-straight-legged-parallel-to-the-ground-but-at-his-shoulder-height kick/ram/plunge/lunge thing. Never been executed by a human being in quite that way before. I also had to pick myself up off the ground. Rick went flying. Didn't know what hit him because his eyes are in the right place—at the front of his face—not like some of the other football players who got even more messed-up playing that game. Rick figured it out—not as fast as a soccer player would have. He was pissed. Think of a Vice Presidential Henry A. Wallace (later) bull charging you, swinging a football helmet by the face guard—helmet aimed at your head if possible. Luckily we were not too far from the locker room door. It took Coach Todd, Doug Owen, hairy Fitzy, and half the athletes in the school, representing all the athletic teams in the autumn sports program, to hold Mr. Walker back from killing me. In Japan we hear that people hold grudges maybe more than in some other places. Actually, my relationship with Rick improved after that. He stopped sticking his chin up every time our eyes met. I probably still stick my chin up. But I try to keep my chin down so less of the white space between my 79 hairs on the crown of my head can be seen by people walking behind me.

The Hawthorne Brothers, Stars of Our Gymnastic Team, Decided to Cut-Down and Prune Trees, rather than Young Girl Witches the Way Their Great GGG… Grand Daddy Did at the Salem Witch Trials (1692).

102. Mr. Cutler, our extraordinary and accomplished gymnastics coach, took us to the state meet, and to become Section 1 champions. John and Richard Hawthorne (the above Robinson Crusoe in the White Mountains) are many generations down the line from Judge John Hathorne. He was the toughest judge at the Salem Witch Trials (1692) in Salem Massachusetts, not my town of Lewisboro's Salem, N. Y. Judge Hathorne was the only judge who said he had no regrets about the execution of those 20 people. Thirteen of them were girls, mostly young girls. Very Dick Cheney-ish, the no-regret part. Not the young girl part. The famous writer of *The Scarlet Letter* (1850), *The House of the Seven Gables* (1851) etc., Nathaniel Hawthorne, added the 'w' to his name to get out of the censured and maligned dark shadow of the Witch Trial Judge. It was Richard Hawthorne who got me into gymnastics and also trained me and made me throw scary tricks. Richard and John didn't chase down witches or write novels, but they started one of the biggest 'tree companies' in the New York area—the Hawthorne Brothers Tree Service. They did Central Park for years. I've seen their sprayer and chipper trucks in the background settings of big Hollywood movies a few times. The way you see Fed Ex, UPS, DHL, and Snap-on-tool trucks—all my good past clients!

103. During the summer after my junior year, I started working with Richard and John Hawthorne at Dick

Herz's tree company. Mr. Herz lived on Lake Kitchawan about two houses across the way from my high-school honey, Laura. My dad also didn't let me do the AFS, American Field Service program, because "your (one year older) brother Art didn't get it last year". Maybe it makes my dad sound bad, but I understood. He also didn't want me to zig-zag off course. I was happy because my girlfriend Laura was runner-up to me in the vote by all the students (and teachers?). So Laura went off to Belgium that summer. And all I heard from Mr. Herz, and my gymnastic senpai trainers, Richard and John Hawthorne was, "Laura met a big Belgian with a big salam. They're at it right now."

104. Plus the Hawthorne boys were unhinged lunatics. Could cut and prune the trees like chimpanzees. They never even strapped or safety roped themselves in. (They have always maintained impeccable safety standards for their employees. As the Japanese say 'Even the monkey falls from the tree'. And Richie and John did that too when they were kids.) It was scary as hell. I was no match for those crazed maniacs. And they did this all in bare feet, just like the chimps or orangutans. Actually, a bit like my family, Richard Hawthorne's parents must have sold their beautiful big colonial white clapboard house with sky blue shutters. Or maybe the shutters were dark green or black. Actually, I have no idea, what color the damn shutters were. A very old, stately true-colonial house, from colonial times. It was on Honey Hollow Road. Yes, Winnie the Pooh lived down the street. (But in the USA and much of Europe, South America and other places, 'very old' means good, and even premium price. Different from Japan where a typically constructed wooden house has little value after 20 years.)

105. Anyway, we insisted Richard Hawthorne finish his senior year and graduate from John Jay H. S. He graduated the year before me, so I think Richie stayed half of his senior year with us, and the other half at the Gullens' (later!) house two doors down and also on the shores of Lake Waccabuc. Maybe someone else put barefoot Richie up for awhile, but I can't remember who. I nicknamed Richard 'The Squirrel', because as soon as he ate dinner and went up to his room to start his homework on his bed, he curled up and fell asleep like a squirrel. Although, I've never seen a squirrel sleep. Richie still managed to graduate just fine. The Gullen brothers, one year apart, were also stars of our championship gymnastics team.

106. But George Gullen, co-captain of the football team the fall of his senior year, was so big, that every time he did Giants, and went around on the 8-foot-tall high bar, he had to unpoint his toes, and go around flat-footed as he approached the gym floor. How the heck could he keep track of that? The judges must have thought so too, because they just smiled. They couldn't cut back his points for that. I think they were glad such a big guy was doing gymnastics. My sophomore year, John Hawthorne and Jack Gullen were co-captains of our very strong gymnastics team. My junior year, Richard Hawthorne and George Gullen were the team's co-captains. The Brothers Four*—sounds like a music group. I had the captain's job solo my senior year, Class of '68.

107. * Bingo—they were/still are a great music group. The Brothers Four were 4 Phi Gamma Delta Brothers (my fraternity at Cornell—Hail FIJI!!) from the University of Washington in Seattle, where my wife Chika's daughter graduated from. They had the huge 1960 hit

'Greenfields'. Their 4th single was 'The Green Leaves of Summer' from the movie that almost bankrupted John Wayne—*The Alamo*. I loved that movie. Saw it at the Bedford Theatre when I was 11 years old. The Brothers Four sang that movie theme song at the 1961 Academy Awards. Wikipedia says the Brothers Four always did particularly well in Japan, and on the USA hotel circuit. So old panty burpers from both my countries know my four Phi Gam fraternity brothers well.

Another Band of Four Brothers Just one House Apart off Perch Bay Road on Lake Waccabuc—the Gullens, and the Nevins. At some Point I had to Break Away, Leave the Band, and Try and Go Solo.

108. I asked very few guys to sign my yearbooks. Not many more girls either. George Gullen wrote in my 1967 year book, "Tom, it's easy to leave John Jay knowing that it's in the hands of another Perch Bay Road boy [the name of the street our 150 or 200 meter long driveways started from]. I know you will do a fine job and even go farther than your brother did. Enjoy yourself senior year. It's really the greatest. Make sure you leave enough time to frog around. Have a successful year! Best of everything, George." That year George was senior class president. My brother Art preceded me as president of the Senior High Student Council. The Gullen and Nevins brothers, separated by just one other lake-front house, tried to make Waccabuc proud. I know I learned a lot from watching and growing up with my brother and these very impressive and talented older guys.

109. I sometimes wondered is it me or them? After also following my brother to the same fraternity at Cornell, Phi Gamma Delta/FIJI, I did have to make a break at some point. My freshman year, I was the fraternity pledge class president the year after Art had it. Art was the fraternity president his senior year. I wasn't. I finally had to 'make a move'. All the way to Japan. Even my girlfriend Laura told me that I shouldn't follow my brother to Cornell: "You should go to Princeton." Our guidance counselor, Ms. Loretta Servodidio said she could get me into Princeton. 'A Princeton Man' sounds okay, but I was better off having a trade, and being a Cornell ILR'ie, whether I stayed at the Department of Labor in the USA (later), or been this Labor Consultant in Japan.

110. I was always making little moves. Little adventures on my own. Now I wish I had done much more of that. But playing with my friends, going to and staying over at each other's houses, and getting into some mischief and monkey business together was also important I guess. On windy, clear fall days, I would crisscross across Lake Waccabuc in our one-sail Sunfish sailboat. Especially when strong westerlies were coming. Facing west was a treat with Waccabuc's breathtakingly stunning sunsets reflected over the lake. We were in our own cove, blocked a bit by our P & G neighbor (Mr. Guitellious's) point or mini-peninsula. They and the Gullens had great views of the sunsets. Right from their own dock. We were in better shape to see the sunrise from the east over Dickens' boathouse with his gold teeth flashing (later). But were never out of bed and down at the dock early enough for that. From the house? No way. Blocked by the surrounding forest. Maybe it was possible to get out early enough on the dock for the sunrises on school days but it never occurred to me.

Getting More Romantic and Dewy Eyed about Lake Waccabuc with Its Tons of Bat Meat and Star Streaked Dome. Shimmering Celestial Heavens in Yamanashi too—'From Dusk till Dawn'.

111. At night in the canoe there were hundreds of 'somethings' flying right past my ears, sometimes messing and pulling my hair if I moved my head quickly. If you shined up a flashlight, either more would come by, or for the first time you would see just how many were streaking by. We didn't even seem to care what they were. They were part of our life on Waccabuc. They did us no harm. Now I know that except for much larger owls, or nighthawks, very few bird species can see well enough to fly at night. Some of that hoard in flight may have been whip-poor-wills, but surely most would have been bats. I once read that the weight of all the bat meat in the world is far heavier than the meat of all the edible livestock on the planet. Apparently there are lots of underground caves with small entrances. We don't even know those caves exist. I'm starting to get into my raw intelligence here— distant, unsubstantiated memories. Stuff I read in the past. Maybe some people on the lake knew they were bats. Could that be the reason I was always the only asshole out on the lake late at night? I was probably famous back at the bat cave as they sonar each other: "Watch out for aluminum canoe paddle boy. Very large, hard head." It's true. To this day I don't wear hats. I can't find any that fit. There's not enough shelf space at the stores for my size.

112. When I was out in the canoe in the middle of the pitch-black lake, down on the Western end by Castle Rock where there were no houses and lights, and on moonless

nights, the starlit sky was 3.13 times more impressive than the Hayden Planetarium. The next times I saw stars like that were in Alaska between Anchorage and Fairbanks, and one clear New Year's Eve night when I drove to our gassho zukuri minka thatched roof besso/second house on the Yatsugatake Mountain slope in Yamanashi Prefecture. This old house was supposedly going to become a Juyo Bunkazai/Important Cultural Property if we didn't buy it in a hurry. Maybe. This is the first real estate I bought in Japan, probably in 1974 or '75. I bought it with Peter, not the pumpkin eater. I let him use it.

113. If I go to the besso, Peter pulls out buckets, mops, rags, and Windex and makes me do heavy-duty cleaning! We had gone to kindergarten, 1st, and maybe 2nd grade together at Alden Terrace Elementary School in Valley Stream, Long Island. We met 14 years later at Cornell. But it took a few months to realize we used to be much shorter classmates. He was already studying Japanese, and I had already been to Japan. He was hitting on and trying to pick up as many of the Japanese Cornell chicks as he could. They were nice and slim, but slim pickings. There were only 67 Japanese foreign exchange students at Cornell. Most were male graduate student guys sent by their companies, banks, or government ministries. Like the Mormon missionaries, I figured, same roots—if Peter can get that good at Japanese, I can too. So that was another reason I studied Japanese my senior year at Cornell.

114. That New Year's Eve, after showing my friend (main squeeze) the besso, and waking up Peter, who was sleeping with a noisy mini-dachshund, and not sure what else, I was too sleepy to keep driving on that scary mountain road. If you went off the shoulder, with no guard rails, you would often go down a sheer mountain cliff. So we stopped in one

of the 37,000 love hotels (used by 2,500,000 Japanese per day—2% of the population everyday (although could be virile repeaters)—Natalie Paris, September 17, 2012 www. telegraph.co.uk.) Seems to contradict the prevailing view that Japanese don't have sex anymore. Maybe that is more true of long-term relationships. Some people obviously have a lot of it! The hotel was in a hollow, down a lonely, dark and scary dirt road off this winding mountain road which used to be Koshu Kaido.

115. This was one of the five old Edo-period roads out of the Edo/Tokyo capital. All 5 roads started from Nihonbashi in the middle of downtown Tokyo. This was a few years after we saw George Clooney and Quentin Tarantino for the first time in the 1996 Robert Rodriguez-directed film *From Dusk till Dawn*. They both made a big impression—cool guys and Tarantino was unglued crackers. But I didn't fall in love with those guys. I still have a big crush on the Salma Hayek's snake and table dance. Salma, not the gross and grotty white snake. I wondered where they all came from. I had never seen *ER*, hospital emergency room drama, so knew nothing about Mr. Clooney. *From Dusk till Dawn* was George Clooney's first breakthrough movie. Mr. Tarantino went on with his *Kill Bill* film and so much more.

*Why would the Secret Service Protecting President 'Bill'
Clinton Let Mr. Clinton Dine at the Kill 'Bill' Gonpachi
Restaurant? Who Protected Lake Rippowam's
Lady of the Cave?*

116. That iconic *Kill Bill* crazy sword fight restaurant scene was inspired and completely modeled after the Gonpachi restaurant in the hollow of the Nishi Azabu (formerly

Kasumicho) intersection. It's about a one or two-minute taxi ride, or 400-meter walk from our building. It's one of the 70 or so restaurants owned by our next-door neighbor. We were at Gonpachi the other night with 20 friends. It was packed even on that Wednesday night. We are lucky. We can look out from our north-side windows at our neighbor's inner garden with its lawn and trees going up to our 5th floor. Presidents Bill Clinton and George W. Bush have dined at the Gonpachi *Kill Bill* restaurant. When Bill Clinton went, not sure how the Secret Service felt about the name association. But it is protected on 3 sides by castle-like stone walls.

117. Another of my neighbor, Kozo Hasegawa-san's www.global-dining.com early and classic restaurants is Tableaux in nearby Daikanyama. For about 20 years the Australian wine drinking and dining club, Beefsteak and Burgundy (looks like there are 271 clubs around the world, www.beefsteakandburgundyclub.org.au), did their Christmas lunch at Hasegawa-san's Tableaux. At the most recent 12/12/2014 lunch we had 90 members and guests participating. Tokyo was the second international chapter, following New Zealand. Tokyo was founded in 1972, the year I came here! If you're an Australian with no sheep in your city, settle for your mates, and start a new B & B chapter!

118. Off that dirt road, and out of the Yamanashi mountainous darkness came this brightly lit and gaudy love hotel. Pretty tacky inside as well. We expected that *Dusk till Dawn* Chet Pussy character to be out front screaming "Give us an offer on our vast selection of pussy! We got white pussy… Spanish pussy, yellow…" and goes on using the pussy word 26 times in one continuous quote! We are not talking about 26 different breeds or colors

of cats. Credit to Wikiquote. Japan is also convenient with about 43,000 usually 24/7 open all night Konbini/convenience stores. Seven-11, Lawson and Family Mart are the leaders. Almost everything can be bought or done there, including paying bills, banking, and free restrooms. The only thing you can't do is covered by the over 40,000 very reasonably priced 2-hour (or longer) short-stay, or overnight-stay love hotels. With rooms, and baths much bigger and better than normal hotels. 'Discover Japan!' says the tourist authority.

119. Back to my hometown. I would canoe through the two swampy channels to Lake Rippowam, hide the canoe behind some clean, gray boulders, and climb to the top of the hill and over into Connecticut. I would look for the highest hill/mountain, and climb it. So without knowing it, and before there was a Mountain Lakes Park, I climbed Bailey Mountain, the tallest elevation in Westchester County at 982 feet/299.314 meters. I'd pick a clear day and look out with a bit of wistful nostalgia toward Long Island, 20 miles away as the bats fly. That is where I spent my first seven winters. This last couple weeks I realized I had discovered Sarah Bishop's cave, high up on the mountain. I saw a picture of the cave in a book about our area written by Maureen Koehl. I had no idea that it was a special cave at the time. Sarah had also looked with her melancholy blue eyes toward Long Island—the place she had to leave. When she came to the area in 1780, she was attractive, well-spoken, but reticent about her past. It was speculated that perhaps British soldiers toward the end of the Revolutionary War had dealt out harsh treatment to her or her family. She may have suffered from what war-zone soldiers with too much drink can be prone to do. I suppose, not all were British gentlemen.

120. Unless she had a wooden structure at the mouth of that shallow cave, I don't see how she could have survived the cold winters. Unlike the famous Leatherman (later) she was not on the move in thick leather clothes. Ms. Koehl writes that Sarah Bishop did sometimes attend the Church of Christ in nearby Salem. She would change from her cave rags to a nice dress that the Hoyt or Benedict family (names I remember) would keep for her. I imagine they also let her clean herself up. She did some chores for others in the neighborhood too. I am sure there were people happy to take her in when very cold weather was expected. Sarah died of exposure or sickness in 1810.

121. I would go off on walks. No one else in the family was into that. There was a good-sized pond, maybe 30 meters across. More like 40 meters in rainier weather. It's the only nearby, lakeside pond you can see on Google satellite. It was pretty much split between our land and our neighbor's land. In dry weather it would be more like a large deep swamp. I was the only one who knew about it. I never mentioned it. It was there. I took it for granted. What's there to say about a swamp? When it was a pond, and combined with a couple of rainy days, a torrent of water flow would go down 'the stream' on our property down toward Lake Waccabuc. There would even be considerable white water at times but only enough for a good thrilling toy boat ride. Still we had our own little Grand Canyon beginning about 30 meters from the swamp/pond. I never mentioned that I knew the source of 'the stream'. The subject never came up. In those days gentlemen didn't talk about swampy ponds. There are two incoming sources of water to Lake Waccabuc that are visible on maps. Our stream is not one of them, but it had to be the closet 3rd source, other than the springs. A little bridge was required to cross our private stream.

More on My 4-Acre Forest Fiefdom, and this Beautiful Lake Waccabuc—the Largest Lake in Westchester County, other than the Reservoirs Feeding New York City. A Two-Legged Horse by our Swamp/Pond was set on Fire. A Four-legged Bio-Hazard Horse in Omotesando.

122. In those days, as kids, you could walk along the Lakefront shore, crossing everyone's private property without getting shot. It would be a good idea to stay away from the houses. But except for a couple houses, we knew and greeted each other. Our P & G neighbor's house was built over the water on a steep cliff-like hill. So there was no place to walk in front of the house. So a route around the back had to be taken. Actually that must have cut down a lot of lake-shore walking traffic. I knew every inch of my side of the lake. I would say that our stream was the only functioning stream between the Waccabuc Country Club beach, with its snack restaurant and boathouse, and between the Waccabuc River, which we also called 'the waterfall'. So I guess the Nevins' stream and canyon made our property pretty special. Didn't realize it at the time. Melvin and Marian Ringstrom's (later) land may have gone right up to the waterfall. Unless the state or New York City waterworks authority owned all such parts of the watershed. The Waccabuc River seems to be the only outlet for all three lakes—Waccabuc, Oscaleta, and Rippowam. Across from Castle Rock on the western end of the Lake Waccabuc was 'the sand bar'— that's where water flowed into the lake. These are also spring-fed lakes. We used to group down at the sand bar, party, and take off on our water skies form there. Now it has all been bought up by some Waccabuc residents to form the 39-acre Long Pond Preserve. No more such freedoms.

Maybe good but sucky progress.

123. You enter the preserve trail from Mead Street across from the Mead Chapel. Although it is okay to walk the trail through the preserve, it is actually forbidden to go down to the water to swim. Also forbidden to walk on the private Tarry-A-Bit drive. Breathing as you walk is permitted. Castle Rock is off limits and is privately owned. The police patrol the area, and there are $250 fines, and maybe community service time for swimming, going on Castle Rock, or launching a boat. Boats from elsewhere can introduce invasive little muscles and unwanted yucky things. Anyway species that can mess up the lakes' natural habitat. There is no swimming, boating, or fishing public access to any of these three lakes connected by the two channels. So you're best touring this spot on Google satellite.

124. When my 4-year-older big sister was little, she used to neigh like a horse, and even do that horse snort thing as she shook her head and long flowing mane. No, she was not mentally retarded, just loved horses—big time. And maybe a little lonely, because me and my one-year-older brother were so close. We all had to go to Assateague Island to hang for much too long with feral, inbred Chincoteague ponies. All because of some dumbass book that Marguerite Henry wrote in 1947. Had to suffer through the 1961 family film too—got all 'misty' over it. Kathy must have been in the middle of the bush near my pond/swamp. The brothers next door, Bobby and Dickey Stewart, just a little older than Kathy, heard a horse.

125. They came charging down shooting with their BB guns. Kathy was hit in the back and the hindquarters as she galloped home. We never knew our Beebe gun brothers

and neighbors to the east that well. I guess because the kids were maybe a handful of years older. Also never in the same school district. The Walter Stewart family, to our east, like the Gullens to our west, also ran grocery stores, but over New Canaan, Connecticut way, so did not compete with the Gullens and Mr. Gullen's Partner Mr. Ralph Felice. Gail Felice was in my class at John Jay. Mr. Felice and Mr. Gullen were high school classmates, war buddies in Germany, and named their market the Fifth Division Market. The grocery and, later separate, liquor store were near the Cross River Reservoir where Route 35 intersects with Route 121. They supplied food and made home deliveries— something important and useful. Hopefully the Stewart family also are still in the hood. Hopefully not replaced by investment bankers, or hedge fund guys. These are good people too. But some aspects of financial services seem to be set up such that at times they are delivering, not sustenance, but rather their share of financial pain and unnecessary misery to too many people.

126. Once I smelled something really bad. Big sister equestrian Kathy was leaned up against the fireplace protective screen. She was pushing it and her hindquarters too close to the big field-stone fireplace the Moore brothers (later) built for us. The fur trim on her winter coat caught fire— burnt horse hair. She was okay. Just a little shaken up. By the way, today, Sunday January 11, 2015 (1/11/15) for the first time in 43 years, I saw a beautiful Japanese lady walking a handsome, short, husky, gray, thick-haired 17 year-old horse. We were walking the dog around 2 pm. We met up at the huge, 60-meter-long, 4-storey-tall white house with the Mansard roof. I get to look at it from my 5th-floor bedroom. They also have red flowers in flower

boxes below all the balconies on every floor. I don't know what those flowers are. Maybe some type of carnation. The house is on the corner, just behind our building and on the street behind us. Now we know our little sausage doggie with the ridiculously short legs has no problem with short-legged horses— just other dogs if they start to run, and make that paw slip sound, simulating an attack on our blind dog. It's a stretch of the mind to think that all dogs originated, and were bred from more friendly and maybe weaker, hungry wolves. They needed our scraps. They guarded the entrance to our caves. They barked to protect us, and to make sure the scraps kept coming.

127. We did not catch the horse's name or the beautiful young lady's name. We did talk. She looked like our kids, so I started in English. She was not getting it or preferred Japanese. My wife Chika has also never seen a pet horse being walked in Japan. Not in Kobe. Not in Tokyo. There is an interesting Japanese fellow who walks our nearby Omotesando Avenue with a couple of hissing monkeys— one on each shoulder. Hopefully he doesn't live here, and takes the subway in. Who says you can't lead cats. One young man keeps a cat on a leash. Another walks with a ferret (*Mustela putorius furo*)—shorter cuter snout than, and hopefully nicer than a weasel. And luckily also on a leash. I guess the animals help them meet chicks or offer them companionship in a city teaming with nice people. This maybe can make it all the lonelier, if all you have are hissing monkeys or a weasel to keep you company.

128. In Japan, or at least Tokyo, there is a law that dogs have to be leashed. And you have to have special plastic bags with a paper towel inside. You can grab the doggie doo doo and wipe up with these special bags you must carry with you. You then tie a not in the elongated plastic bag part, and

put it in your pocket. Back pocket before sitting down is not a good idea. I once left one in a coat pocket for 3 or 4 months. Ever see mummified doggie poop? Not that different from mine. Recently for the first time I saw a guy with a dog toilet—green, plastic backed big square diaper— out on the street walking his dog. These plastic-backed diapers are usually spread out on the floor of the house's designated canine pee-pee zone. The diapers just sit there patiently waiting for the dog. But this guy spread it under his female dog's butt just in time before pee-pee. Maybe not to be tried with long-legged male dogs, unless you wear a raincoat and safety goggles. Walking Diaper Man was a pet owner with fast reflexes. This is not legally required. But most people have a bottle of water, and dilute the pee on the sidewalk or pavement.

129. The pet horse… At first, at a distance, we assumed it was a biohazard-type big deformed dog. Chika loves Milla Jovovich, *The Fifth Element* (1997) with Bruce Willis, *The Messenger: The Story of Joan of Arc* (1999), and most of all the 2002 *Resident Evil* 'biohazard girl', with its 4 or 5 sequels. Milla has been given the title of "reigning queen of kick-butt", which is a little scary, because my wife worships her. There is a story here. Chika's dad could marry a Takarazuka star because he had a family box/carton-making business, which he wanted to stick on Chika. So she ran away to Tokyo to supplement her four-year university degree with executive secretary skills at the YMCA for girls in Ochanomizu. She went on and did much more in Tokyo—another story. But in today's paper it was written that Japan has the fewest corporate members of board of directors than any other top-20 developed nation. Prime Minister Abe keeps talking about trying to change that. Chika's dad was on

the Japanese Olympic Skeet Shooting team, and taught the Kobe police how to shoot all kind of guns. But he wouldn't let Chika shoot guns, learn karate, ice skate, and play volleyball, dance ballet, or kick-ass in general. And I am forever thankful.

130. Our really cool Japanese next-door neighbor, Mr. Hasegawa, the restaurateur, is 3 weeks younger than me. He is also married to a beautiful Ukraine born lady like Milla. Even nicer than Milla Jovovich! I was the only non-Russian or non-Ukrainian-type white guy at the wedding held at his Tableaux (above) restaurant. I think it's a Russian thing. They make an older guy prove he can take care of his younger bride. With noisy, smoking, laser shooting machine guns a 2.7-meter-tall Russian guy and 2.3-meter-tall girl with long legs suddenly entered the room. When she passed by our table her belt was just above my eyes. I was standing. They were both in army camouflage uniforms. They made Hasegawa-san do push ups. He rattled off about 60 of them. He also runs from here to the Imperial Palace Moat, runs around it twice, and runs back here to his house. One of my friends said that is about a 25-kilometer/15.6-mile run. Kozo is my age. I'll drive it in my Prius Alpha anytime. Stay cool and green. I get 15.8 kilometers to the liter. The guy in the Ferrari gets as much beaver as the first non-native guy who settled into Manhattan (later).

131. Back to the short, cute, thick, hairy horse. The horse is kept on the terrace of the pretty lady's company nearby. Probably a set-up like our Omotesando building where they live and work in the same building. So the horse lives nearby in Minato-ku. We are amazed we have never crossed paths before. I asked, "This has to be the only horse pet in Tokyo, right?" She seemed to agree, but did mention

one, or some in some part of the city out in the 'burbs that I never heard of. "I believe there is a horse there," she said. I was thinking that little horse would be happy up on our wrap-around 5th-floor roof terrace. She could see Roppongi Hills and Tokyo Midtown at sunrise, and the Shibuya station and the Shibuya skyscrapers at sunset. Could probably fit in our 4-person capacity elevator. Anyone buying the building, don't worry. There won't be horse manure under the redwood roof terrace tiles. What kind of poop clean up bag could work for that little horsey? One of my buddies, Clark Griffith, who resurrected the Tokyo Goode Grubbe Clubbe from near death (begun in about 1955), has a huge Great Dane. I've seen 'Take-chan' in action. The doggie poop bag is large enough to pull over your head—best done before not after.

The Leatherman––Talk about the Marathon Man. For 33 Years this Cave-Dwelling, Grunting Frenchman Walked 16.6 Kilometers/10.4 Miles Every Day. Tougher than Tora-san sans/*without the Japanese Bathing. Unlike Tora-san, never earned a Dime.*

132. The Leatherman. This is the Japanese Tora-san, Atsumi Kiyoshi (more later) Tekiya (man who sets up *yatai*/ outdoor tent booths to sell usually food or toys at Japanese *omatsuri*/festivals) guy on steroids. And much more footloose, fancy-free, primitive, untamed, and smelly. You can see on Wikipedia a picture taken of the Leatherman on June 9, 1885. He's either eating or biting his nails. Tora-san, Yasuo Tadokoro was clean and clean-cut in all 48 Tora-san films starring him from 1969 to 1995, the year before his death. Later you will see that I sang his song to

him in front of his *tsukibito*/entourage and my parents at Haneda airport before they even had a Narita airport. The Leatherman was totally wild compared to Tora-san. He did not just belong to Waccabuc, or even just the town of Lewisboro, of which Waccabuc is one of 6 hamlets. He lived from 1839 to 1889. (So died at 50 years old.) Roughly from 1856 to 1889, he walked a circuit between the Hudson and the Connecticut Rivers. Every 34 to 36 days, without fail, he walked a 365-mile/584-kilometer route. That means he walked on average 16.6 kilometers per day. This was no Lily-white Sarah Bishop, content to stay in one Rippowam West Mountain cave overlooking her Long Island 20 miles away. The Leatherman had caves all along the route. On his Wikipedia entry it indicates that he visited 48 different towns like clockwork. The towns are named. No one is sure of his origins. I can see how he got through the winters. Me too. As long as I'm moving I don't wear or need clothes.

133. One story has it that he was from Lyon and worked in a glass-making factory. He was to marry the owner's daughter, but got ditched by her—or kicked out by the father. Old man wasn't into smelly leather? So he came to America to live the American dream of being probably the hardiest beggar in the history of the world. Unlike Sarah Bishop, he entered no one's home. Did not talk. Only grunted and pointed to his mouth. Everyone came to know what that meant. They knew his schedule and had *bento*/box-lunch-like food ready for him that he could take away. If hot food and the family utensils, he ate it at the door step and would never go inside the homes—thank God. He made his own leather clothes. In the winter he made sure the top and sides of his cave were well heated by fire in advance so that it was warm enough when he wasn't

moving and when he slept at night. I have a feeling this Frenchman ate about 12,000 calories per day. A walking Michael Phelps, who hopefully also swam in that foul leather kit whenever he came across a body of water. Even the cows politely moved away from this bloke.

134. One of his favorite caves was on Ward Pound Ridge Reservation, (the largest public park in Westchester County) near John Jay H. S. Remember? The place that triggered my 'four eyes' and waterboarding of another youth. I have only seen pictures of that Leatherman cave. When a kind family saw that after a bitter cold storm, the Leatherman had white frostbite markings on his face, he was forcibly hospitalized. But before he could be treated, he escaped the hospital back to the life that he loved. People loved to help this grunting Frenchman. Kind of like today in Paris; Sunday January 11, 2015, when 3.5 million Frenchman and leaders throughout the world are rallying in Paris behind the French after the brazen and bold Charlie Hebdo satirical weekly newspaper killings of 12 people, including 10 journalists. The Leatherman's 365-mile monthly loop and legend was so respected, that 10 towns along the Leatherman's route passed ordinances exempting specifically him from the New York State "tramp law" (against begging and being a tramp). That law had been passed in 1879. Probably because of the Leatheman's monthly aromatic visits!

From the Lake Waccabuc Boys to the Famous Walden Pond Boys. Nathaniel Hawthorne Wrote that Henry David Thoreau was "Ugly as Sin", but in his Character and Nature, Thoreau was much like Nathaniel's Descendent— My Good Friend Barefoot Richie.

135. Richard Hawthorne, Nathaniel's great, great grandson went barefoot all the time, even to school. Bathed every day but barefoot by choice. Didn't beg, and no leather clothes. His dad had a big writing and editing job at NASA, and helped us reach the moon two years later in the summer of 1969. Even in the winter, in the snow, Richard went barefoot. My father didn't mind his clean feet after a pure white snow storm. But otherwise made him wear shoes in the house, "Because a smooth leather shoe sole does not pick up and keep as much dirt as your oily foot prints." Probably accurate. But what does that say about the Japanese who never wear outside shoes in the house? Usually socks and slippers. Interesting but smelly stuff. Richard's famous ancestor, Nathaniel Hawthorne (1804-1864) was really handsome like Richie. But seemed to be more of a dandy. I'd say he wore shoes. He did enjoy swimming in Walden Pond, but mostly alone. Probably Commando.

136. Undoubtedly, not swimming together with Henry David Thoreau who Nathaniel wrote was "ugly as sin" in his September 1, 1842 private journal entry. A detail on those famous Walden Pond fellows. Nathaniel Hawthorne was one year younger than Ralph Waldo Emerson (1803-1882), and 13 years older than Henry David Thoreau. It's ironic. In that day's journal, Hawthorne's description of Thoreau is exactly what Richard Hawthorne was like as a teenager—knowledge and love of animals, snakes, plants, berries...

137. I was always kind of in to Henry David Thoreau (1817-1862), the star of the Transcendentalism movement—the inherent goodness that comes from people and nature. A belief that people should be self-reliant and independent. That in particular, government, political parties and

organized religion can corrupt the purity of the individual and his or her rational logic and better sensitivities. I wrote a book about living our lives. I don't like to say it is a personal growth book. My book is light, and not that preachy. It is not about Japan, or my labor relations consulting. It is titled *Know Your Own Bone*. That comes from Henry David Thoreau's quote, 'Do what you love. Know your own bone; gnaw at it, bury it, unearth it, and gnaw it still'. Put simpler, it is also about, 'Do you stay put? Or do you make a move?' Physical location and things around you, as well as what is going on in your head.

138. When Richard lived with us for a few months so he could graduate from John Jay High School, he saw a snake on Post Office Road as we got off the school bus at the top of Perch Bay Road. He knew it wasn't a copperhead, or anything poisonous. So he brought it back to our house. We got mom's typical comment: "Let's wait till your father comes home." Dad, always drove down the driveway at 6:15 pm. Can you imagine what time he left his office at Rector and Wall Street on Manhattan? The good old days. Before email and workaholic Americans. I was worried for the snake. Just hoping Dad wouldn't panic and reach for that axe again (later).

139. Nathaniel Hawthorne (1804-1864) also did love the wilds of Lake Sebago where he lived from age 12 to 15 between 1816 and 1819. Lake Sebago is the second largest lake in the State of Maine, with a surface area of 30,513 acres, or 335,643 sq. meters—so 221 times more expansive than our Lake Waccabuc. It is the deepest lake in Maine at 96 meters or 316 feet deep. That puts the bottom 46 feet, or about 15 meters below sea level. Our Gullens on Lake Waccabuc hunted moose and bear every year in Maine. They probably know Lake Sebago well.

They would not waste gas bringing hunted and dead deer back home. Especially, the last 20 years, as the deer population has exploded. They would be able to lasso deer off their second-floor redwood, or cedar, or oak— anyway a terrace made of wood.

140. I wonder if Nathaniel wore shoes around Lake Sebago. Nathaniel also lived for a while in the country in a house on Walden Pond. This was during July 4, 1845, until September, 1847. Did you ever wonder what Walden Pond, the most famous pond in the USA was really like? How does Walden Pond compare with Lake Waccabuc? The Pond is only 61 acres while Waccabuc is 138 acres. But Walden Pond is 31 meters/107 feet deep compared to Waccabuc's 14.2 meters deep, so it is about twice as deep as our lake. A very deep glacial pond for sure. Anyway, I couldn't compete on the nature boy level with the Tree Skinner Hawthorne brothers swinging barefoot from the trees with a saw, and pruning shears—right over my head.

141. Here is Richard's Hawthorne's description under his senior graduation picture in the '67 John Jay H.S. yearbook: "Richard!…Richard Herz Flea Circus… a blue-eyed blondie…king of the parallels and high bar… famous for handstands on cars, bridges, waterfalls, and crutches…jazzy pianist…likes girls, music, dough, and life." Richard could climb up a whole flight or two of stairs on his hands. He once walked around the quarter-mile track on his hands without putting his feet down. Our good gymnasts could all walk pretty far on our hands. But not that far. As it says in the yearbook, Richard was a great jazz, classical and all-else pianist. So were his mom and big sister. I think his big sister Rosaline was campus queen in '63 at John Jay. She looked just like her mom. Little sister Allison was also a knock-out; a turn-your-

head-around twice beauty. A year or two younger than me, she used to feed me my balls during volleyball games in the Lewisboro Elementary school paved courtyard area. Unfortunately she married a rich guy in the D.C. area who owned radio stations, and maybe a newspaper. Never met him. I heard he was a nice guy.

142. After the gymnastics season his senior year, Richard lost about half of a couple fingers in the wood chipper. Richie was good enough to do really well in his university -(Indiana U. I think) level gymnastics. But because of the missing digits he had to quit the high bar and rings. Mostly he did floor exercise and the long horse. Also he had to quit the piano. Nothing got Richard down. He switched over to the bass fiddle. For years he has been a key man in Bluegrass Bands such as The Mountain Oysters band. On ctpost.com you can see him jamming in a duo with Roger Sprung, a very famous banjo player who has played at Lincoln Center, Carnegie Hall, and lots of TV appearances such as the Dean Martin Show. Mr. Sprung has about 20 more years of wisdom and experience than Richie and me. I never met Mr. Sprung— just heard about him from Richie.

143. On the subject of hand walking and climbing stairs, the most embarrassing time of my life was when my big sister brought home for the first time the guy she ended up marrying. Now it was guys, not horses. And Kathy is still married to him today! I guess I wanted to show off. I walked on my hands up the 5 steps separating the dining room from the living room. I was in my bathrobe with no underwear. The "Thomas!" scream came out from my sister. I threw a nearby couch pillow frisbee style at her and ran up to my room. Not one of my finer moments. Luckily, about that time, Mr. Attridge, who had been the

assistant scoutmaster invited me to the above mentioned barbecue, and we agreed to do the Boy Scout challenge together. So I quit being a Tree Skinner, and decided to lead the clean life. I did not die falling on my saw, tumbling out of a blighted Hemlock tree Commando style.

My First True Love, with a Grandfather in China Fighting His Private War along with Chiang Kai-shek Against Japanese Zero Planes, and Later against Mao Zedong (Mao Tse-tung).

144. A little more about Laura, my girlfriend junior and senior high school years. She was a new kid. The first time I saw her was when we were doing something in the shop class workshop facility. I have no idea why a mixed group of us were there. Maybe making student, or class posters or planning the post-sophomore-year summer trip. Then a couple weeks later as President of the sophomore class, I had to lead us in our end of the year summer school trip in buses to Jones Beach out on Long Island, New York. Blasting on the beach all summer long was the Four Tops' song, 'Reach Out I'll be There". Undisputable #1 all summer on all the charts in the USA and UK. On the bus and at the beach, I finally had a chance to talk to Laura. For the next two years we were like *kingyo no fun* as the Japanese would say. According to www.urbandictionary. com always together, "like 'goldfish poo' specifically, a string of expelled poop that has failed to detach from the fish's anus so that it trails behind the fish as it…" How much dirtier can it get? Anyway, I would have trailed Laura, not the fish, anywhere. Luckily we could swim

and walk hand in hand. Now you are surer that this is an unholy Bible.

145. There are a couple of pretty neat stories here. At Laura's house up above Lake Kitchawan, there was an upstairs play room. It was equipped with a pool table and everything. There was a huge, 5-meter-long banner of red tapestry with huge gold embroidered Chinese character letters. After maybe a year or so, I asked her what it was. She just said, "Chiang Kai-shek (1887-1975), the Chinese leader, and President of Taiwan, gave it in thanks to my grandfather. My grandfather had textile factories in China. He helped Chiang Kai-shek fight the Japanese. And after the Japanese lost the war, together they fought the Communists under Mao Tse-tung (1893-1976)."

I'm like, "Okay, cool."

146. My dad's parents were from Ireland or some unknown place. A couple years later at Cornell, Professor Walter Lefevre devoted a whole class to his Alfred E. Kohlberg lecture. Professor Lefevre sat on a stool with no notes and just talked. He always filled Bailey Hall with its 1,324 seats. I went up after his lecture, and sheepishly said, "I think Mr. Kohlberg is my H.S. honey's grandfather. Although her name is totally different. I know her mom was the oldest child."

Professor Lefevre cleared his throat, and said, "The Kohlberg papers would be very interesting." He winked down at me from his stage stool. Laura's mom talked to Professor Lefevre. We delivered a couple boxes of papers after I made some copies. I wrote a paper and got an A in the course. I did not get A in all my courses. I studied hard my first semester freshman year. But alas not all As. My reaction was what you have here is not what you want. That is when I took up everyone's unwanted shifts at the

Willard Straight Hall (student union building) Straight Desk. I worked about 40 hours a week the rest of the time I was in Ithaca at Cornell. More on that later. My parents paid full room and board, and gave us some spending money. So my money was always saved for my adventures.

147. After I wrote this paper about Mr. Alfred E. Kohlberg for Professor Lefevre's class, I got the challenge by fraternity *senpai*/seniors to go to Katmandu. It ended up that I would travel around the world for 7 or 8 months. One of my stops would be Taiwan. I knew that on Laura and her mom's introduction, I would have been able to meet Chiang Kai-shek, who would be President of Taiwan for another 5 years until his death in 1975. Or at least I could have met the famous Madame Chiang/Song May-Ling (1898-2003) who had been the President's wife from 1927 to 1975 when her husband passed away. She lived to be 105 years old. That's pretty good chop suey. She would also know the Kohlberg family very well. But I never try and do things like that. What's the point? They are so far above me. Just because I was fortunate enough to chat up, and lucky enough to be buddies with the prettiest, smartest and sweetest girl on the John Jay H. S. campus. So instead, I spent about 10 days in Taiwan hitchhiking on the road that goes all around the island. I also got into the center of the country to Sun Moon Lake etc. Good or bad, I'm not sure, but I never tried to get up close and personal with any of our heavyweight ambassadors out here in Tokyo. It always seemed like there were enough guys nervously jiggling the change in their pocket, hoping to shake hands and get a word in.

148. Princess Diana is my exception! Later. Tokyo's ambassador line-up is indeed impressive. Ambassadors such as Mike Mansfield, Senate Majority Leader; Walter Mondale, Vice

President under Jimmy Carter, and 1984 Democratic Party Presidential Nominee; Thomas S. Foley, Speaker of the United States House of Representatives; Howard Henry Baker, Senate Majority Leader, and White House Chief of Staff under President Reagan; and today we have the very bright, beautiful, and charming Caroline Kennedy. That iconic image of her saluting at her father's funeral 3 days before she turned 6 years old. I was 13 years old. I cried throughout the funeral and then some.

149. A couple of highlights of the Kohlberg personal papers that are easy to remember is that Alfred Kohlberg learned to fly. He bought a couple airplanes and actually attacked the Japanese Zero fighters. He shot a couple down, but was also shot down. He was wounded in the leg and had a limp the rest of his life. He was an active member of the China Lobby, and an ally of Senator Joe McCarthy, with his anti-communist campaign. Mr. Kohlberg was a member of the original National Council of the John Birch Society. He was on the board of the Institute of Pacific Relations, but later on thought it was infiltrated by Communists. Laura's grandfather was the financial backer of *Plain Talk* which merged with *The Freeman: Ideas on Liberty*. Mr. Kohlberg was smart, but Laura was smarter than Grandfather Kohlberg and me put together. She also looked at the world a bit differently and in her own perceptive way.

150. Laura went to Mount Holyoke as her mom had. It was this dolt's nincompoop recommendation not to have Laura come to Cornell. 'Because we have to grow as people in independent ways', or some such trash. Ends up I had almost no girlfriends at Cornell! Indeed, I was a focused, callow and featherless youth—very few feathers in my cap. Very few notches on my gun. From

high school, Laura got into every school she applied to, including Cornell and Harvard. Later on she got a Ph.D. at Harvard and worked there for years. But she wanted to start her own chartered school, which she did. And get this—Nothing to do with me—Laura would not have even known I had made my life in Japan but she married a medical doctor named Tom who was half Japanese. But that Tom did not speak Japanese, and had not been to Japan yet. He had 'stayed put' in the States. Life does work in mysterious ways.

Blessed by More Smart Angels from Heaven, and Madonnas of Charisma and Power.

151. As devastatingly cool and beautiful as my high school Laura was, I must say that like Laura, I never seriously dated or married anyone who was not considerably smarter than me. I took some girls who were "not the sharpest knife in the draw" (learned this from my son Johnny who wanted to get far away from being half Japanese, so set himself up in West Virginia and then the Outer Banks of North Carolina) to the movies, or maybe a place where the lights were low. There was no more stimulating conversation required. Yeah. Places where you would never put a pillow case over their beautiful faces. But you also would not have to talk. All the ladies I got spiritually close to were much smarter than me. Laura, both wives, Louisa McDonald, and many unnamed smart beauties who trained me and groomed me. Yes. I'm brushed, trained, groomed, and have been tick-free for years. They taught me more about life, and how one should live one's life.

152. No. Louisa was not Ray's daughter. She ate very few hamburgers. And she has become a good friend of my second wife Chika. That is actually my wife's Christian, err Shinto, Buddhist, or whatever name: Chika—a Chick— easy to remember, right? Louisa was a Miss Teenage America, or some other major beauty contest her Mom (also a beauty contest winner) subjected her to. Then she was a pompom cheerleader girl for the Stanford football team. Got a PhD at Stanford in Art History, and had a lot of trips in and out of Japan. I first met her in 1980 during my separation from my first marriage, and shortly before my divorce from my first wife. We met at a party with my leg in a full plaster cast and on crutches. Broke my ankle playing paddle tennis on the roof over the Tokyo American Club parking lot. Mr. Dick Reilly, my Scout Master and pioneer of spreading paddle tennis (above) would not have been proud of me. I think the party was celebrating my 1980 book being published by JETRO, so Louisa didn't just see me as a crippled mess—she thought maybe I had a brain. That book got me on NHK, and all the main TV networks discussing in Japanese with the TV host about my book. With my white leg cast, and crutches at the side of my chair.

153. I was not allowed to meet my kids until 1981 or 1982 after my divorce was finalized, and my first wife had clear legal custody. That is a unique Japanese thing. Quite different from the States, and many countries I suppose. Mothers get unshared custody almost all the time. But after I met my two boys I always took care of them with real estate, private school tuition, boarding school in the States from age 10 and 13, trips all around the world—often just the 3 of us. Even when they were very young. I don't really buy that line about, "They are too young. They won't

remember anything." I remember everything. My boys are sharper knives than me. If you wait for them 'to be old enough', they would rather not travel with you. They would rather stay home with the dog and cats. We had a lot of goofy fun and laughter together. I was close to my boys.

154. By the way, my boys' mom, my first wife, was very charismatic and powerful. Almost no one saw, or thought, and came up with the same concepts, and verbal descriptions. Her unique way of expressing herself. Also for my benefit, she never worked on her English. She had more power in Japanese. I did learn a lot for sure. She was an only child. At the very beginning of the marriage we lived in Ichikawa, the first Chiba-Ken/Prefecture city when you cross the Edo River from Tokyo. It was another age. Ichikawa was not Omotesando, or 'the Banchos' by the Imperial Palace in Chiyoda-ku.

155. So walking together in Ichikawa, or if I talked in a restaurant, you could feel she and her Mom would rather be somewhere else. Unlike the wives or families of most *gaijin*, they expected me to toe the line as a Japanese man in both verbal and behavioral expression—a big but helpful challenge. It did me a lot of good, and I have always been thankful. If she had joined Aum Shinrikyo cult (Tokyo subway sarin gas attacks and more on this later), she would have given Mr. Shoko Asahara (1955-still with us), the babbling, half-blind leader, 4 or 5 months of respite. She would take some time to figure out who the smart power players are. But once she would decide to move in on him, Mr. Asahara would have been permanently placed out in the Matsumoto woods outside the compound. She would see to it that he came up to the fence at the appointed hour. He would be given ample

warm meals each day. Also a periodic change of robe. It worked out like that for me too.

156. As of fairly recent info, there have been 192 trials of former Aum cult members. All but one were convicted. Thirteen of the cult leader Shoko Asahara's underling disciples, have been hung by the authorities. Mr. Asahara tried to appeal to the Supreme Court in a trial that has gone on since 1995—20 years!! He is still trying to hang on to his precious life. Taxpayers pay. He appears to be no Alexander the Great, Peter the Great, Joan of Arc, Napoleon, Hitler, or native sons Sakamoto Ryoma, Saigo Takamori, Tanaka Kakuei, or Koizumi Junichiro. The source of Asahara's charisma and leadership would make an interesting study. He clearly did not make it on his looks, or the profile he cuts. He started in 1984 in a one-room apartment. In a 1992 book he declared himself Christ, and the only 'Lamb of God' in Japan. That main subway sarin gas attack killed 12 people, seriously injured 50, and about 1,000 people had temporary impaired vision. I used the allegorical story about my first wife and the Aum Cult's Mr. Asahara facetiously. Indeed, there must have been something very special about him. Mr. Asahara was able to attract and keep a large number of very smart and highly educated holders of advanced degrees as his followers. History is made by people with strong beliefs, and an unyielding commitment to a passionate or a fierce concept or plan.

157. Back to Vegas and Louisa. I was close for a while to Louisa. Not the hamburger heiress, but that same name. We were together about a year in Japan, and a little time in Las Vegas. That's where Louisa was born and raised. Her whole family had 'stayed put' in Vegas. But alas, Louisa was not going to spend her whole life in Japan. She taught

at the famous Seven Sister universities in New England, and then went back to her roots in Vegas. She bought two houses next to each other. One for her mom, and one for Louisa. She has been a professor of art history for 15 years at the University of Nevada, Las Vegas, and chairman of the history of art department since 2011. A truly great and classy lady, well loved by her students. Some of them don't like her pop quizzes. Really knows and loves her subject.

Not a Gambling Man, but I Always Loved the Las Vegas Shows. Louisa has Great High School Buddies too.

158. I always loved Vegas. Louisa must have gone to Bishop Gorman High School in Las Vegas. I believe she was classmates with Bob Miller, and probably his wife of many years, and still today, Sandy Miller. They were all great friends. When I was visiting Louisa's family, the four of us went to a dinner show featuring Captain & Tennille performing. One of their big songs, 'Love Will Keep Us Together' won the Grammy award for Record of the Year in 1975. 'Do that to Me One More Time', 'Muskrat Love', and the 1979 hit 'Make Your Move' were also gold records. Sounds like the title of this book.

159. Bob Miller was the nicest gentleman you could meet. I wondered why we could decide last minute which show to go to. Yet when we walked in, we were taken right up to one of the best booth seats, just the right distance from center stage. Not by one staff member. A couple other staff popped up out of the woodwork. And this is before cell phones were invented! So I know no advance notice to the dinner show folks. Well it ends

up that at that time Bob Miller was the Clark County (Las Vegas) district attorney (1979-1986). Mr. Bob Miller was the first holder of that office to be reelected (1982). He was also elected president of the 3000+ National District Attorneys' Association. Mr. Miller went on to be lieutenant governor of Nevada. Always clean as a whistle, we went Dutch and paid for the dinner show with our credit cards.

160. Next he was elected to two full terms as the Nevada State Governor (1989-1999). His 10 years as governor make him the longest serving governor in Nevada's history. Between 1997 and 1998, Bob was chairman of the National Governors Association. That was a position Mr. Bill Clinton was also honored with in 1986-87, while Mr. Clinton was governor of Arkansas and before he became President. Nowadays Governor Miller is the Principal of Robert J. Miller Consulting (www.rjmillerconsulting. com) which develops business for government. He also provides business-to-business advice and assistance. Mr. Bob Miller is also a senior advisor with Dutko Worldwide, a bipartisan Government Relations Company headquartered in Washington, D.C.

161. Governor Miller has written a highly acclaimed autobiography entitled *Son of a Gambling Man* (Thomas Dunne Books, 2013). On Amazon you can find many positive reviews from various media: Steve Forbes, CEO of Forbes; John Walsh, host of the popular TV show *America's Most Wanted*; Harry Reid, Senate Majority Leader; Wayne Newton, famous singer and perennial Vegas showman; and James Carville, Bill Clinton Presidential Campaign Lead Strategist, and co-host and commentator on CNN. I see them all a lot on CNN here in Tokyo. Now with Japan considering getting into casinos, Mr.

Miller can be a great resource. He goes around the world on other business and consulting gigs too. We briefly met up for a second time in Japan about 15 or 20 years ago. A very connected and also very nice gentleman. I read somewhere on the web something like, "at 6 feet 5 inches, Bob is a great basketball player, who until the end without giving up, would/will make the winning shot for you". So a good man to have on your team.

162. I finally got remarried on Christmas Day 2007, after 25 years of not being married. It's not a public holiday here so you can register at the local Japanese government office. There was some procedure at the US Embassy here as well. The American Consular Services person blurted out, "It's about time!" Not sure that was in her job description. Anyway, the next day we got on a plane for a small family wedding at the Cornell Club on 44th street in Manhattan, NYC. It's pretty much within view of a lineup of university clubs all on 44th Street—Harvard, University of Pennsylvania, Yale and Brown. Princeton and Columbia are on 43rd street. I guess they want to be near the theatre district, or something? I was a founding member behind the construction of the Cornell Club in Manhattan when I used to make money. I think TAC Tokyo American Club members have a reciprocal relationship with the Cornell Club. Tom Inglis, the general manager, is a good friend, and has been there forever (later).

How to Remove Bloody Mary, Wine, and Bloody Tom Blood Stains—Few Men or Women Know this. Manila, Philippine Experiences—Audience with President Ferdinand Marcos, and Getting to Know a Little Bit Gary Valenciano, the "Michael Jackson of the Philippines".

163. At our Cornell Club wedding dinner, the maître d' spilled a whole very large carafe of red wine on Chika's white wedding dress. We had bought it at Printemps Department store in Ginza a couple of weeks before. I remembered an old trick Barney Williamson, Hercules Japan CEO, and a former president of the American Chamber in Japan, taught me 30,000 feet up in the air. We were in a plane—dah—funny joke. We were on our way to an APCAC/Asian Pacific Council of American Chambers of Commerce meeting in Manila. I think it was 1979. The event included a visit to the Malacanang Palace, and a meeting with Ferdinand Marcos, Presidential Dictator of the Philippines. I managed to spill a whole glass of Bloody Mary all over the only suit I brought with me—A very light blue one, almost white. I looked very cool in it. Mr. Williamson asked the air hostess for 2 bottles of tansan/carbonated water. He poured it generously all over me. Stunned by the cold, but all the stain completely left my suit. No streaking at all. He also knew the jet's rug would be fine. It was.

164. So I startled the Cornell maître d' by asking him for his largest bottle of club soda. He had not been a marine officer. Barney said the marines soaked each other in club soda all the time. By Brother Art, who survived without food for that week with us in the White Mountains was calmly surprised. "I'm impressed, Tommy." First time I ever got that from him. Everyone was amazed. My new wife Chika's wedding dress came out without a mark or a streak on it. She can even use it again if she leaves me like a dog and remarries. Something I learned from Chika lately: for any cotton and maybe other textiles. Even if a thick, fluffy full-size bath towel is totally soaked in blood, detergents, washing machines, dry cleaning etc. won't

work well. You know what will? You get a big old bucket. You just soak it in cold water. Maybe change the water a couple times. Please don't ask me why I know this. After New Year's Eve together with the family at the Cornell Club near Times Square, we spent our honeymoon in Las Vegas at the Bellagio. We didn't want to barge in on Louisa or Governor Miller. No gambling. Just walking, the shows, and some great food.

165. On another New Year's Eve in 1985 we flew into Manila on December 29 and checked into the iconic Manila Hotel, where General MacArthur stayed before the Japanese booted him out. With the, "I shall return," he meant to the hotel, which he did. I was on top of things for a change. So right away reserved good seats for the New Year's Eve show in the hotel ballroom. Gary Valenciano was performing with a famous female singer. Gary was 21 years old and pretty much at the start of an illustrious career. He has released 26 albums; 5 platinum, 4 double platinum, 3 triple platinum, and 2 sextuple platinum. Hmmm... Mr. Valenciano was the sixth of seven children. Gary has won the Awit Award for "Best Male Performer" 11 of the last 21 years. He is nicknamed Gary V., or Mr. Pure Energy. In 1998 he became UNICEF's first Philippine National Ambassador. And held this position over 10 years. Also an actor. Won the "Best Single Performance By an Actor" in the 22nd PMPC Star Awards for TV in 2008. So still going strong, despite his well-publicized and famous struggle against his diabetes.

166. After the fabulous show, when we got in the elevator, an attractive Filipino lady was carrying four drinks in her hands. She said, "Your little boys are so cute. I saw you upfront watching the show. That guy dancing and singing is my husband." I thought, yeah right lady. Tip

down a couple more. But it ended up that it was true. We exchanged cards and info. Three months later Gary came to Japan representing the Philippines in some big International Music Festival. I think it was at the Budokan right along the Imperial Palace moat in Kudanshita. On Friday, March 29th that year, before or after his show, Gary and his wife came over to our apartment facing the Imperial Palace in Ichibancho.

167. The same apartment that later on might have been the launching pad for the poisonous chemical attack on the Japanese Emperor and Imperial Palace (later) by the Aum Cult (above). We made homemade sushi together. Then, now, and forever, this shining star's fame never went to his head. Mr. Gary Valenciano was the nicest, humblest person you could possibly meet. His wife's dad was also in the staff supply business. Sending Filipino workers all over the world. I had lunch with Gary's wife's dad when he came to Japan on business. I remember the dad gave me some candid advice. He said I should have a separate secret lair/hideaway somewhere to be able to go off line and think, chill-out, and… I guess he did not know much about our 40,000 reasonably priced and very comfortable short-term stay love hotels.

168. Have you Googled Lake Waccabuc yet? Just check out Wikipedia. I didn't think it was that ritzy glitzy in those days. As Wiki states as of 2010, even though that was long after the Lehman Crash, the median home value is $1,375,000; the highest of any zip code in Westchester County. That amount is double the town of Lewisboro average, and 4 times higher than the average for Westchester County, which is not a shabby place. We sold our over 4-acre house on the lake after I graduated from high school, so it was soon after June of 1968. My

dad had already been spending weekdays in a Summit, New Jersey apartment because his company moved from downtown Manhattan to its own campus in Berkley Heights, New Jersey. They let me stay on in Waccabuc for a year with my mom to finish H.S at John Jay. And I did have responsibilities for sure. Probably more pressure, tension and hard work than any time since. I had to run Lewisboro (Boy Scout) Troop #1 and wanted to make it #1 in the Muscoot District (out of 15 troops), become an Eagle Scout in a flash, run the Senior High Student Council, and captain our championship gymnastics team etc. That year at our traditional tri-school concert with Bedford and Mount Kisco's Fox Lane H. S., and Chappaqua's Horace Greeley H. S., my school John Jay H. S. in Cross River had to host this three school joint concert in our John Jay gym.

169. The mod kids who went down to Greenwich Village wanted the Cream, or Paul Butterfield Blues Band. I think we won the vote for the Lovin' Spoonful and John Sebastian 'Do You Believe in Magic?' (1965), the all summer #1 hit 'Summer in the City' (1966), and 'You Didn't Have to be so Nice' (1966). We paid them $5,000. I believe in cash. That may be too much. It was a long time ago. A $1,200 figure is also in my head. I think I recall feverishly counting the money with my girlfriend, Laura, who was secretary of the Student Council, and with the incredible-in-every-way Cathie Gordon, who was our treasurer. We didn't get to see any of the concert. But we heard it. Lovin' Spoonful went into the Rock and Roll Hall of Fame in 2000. This was 15 years before the Paul Butterfield Blues Band were nominated to be inducted in 2015. That's why the mod pot-smoker lost the president of the Student Council election to me ☺. Actually, Steve

was a good guy and a friend, and we played at each other's houses back in Lewisboro Elementary School.

Could have used a Couple More Lovin' Spoonfuls of Gold when We Sold Our Waccabuc Estate.

170. Back to selling our rambling two-storey house along the shores of Lake Waccabuc. It was just across from "the island" with its centuries-old "Indian Ovens"—2 of them carved 8 to 12 feet deep into a 10 to 12-foot-tall sandstone rock. This is where most of us first saw a coed schoolmate's torso—more native than Pocahontas. The only approach to the island without breaking a leg was close to the ovens, and even canoes (aluminum) are noisy, so it was very private. There were straight ridges in the flat sandstone areas made by the Lake waves over the centuries. The only smooth place to lie down was on top of the large sandstone rock with the ovens below. It must have been worn smooth by the Indian Baker on his breaks. And a lot of lovers after that. Maybe the chief of the local tribe sat up there surveying his lake and getting first dib's on the warm bread. It was also a safe look-out point.

171. And above the vision line of anyone but Phil Silvers if he used binoculars from his living room. (More on that later.) The sale… We got $69,000 for our 4-acre estate with our own shoreline, and with two stone columns my dad built at the entranceway. When still on my driver's permit, I knocked two stones out the first time I was behind the wheel with my mom in my mother's sky-blue Mercury Comet. "Thomas, this is not your fire truck!"

she screamed. I had been a very cocky driver in my fire truck. I helped my dad cement the stones back in that weekend. The $69,000 was from an IBM gentleman who held on to our home until about 2007. The next year in 1969 our neighbor, a father that worked at P & G/Proctor and Gamble, with Teddy who went to Princeton, and Paul who went to Northwest, sold his 4-acre estate for almost twice as much $122,000.

172. Before the sale of the house is complete, and while on the subject of bare-chested Indians, for the history lovers… On February 24, 2013 at the Waccabuc Country Club, an amazing Renaissance gentleman named Alex Shoumatoff delivered a fascinating talk at the Club. I was not in attendance. They would not have let me in. I read the script of the talk on Mr. Shoumatoff's very interesting website, www.dispatchesfromthevanishingworld.com, 'Dispatches From the Vanishing World'. I never looked for a Renaissance man before. I thought they all died off a few hundred years ago. I did try and find a few Renaissance women. Mr. Alex Shoumatoff also has a very large Wikipedia profile. As far as I have experienced, it seems to me that Mr. Shoumatoff has written books and articles on the widest range of subjects, and also on the most remote places on the globe. I don't know who could possibly beat him on that.

Discovered this True Renaissance man, Mr. Alex Shoumatoff, Speaking at the Waccabuc Country Club. His 1986 Vanity Fair *Article Led to Sigourney Weaver's* Gorillas in the Mist *film—Nominated for 5 Oscars and Won 2 Golden Globe Awards—Just the Tip of One of Mr. Shoumatoff's Many Icebergs of Accomplishments.*

173. Mr. Shoumatoff was a magazine staff writer or writer for *Village Voice*, the *New Yorker*, *Vanity Fair*, *Conde Nast Traveler*, to name a few. He has had books about the remotest places in Africa, South America, Asia, and everywhere on an incredibly wide area of subjects. His many books have been published by fine houses such as Knopf, Avon, Vintage, Simon and Schuster, Little Brown, Sierra Club Books. Just one example of Mr. Shoumatoff's impactful articles is a 1986 *Vanity Fair* magazine article about the mountain gorilla advocate Dian Fossey in Rwanda. It became the film *Gorillas in the Mist* with Sigourney Weaver playing Ms. Fossey. This 1988 film was nominated for 5 Oscars and won two Golden Globe awards.

174. It looks as though Alex Shoumatoff was born at Mount Kisco hospital, where my big sister was a candy striper (not stripper). In the States, I think a candy striper is usually a young female volunteer who, more commonly during summer breaks, helps nurses with their duties at hospitals. I guess their uniforms have some stripes. Kathy's were red. Kathy is just 3 months older than Mr. Shoumatoff so she did not assist with that birth. Alex Shoumatoff grew up in Bedford where we would go to the movies and church, almost as often as our trips to Ridgefield Connecticut, just across the state border.

175. By the way, whereas in all of Japan, the drinking and smoking age is 20, when I grew up in New York State, New York's drinking age was 18, and Connecticut's was 20. So a lot of kids from Connecticut would cross the border. It seems in the 1960s there was a movement to lower some states' drinking ages. But then with some 1984 federal law effecting federal government highway subsidies, states have tended to increase their drinking ages to 21. Including New York State. I once went to a

home party, where the family was seriously saying that half their home was in New York, and the other was straddling the border with Connecticut. No. There was not always a state trooper with his nose to the glass, making sure the high-school kids drank on the N. Y. State side of the house.

176. Young Alex went to the Rippowam School, a private school that I knew about. The school is not so close to our Lake Rippowam, which is connected to Lake Waccabuc by a channel after a paddle on Lake Oscaletta. After that, Mr. Shoumatoff went to Harvard, and then on with these larger than life accomplishments, including as a gifted guitar player and musical score writer—some catchy tunes in his *Suitcase on the Loose* album. He is fluent in of course English, French, Portuguese, Spanish and Russian. Mr. Shoumatoffs' website says he is nearly fluent in German, Italian, Modern Greek, Kiswahili, and speaks 'serviceable' Kinyawrands, Kirundi, and Rugenda. And he has rudimentary Cayapo. Living in many of these areas helped, but truly amazing. He also climbed many mountains, white-watered many rivers, and played a lot of golf around the world in the middle of these other attainments.

177. The USA is one of the worst countries when it comes to the perceived need or effort to learn foreign languages. Japan also needs to get much better. I always thought one reason Japan was weak in English and other languages was that there was no need to speak or really know a foreign language to reach the top of most organizations. Including government office. The majority of the population did not have good English, and perhaps the majority and the elites did not want that situation to change. In so many other countries, having foreign languages goes hand in

hand with reaching the top. Hopefully this situation can improve in Japan, with companies like Mr. Yanai's Uniqlo and Mr. Mikitani's Rakuten insisting and testing whether or not employees are learning English.

178. I recall reading on Mr. Shoumatoff's website that he got the highest college board scores in the nation on the Homeric Greek and Attic Greek tests. I suppose like my writing in this book, it is written that Mr. Shoumatoff likes to write on a wide variety of subjects, and with a lot of facts and details (except mine are all in the same book☺)! So he is a good hometown neighborhood *senpai*/ senior for me. Next to my senior picture in the 1968 yearbook, the editor's last phrase was 'Great mind for trivia'. My dad did not like that. "Why didn't you control those guys?"

"We don't get a sneak peek, Dad." It didn't bother me. Because it's true.

As Mr. Shoumatoff Knows from Learning Many Languages we have never even heard of because He lived in those Exotic Places, Traveling, and 'Making Our Move' can Open Up our Eyes, Our World and Help Us See and Think Differently. The Yen is Cheap Now.
Time to Come to Nihon!

179. I don't know how many others did it. But on Princeton Educational Testing Service Scholastic Aptitude American History and World History Achievement tests, I got the perfect score of 800 on both of those college board tests. I think a big reason for that was that our parents took us to some historical sites on the East Coast and Canada. Also when I was maybe 13, we went on a

Cook Tour of Europe. Travel can change us in interesting ways. Travel can never be taken away from us. Unless we bang our head or something. I banged my head on the Great Pyramid of Giza. The pyramid won. It's the largest one of the 3 you can see from your Cairo hotel room. Be careful. It happened as we reached the top, and as I turned too quickly to enter the open chamber. Too dark—needs a couple more light bulbs. We were lucky on our timing. It was just a few months before Egypt's Arab Spring when Mr. Mubarak stepped down. No time in this book for the amazing things that happened in Egypt.

180. I believe my age 13 European tour was something like 8 European countries in 21 days. As Mr. Alex Shoumatoff so well shows us, a decent memory can be helpful. Our lives and days are determined by the details of how we spend our minutes and seconds. I have found on the web, no evidence that Alex Shoumatoff has been to Tokyo. I hope he, and any of my old friends in this book, or those not in this book, will be in touch with me and meet up if they can get over this way. The last 9 months, as of about mid-2014, the yen has become weaker. So please get over here before it cycles back up!

181. Now for my first insight into this remarkable Renaissance man from the land of my roots. I came across Mr. Shoumatoff's Waccabuc Country Club talk in transcribed form on the web. I didn't even know who was talking, when the talk took place, or where it took place, until I 'listened' to (read the entire transcript of) the talk, and wanted to learn of its origins. This is a great thing about trips into cyberspace on the web; it is a bit like Alex Shoumatoff's description of the uncanny, serendipitous, accidental discoveries that change and alter our lives when we physically travel, and expose ourselves to new places, people and their influence.

Some of his stories in his Waccabuc Country Club talk, I found repeated in other sources.

182. But one story from Mr. Shoumatoff that I will search more into from this moment, is the story of an Indian massacre ordered by the then Dutch Governor of New Amsterdam in 1644... After a few hours on the web, I confirmed the site of the massacre, and read all about the history of the Dutch discovering the Hudson River, the first settlements on Governors Island etc., and as far north as Beverwyck (Beavertown?) now Albany. Also many other very interesting insights about New York City—a city that I know fairly well, and very much enjoy visiting. For instance who ever was the first non-native American to trap beaver pelts had the beaver all to himself? Had as much beaver as he wanted, while informally representing the Dutch? Of course! It was the Dominican trader Juan Rodriguez born in Santo Domingo of Portuguese and African descent—the first New Yorker, err, New Amsterdamer. (Santo Domingo was discovered by Christopher Columbus in 1492, settled by his younger brother Bartholomew Columbus in 1496, and is the oldest continuously populated settlement in the New World. Santo Domingo is the home of the first castle, church, monastery, university, and fort built in all of the New World.)

Now You Know the Name of the First New Yorker. Who Was the First Geek, who Got Sucker Punched by the Indian Who Sold the Manhattan Island that he didn't own?

183. The first non-native New Yorker, Juan Rodriguez, arrived during the winter of 1613 to 1614. The 1620 Plymouth Rock Pilgrims were actually aiming for the Hudson River, however

the *Mayflower* instead reached Cape Cod, Massachusetts on November 9, 1620, after a 64-day cruise. They were beat. No more supplies. Better set up camp here. Back to New York. Between 1621 and 1623 orders were given for the private, commercial traders like Juan Rodriguez to vacate the New York City area of today. This allowed laws and ordinances of the State of Holland to apply. So Juan no longer ruled. The first family men came in 1624. According to writer Nathaniel Benchley, about that time, Peter Minuit bought the Manhattan island from the Lenape chief Seyseys for not the '$24 dollars', but more like 60 Dutch guilders. At the 2012 exchange rate more like $1,100. Seyseys was a happy Native American Chief because it was not even his island. It was controlled mostly by Weckquaesgeek Native Americans. Maybe where the name geek came from?

184. So no wonder there were the Indian wars—Native American against Native American with no direct round eye involvement. In fact the Mohawk-Mahican War in the Hudson Valley was already getting started. This was a war fought only between Native Americans. In a word it seems like the more warlike Iroquois nation tribes were moving in and taking over the land and the beaver from the geekier Algonquian tribes. This was a precursor to the Beaver Wars of the mid 1600's. They took place throughout New York State, further west in the lower Great Lakes and up the St. Lawrence River. It was triggered mostly because of this new demand for beaver skins from Europe. Pounded into felt they made great waterproof hats. Naturally—ever see a leaky beaver? They held their shape. Umbrellas for protection against the rain were not yet used in Europe. Indians had already become dependent on some European goods. I suppose this included guns. Man's pursuit of beaver continues to influence history and our lives. It is man's great

blessing but can also be his downfall. (For Puritans, Pilgrims and readers across the sea, beaver has a different meaning than the dam building furry animal. Think *"From Dusk to Dawn"* and the 26 pussy cats.)

185. New Amsterdam changed to New York when on August 27th 1664, four English frigates sailed into the harbor and demanded New Netherland's surrender. Kept it simple. This came like a lightning bolt out of the blue, because England and the Dutch Republic were at peace. Peter Stuyvesant might have been inclined to start shooting his cannon from Fort Amsterdam, but the majority of his citizens pleaded with him not to fire on the British. Instead on September 6, 1664, the Articles of Capitulation/ surrender were signed. In June 1665, the city became New York City under English law. It was named after the Duke of York. (He had his own Beaver Wars break out in January, 2015. Andy was always Randy, and he was still single. Beaver entrapment? Young beaver, just like undersized fish on Lake Waccabuc, best be returned to the pond.) New York's namesake, the Duke of York, went on to be King James II of England. The New York area had been granted to his brother, who was the English King Charles II, before James took over and got the kingly crown.

186. Having fun here, but still can only find Mr. Alex Shoumatoff's words on a horrific Native American massacre ordered by the Dutch Governor of New Amsterdam 20 years before the name changed to New York. It was 1644. Some Indians had attacked and killed some European settlers. Presumably near or around Lake Waccabuc and Katonah, and probably places south of that in current day Westchester County. John Underwood was engaged by the Dutch Governor to hire 200 mercenaries. They went to a spot where Pepsi

Cola has one of its Westchester offices. It is not the head office further south in Purchase, New York. It looks like it is a Credit Union building for Pepsi staff. On Google satellite, as Mr. Shoumatoff tells us, you can see that this Pepsi campus is very close to the Muscoot Reservoir, on a street called Pepsi Way—dah. A good-sized building with a large partially filled parking lot. At least it was so when the Google satellite snapped that shot.

187. Where do the Google satellite pictures come from? Well, soon they will come from Google! According to Elyse Wanshel in an August 11, 2014 article on *Motherboard*, in June or July 2014, Google finally acquired its own private satellite company, Sky Box Imaging. This was shortly after the US government relaxed its satellite imagery restrictions in June, 2014. Imagery moved from 50-cm resolution to 25-centimeter resolution. Up until this point Google satellite shots were rented or bought from a company called DigitalGlobe. In August, 2014 this company had five satellites in the sky. Google intends to launch a constellation of 24 satellites by 2018. Actually, competition from other countries' companies is pushing this. It is certainly not just a USA game.

188. More on the 1644 Indian Massacre taking place where Pepsi has its employee credit union. About 180 Native Americans were shot as they tried to run away. Then their douchebag, dumb-as-a-post leader ordered them to 'flee and hide' in their residential lodges—huh? Maybe leader not sharpest knife in teepee. Underwood's mercenaries set fire to those lodges. The 500 Indians were very obedient. Women, children, and braves stayed put in their lodges. There was not a sound of screaming, or even crying or weeping. Mr. Shoumatoff read the diary of one of the mercenaries who wrote that those

burning Indians' silence, strength of spirit, and his own cruelty, haunted that mercenary the rest of his life. Such cruelty among men has always been with us. Stories like this make me feel good about the Native American reservation casino phenomenon in the United States. It had not started when I lived there. At first I was puzzled and surprised when I heard about it. And I didn't even know there were Native American lands and reservations nearby in New York and Connecticut.

Some Parties in Tokyo and Japan are Hopeful that There Can be Casinos Here, as there are in Macao and Singapore. Since I've been in Japan, in the USA, 240 Native American Tribes Started-up and Ran 460 Casinos on their Indian Reservations!

189. There was a unanimous Supreme Court decision authored by Justice William Brennan in the 1976 case of Bryan v. Itasca County. A county in Minnesota had tried to tax a Native American's mobile home located on the Indian reservation. The court ruled that the state did not have the authority to impose such a tax. It also held that more generally the state had no right to regulate behavior on the reservation. This led to Indian gaming on reservations. As of 2011 there were 460 gambling operations run by 240 Indian tribes, with total annual revenue of $27,000,000,000 dollars. It was further confirmed and codified by the Native American Gaming Regulatory Act of 1988 that the reservations have tribal sovereignty. New York State has 8 Native American Casinos owned by the Oneida Indian Nation, The St. Regus Mohawk Tribe, and the Seneca Nation of Native Americans. The Geeky tribe (above) got

elbowed out again! In the November, 2013 state election, New York voters approved a Constitutional Amendment to authorize up to 7 new casinos. Connecticut has two Native American Casinos—Foxwoods Resort Casino, and Mohegan Sun Casino. There are also often racetracks on the reservation properties.

190. In 2007, just before Lehman, I wanted to show my 26-year-old son, Johnny, my Lewisboro elementary school. We met a nice lady in the playground playing with her little girl. This nice lady, when she learned about my Waccabuc and Japan thing, told me in front of her child, and my son that she had considered buying my house, which was largely built in 1956 or 57, "But we didn't have time for a teardown. It's on the market for $2,200,000." So maybe Puff Daddy, or Keith Richards, or some guy who caused Lehman to crash, also crashed my house down. Yes. Google Satellite shows something better. But why do some of these lake houses need a big swimming pool when you have potable lake water just 100 meters down your own hill? We didn't drink the lake water. A Mr. Stone, as mentioned above, most definitely the Republican politico Roger Stone's dad, dug our well. Before that we took our first boat, a heavy, ugly, gray wooden row boat, over to 'the spring', past the Gullen's place, two doors down, but before the Waccabuc Country Club's lake shore swimming and boating facility. A small town—Mr. Stone dug everyone's well. After that, we didn't have to row to fill jugs at 'the spring' anymore. It took two Vikings to row that boat and make ripples.

191. It was the Moore Brothers who later on built our summer cottage's stone foundation, fireplace, chimney and patio. Maybe the rest of the cottage too along with George what's-his-name? Can't quite remember. Maybe

Cunningham. All the stones were right on site. I need to mention that all through our 4 acres, periodically there were heaped up stonewalls. No cement, just nicely piled-up stone fences. As a boy, all I could think of was colonists wanting protection from fighting the Indians or fighting the British Redcoats during the Revolutionary War. The perennial mostly hemlock tree canopy was so thick that no light would hit the forest floor. This was good because it meant there were no scrubby plants or bushes. You could run between the trees really fast. Kind of like in a Robin Hood movie chasing Maid Marian in her knickers, or *Game of Thrones* being chased by pure weirdness. It also meant there would be snow on the forest floor, yet clean white snow the whole winter. Hard to picture those 2 to 4 feet thick tree trunks having once been farmland, or even grazing pastures. Stonewalls? Maybe they didn't want their cows or sheep to get away. And maybe they wanted to remove the stones so their farm animals would not sprain their ankles and break their legs on all those rocks. There also were some pits full of stones.

192. Now I realize those pits were probably houses or sheds with root cellars. The houses disintegrated, or somebody used the wood. Only the chimneys and fire places collapsed into the cellars. Tenant farmers could have been leasing the land from Lord Stephan Van Cortlandt or his progeny even before Enoch Mead came and bought the land in 1776 (later). You take the stone walls for granted. You don't discuss something like that with your parents. Not with anyone. If a kid wanted to get bullied at school he would start having serious conversations about stone walls, secret swamps, and root cellars. After I left the area, and as confirmed by recently seeing old paintings such as on the Waccabuc Country Club website, all around all

three channel-connected lakes, except the steep mountain sides of Waccabuc and Rippowam, there was farming land or pastures. No trees! No forest! Lately we have been reading that while the Brazilian rainforest gets smaller, forests all around the US, Europe, and many other places are growing much larger. More bears, wolves, and other wild animals are coming back into old civilized Europe. This is happening at even a faster rate than the wild animals are increasing in the USA and Canada. But it is happening there too. In Japan too, people nowadays are getting attacked and eaten much more frequently by bears and inoshishi wild boars. So there is still hope—huh? You know what I mean. The world does not necessarily have to go in the same bad straight-line projection. Japan's population of hunters are very old, and decreasing—from 600,000 down to 200,000. Many local areas are providing subsides to have young people go into hunting.

193. The Moore brothers would have done the cottage about 1954 or 1955. I think it was at that time that the Moore brothers left an old black jalopy on our land for many months. I know the cottage was finished because I remember getting my only beating from my dad on the Castro Convertible Sofa my parents and probably the rest of us all slept on together. My 5-year-old, 14-month-older brother, Art Jr. and I decided to gas up the black jalopy car with Mr. Stone's well water, and drive it off our land. It was a bit of an eyesore. I think even my brother disapproved when I added some stones "so we could rock and roll on the way down" our 150-meter long drive way. But big sister Kathy was 8 years old and snitched on us. Therefore the Castro beating. And I think no one drove the car away. If anyone could, it would be Sam and Rube Moore. On a cold snowy weekend we came back and noticed the car was

not there. Maybe our dad took care of the problem for us with the Moore brothers. Luckily I was too young to have an allowance. So damages to the car could not be taken out of my allowance. I think we offered to hand back our toothfairy quarters. More about the Moore brothers later.

It was a Dark and Foggy Summer Night. Tales of the Ghost of the Crazed Naked Waccabuc Axe Man Must have been told for Years at John Jay High School before I Went there.

194. Our tent life on the lake before the summer cottage... It must have been part of just one summer, when we were starting to get work on the cottage off the ground. You already heard about a couple legendary characters, Sarah Bishop and her cave, and the Leatherman and his 584-kilometer/365-mile monthly round of homestead visits. Now for a ghost story that may be in one of Maureen Koehl's books. Our dad's actions one night are probably not in Maureen Koehl's (the Lewisboro Town historian's) books, and maybe not on the web, but I guarantee you our dad scared the daylights out of what was probably one young couple just looking for a quiet place to get to know each other. One dark and foggy summer's night, Dad was shaving over a pot of heated water on the Coleman stove. He used a flashlight for light. He had white shaving cream all over his face. We were in the dark tent but could see through the musty dark green canvas big lights coming down our gravel, muddy, puddled driveway. With a small, young family of 5 to protect, and being a good Catholic boy from Bayridge, Brooklyn, it is a little hard to know what buzzed through our Dad's brain. Dad really didn't know what these country boys were like. Maybe they didn't like city folk comin' in.

195. My dad grabbed a long-handled axe, put the flashlight below his chin lighting up the face of a freaky abominable snowman having a bad trip. All the pure horror and terror he could muster. The loudly growling white rage wearing only his boxer underpants, and holding a threatening 4-foot/120-centimeter axe over his head went charging toward the car. That kid probably just finished his driver's education course. He grazed a couple of hemlock trees as he floored it in reverse up the hill and around the bend. Luckily we probably didn't have the fieldstone pillars at the driveway entrance up yet. I'm sure the kid found a more open spot. No more secluded driveways for him. He probably had to go home early and change his trousers that night.

196. Think about it. When that driver came back during the day with 3 or 4 hardy friends a few days later, as he probably did, there was still no house, no well. The tent was packed up and back in Long Island. What would he think? Is that how ghost stories start? Could Jason Voorhees in 'Friday the 13th' movie series at Chrystal Lake, be based on my dad at Lake Waccabuc?—hah, hah, hah, hah, hah, hah... (The reader having a long belly laugh.) Seriously, if this driver, or his girlfriend are still alive, and get their hands on this book, please email me at tom.nevins@tmt-aba.com. I will send you a box of 3 different types of sake. Just remembered—can't mail booze to the States. How about replacement trousers?

197. Maureen Koehl writes about the Christmas soldier ghost. James Fenimore Cooper (1789-1851) was a very famous New York novelist who wrote 32 novels including the 1826 novel *The Last of the Mohicans—A Narrative of 1757*. This was one of my favorite movies (1992) with Daniel Day Lewis, and Madeline Stowe. A great musical score

by Trevor Jones and Randy Edelman. The second novel Cooper wrote 5 years earlier in 1821 was *The Spy: a Tale of the Neutral Ground*. Also very famous and widely read. In 1811 at age 21 Cooper married Susan Augusta de Lancey, at Mamaroneck, Westchester County, New York. So at the time Cooper was living in Westchester, and getting himself immersed in local history and legends. In history, a real-life patriotic spy was helping George Washington against the British. He lived in a colonial house still in Lewisboro. In Cooper's novel, this spy is the main character, Harvey Birch.

198. The real Harvey Birch was a chap named Enoch Crosby. Crosby died in 1855. Since then, and even today, on Christmas Eve before the clock strikes midnight, whether crystal-clear starry skies, or in howling, below-zero snow blizzards, people see Enoch Crosby, the Revolutionary War-dressed soldier, walking along Route 22 and elsewhere, with his musket over his shoulder, on his way home to that colonial house. Or looking out one of the windows of that house. I have a feeling it might be too much egg nog, or mulled wine. Or could it be one of the Gullen or Hawthorne brothers dressed the part?… My dad gave me James Fenimore Cooper's five part Leatherstocking Tales book series— *The Pioneers*, 1823; *The Last of the Mohicans*, 1826; *The Prairie*, 1827; *The Pathfinder*, 1840; and *The Deerslayer*, 1841. The same ones he read 40 years earlier when he was 10 years old back in 1921. I read them all mostly rocking in the hammock between two hemlock trees near the lake. Sometimes I carried them off into the woods for a read. I would sit on a stone wall, or lie back on one of our beautiful rock outcroppings—dreaming that I was Natty Bumppo/Hawkeye in my own New

York forest. I still use my Boy Scout Pathfinder compass all the time (later).

199. Rock Outcroppings. If you know them, even those in Central Park, Manhattan, there is nothing more virtuous, more elegant, or more inspiring. We would build our forts on top of ours. Or tie a treehouse into a huge rock outcropping. Our two-door down neighbors, the Gullens, have one of the most spectacular rock outcroppings on Lake Waccabuc. Within sight of their dock. They had a dry creek bed, wetting up only with big rainstorms. It was straight down from their house with this 15-meter/49.2126 foot rock towering above the path on the right as you approach the water. Not the scale of El Capitan's Dawn Wall at Yosemite National Park. But even Kevin Jorgeson and his climbing partner Tommy Caldwell would have sighed and scratched their heads. They at least would have wanted a safety harness. Ethan Hunt/Tom Cruise in *Mission Impossible II* wouldn't bother with the harness. We had several great rock formations on our 4 acres almost as spectacular. There was one 10-meter slide run when it iced over, just off to the left of our front lawn. Facing the driveway, it was within 15 meters of the living room bay window.

200. The Gullen family made a huge contribution to Waccabuc coming in from Scotland and designing and managing the Waccabuc Country Club's golf courses. As I recall, after the Club stopped doing the Fourth of July fireworks over the lake, at least for a few years the Gullens at their own expense presented and executed an impressive fireworks display for the Three Lakes' community. They did this off the same float we always played 'King of the Mountain' off of when we wore a younger man's bathing suit. This was an unpretentious game that even

I could grasp. Throw everybody in the water. Who's the last man standing? After Jack Gullen started his high-bar gymnastics a year earlier, it was almost impossible to break free from his grasp. But you could sumo him in the drink. The Gullens' fireworks display would be along with the huge annual 4ᵗʰ of July barbecue party they would throw every year. So a lot of people in our hometown are better off that the Gullens 'made a move' from Scotland, but then 'stayed put' in Waccabuc.

201. Right across Lake Waccabuc from us was 'the Point'. An American comedian named Phil Silvers owned that summer house with its front on stilts. There was about a 60-meter 'channel' between the Point and the only island on Lake Waccabuc. I can't quickly find on the web where Phil Silvers lived, but that was what we always knew. My dad liked 'The King of Chutzpah', Sergeant Bilko in *The Phil Silvers Show*. Maybe it was also because they were both born in Brooklyn the same year, 1911. This was the last year of the Meiji Emperor period in Japan. (Japan's formal dates and legal dates still pretty much go by the Emperor in power, so 2015 is Heiwa 27. Heiwa means 'Era of Peace'—that it has been for Japan. And most of us hope Prime Minister Abe does not change the direction on that. This has nothing to do with the Emperor's name. It is just that now is the 27ᵗʰ year of the current Emperor's reign. Emperor Hirohito reigned for 63 years until 1989. At its start, that 63-year period was named Showa (ironically meaning 'Illustrious Peace'. For complex reasons, and the bombing of Pearl Harbor, there was not always peace.) So all my/everyone's bank checks, bank transfer payment dates, bank account book entries, all formal dates are based on the Emperor's reign!—believe it or

not. Back to Mr. Silvers. Wikipedia writes that in 1996, TV Guide ranked Phil Silvers number 31 on its "50 Greatest TV Stars of All Time" List.

Marilyn Monroe got married in Waccabuc!
I never Talked to or Touched Ms. Monroe.
But I Got Lucky with Princess Diana!

202. Ms. Marilyn Monroe (1926-1962) got married in Waccabuc on July 1, 1956! She married Arthur Miller (1915-2005) in a Jewish ceremony at the home of Mr. Miller's literary agent, Ms. Kay Brown. Mr. Miller was Jewish. So Marilyn converted to that religion for those years of her marriage. Only 30 friends and relatives were there. I was not invited because they had no idea who I was. One of Miller's most famous plays, *The Crucible*, was made into a French language film in 1957, and a Hollywood film in 1996 with Ms. Winoa Ryder and Mr. Daniel Day Lewis. *The Crucible* was a critique of, in particular, our Judge Hathorne at the Salem Witch trials. Also of the anti-communist crusader Mr. Joe McCarthy. Both mentioned earlier. We were probably in Waccabuc on that July 1, 1956 day when Ms. Monroe married Mr. Miller. It was a Sunday. We were probably on our way home from Catholic Church.

203. I didn't get invited to Marilyn's wedding. However, years later in Tokyo, with Prince Charles standing at her side, I had a chance to shake hands with, and talk, oh so briefly to, Princess Diana (July 1, 1961—August 31, 1997). As I reached over the rope, I asked, "Will a Yankee do?"

Princess Diana winked and answered, "A Yankee will do just fine." We shook hands. That night I showered with my right hand in a plastic bag fastened by rubber bands. The next morning too. I was lucky to be with the British Chamber at the Teikoku/Imperial Gekijo/Theater across from the Imperial Palace that evening for that British Chamber of Commerce event. I remember that sorrowful and dispirited day, scorching hot, in a sun-bleached world on August 31, 1997, walking on the Ginza. It was a Sunday. There were guys and girls handing out special "extra- read all about it" one-page newspaper editions on Princess Diana's accident in Paris on all the Ginza street corners. We were all crushed. Years later I would be handed one on Osama bin Laden's demise. Again, I happened to be on the Ginza. The only two such newspaper extras ever handed to me on the street like that.

204. I'm sure you have famous, influential people in your town too. But with a population of 500, give or take, Waccabuc has its share. According to Wikipedia and other public and private sources, in addition to rapper, actor, record producer and entrepreneur Sean Combs; and The Rolling Stones' Keith Richards; there lived or now live, Henry A. Wallace, the World War II serving Vice President and Secretary of Agriculture under President Franklin D. Roosevelt; Stanley O'Neal, former CEO of Merrill Lynch; Alfred Delbello, former Lieutenant Governor of New York; Bill McDonough, former Chairman of the Federal Reserve Bank; and William H. Donaldson, former Chairman of the SEC (Securities & Exchange Commission). (In 1934, Joseph P. Kennedy, President John F. Kennedy's father, got President Franklin Roosevelt's appointment to be the first SEC Chairman.)

205. Apparently, there is also William P. Lauder, CEO and President of Estee Lauder who has one home in Waccabuc. David Marks, is an original member of the Beach Boys.

And sticking with more interesting show business types, there is Blythe Danner, who had a stone cottage with lakefront. I've seen her in movies over the years about as many times as her daughter Gwyneth Paltrow. Gwyneth also has a place in Waccabuc. And even the Japanese will immediately recognize Mr. Stanley Tucci. It looks like he graduated from John Jay H.S. 10 years after I did in 1978. Mr. Tucci is in more movies than just about any actor I can think of. I always thought he was a great number-two character actor. He also has had lots of big leading-man role. Another actor, Mr. Campbell Scott, probably graduated from John Jay in 1979, a year later than Mr. Tucci. And Wikipedia lists about 20 more "Notable People".

206. Like so many places, not everything is perfect and idyllic in the Waccabuc area. In October 2011, there was tragedy with a family in Cross River, so rather close to my John Jay High School. And the 8-year-old and 10-year-old children went to the same Lewisboro Elementary school that I went to. The night before they were to appear in divorce court, an unfortunate 50-year-old Attorney, with the further complications of money problems, bludgeoned his wife with a furniture leg. Then he shot and killed his children with a shotgun as they slept. Went down to the basement, and shot himself in the head. Without the guns over here in Japan, maybe not as many bad things would have happened quite that quickly and easily. A big shock for these sleepy hamlets. His attractive 46-year-old wife had been a vice president of Chase Manhattan Bank. She was a partner in a local American-style *juku*/cram school called John Jay Prep. No such private cram school when I went to school. I think still not very common in most USA communities.

An Inside the Bubble Story. It's a Deafening Burst when
Real Estate Prices Flux 9.6 times in Just 1.5 Years!

207. I think part of the blame for this Cross River attorney's
family tragedy was similar to all the tragedy that
accompanied the burst of the Japanese real estate bubble
in about 1990 and 1991. At the time of these family
murders, his beautiful 1.6-acre (1,958 tsubo, or 6,461
square meters) of land, and 3,000-square-foot (279
square meters) house was on the market for $799,000.
But you can bet that he had not many years before bought
the property for about double that price. That was a very
doomed October. On a cold, dark Halloween weekend,
there was a freak 20-inch (51 centimeters) of snow. It
took down 90% of all of Lewisboro, including Waccabuc's
above-ground suspended power lines and power. It took
a week to completely restore power. Then the same
year in 2011 Hurricane Irene struck. Recall some New
York subways got flooded. Recently, this has happened a
couple times in Tokyo too, with "guerrilla rain" intense
storms that can drop the same 5-10 centimeters/2 to 4
inches of rain in just an hour or so.

208. For people around the world, and even some younger
Japanese, or those who forget, just how loudly the
real estate bubble burst here in Tokyo, I have a true,
inside story. Out of the 43 years I have lived in Tokyo,
the longest time that I have lived in Japan in the same
dwelling is 8 years. It seems I'm never 'staying put', and
always have to 'make a move'! There is a condominium
('mansion' in Japanese) facing the Imperial Palace, just
behind the little park, and the very next building to the
beautiful British Embassy. The Embassy is also along

the Imperial Palace moat, but up quite high. So this is the first building past the British Embassy on the same left-hand side, on the way to the infamous Yasukuni Shrine. This is the shrine also having interred 14 of the 25 Class A WWII leaders accused and convicted at the Far East War Crimes Tribunal. Leaders such as General/Prime Minister Tojo. Their souls are there, along with all the other Japanese soldiers who have died in war. The ruling party politicians' continuing visits to Yasukuni Shrine is the biggest source of friction with the Chinese and the Koreans. Along with those tiny rocky islands, especially since the famous right-wing Tokyo mayor, Shintaro Ishihara, had the metropolitan government buy the islands from private ownership. Then the central government felt compelled to buy them from Tokyo.

209. Back to my big Tokyo real estate bubble. We were renting a 38 tsubo/125 sq. meters/1,380-sq-foot, 3-bedroom apartment, with a second toilet and small sink closer to the living room facing the Imperial Palace. This is no large, luxurious Manhattan penthouse, filled with marble counters! (Later on ritzier but still not such large condos were built in Japan.) It was on the 8th floor. This Ichibancho Park Mansion was constructed in 1973 to 1974, shortly after I arrived in Japan. At the time when purchased new, it was 80,000,000 yen, say US $800,000. In 1989 an identical unit either right above or right below us sold for 1,380,000,000 yen, or $13,800,000. Within 1.5 years after that, an identical unit sold for only 144,000,000 yen/$1,440,000. Now that's a bubble—a flux of 9.6 times within a year and a half. Almost everything in the States between the peak of 2007, and the worst of post-Lehman was no worse than going down to half the price, right? By the way,

remember Aum Shinrikyo? The sarin gas cult that my first wife might have taken over?

210. The Aum cult sarin-gassed the subway lines where all the bureaucrats get on and off in the Kanchogai/government, Hibiya, Kasumigaseki area. It was not publicized at the time, and I can't find anything on the web. But we were first-hand witnesses to something also a bit frightening. Aum was going to use either our unit we had recently left, or the unit below or above us, to launch a missile and a poisonous chemical warfare attack on the Emperor and on the Imperial Palace. The Palace was just across the street and on the other side of the palace moat. To protect only themselves from the sarin gas that would have killed or sickened the rest of us, they assembled huge air purifiers from pieces brought into the condo. When the plot was unhatched, the authorities wanted the equipment intact. So I saw them cutting open the big glass picture windows, and taking the massive equipment out of the apartment using a huge crane operating from the park below. So some bad things can happen in Tokyo too.

Stephan Van Cortland Didn't Know it, but the Land He was granted by Royal Charter in 1697 was Large Enough to Accommodate 211,221,850 Samurai Sleeping Side by Side. Enoch Mead bought some of that Land in 1776 so He could be with His Dead Horse.

211. Now some more background on the Lake Waccabuc area, and a bit more on history. According to Jack Sanders, in *Ridgefield Place Names*, 2005, Lake Waccabuc used to be in Connecticut until 1731. Actually, the quaint and

well-manicured town of Ridgefield, Connecticut, was just over a couple hills, and was closer than the next two closest towns, Katonah (also made famous by Martha Stewart) and Bedford Village. According to Mr. Sanders, Waccabuc was one large glacier lake that was formed about 20,000 years ago. We knew it as 3 lakes connected together with two channels that were easy canoeing. An outboard motor worked fairly well but you would have to tilt the head of the motor down most of the way through the channels. This way the propeller would be very close to the water surface. Slowly, and carefully passing boats would spray each other at times.

212. These lakes were Waccabuc, the largest, and according to the "Three Lakes Council", 14.2 meters, /45 feet deep; Oscaleta, 10.8 meters/35 feet deep; and Rippowam, 5.8 meters/20 feet deep. I was convinced that as the shallower parts of the one large lake gradually filled in over thousands of years, the Native Americans would have wanted to move heavy things by canoe, so they probably kept the channels open. But then again, according to "The Town of Lewisboro, New York" website (Waccabuc is one of 6 Lewisboro hamlets with a total population of about 12,500 in all 6 hamlets), the first Indians were clearly in the area from 8,000 years ago or a bit before. So maybe there were already 3 separate lakes when the Indians came to the area. Maybe there were no channels. The Three Lakes' water was always supplied to Manhattan and NYC, as it flowed into the Cross River Reservoir and on down south to Manhattan. In 1876, NYC had a terrible drought, and the Three Lakes Council website relates that 300 men worked feverishly to lower the lakes drainage outlets, and dig 6-foot-deep canals between the lakes. So I suppose the channels only existed from 1876.

213. Mr. Jack Sanders writes that Waccabuc was called Wepack, Wepuc, or Wequa-paug by the Indians. Maybe depending on the day's magic mushroom omelet, or what they were smoking? The earliest European settlers also got high, a little confused and lazy, and said, "Screw that!" They just went for Long Pond. That was the name until 1860 when Martin R. Mead built the Waccabuc House Hotel. This hotel could accommodate 80 guests until it burned down in 1896. It was just across Mead Street from the Mead Memorial Chapel. The chapel was built in 1905, and is one of Waccabuc's National Register of Historic Places. Mrs. Gullen told me she was really upset that some of the new people moving in were trying to vote to have the chapel converted into a Starbucks so they could grab their coffee on the run. Another registered historic place being the Homestead house built by Alfred Mead (Enoch Mead's son) in 1820 at the corner of Mead Street and Schoolhouse Road. Actually there are older Mead houses in Waccabuc, but I suppose they were more renovated over the years than was the Homestead. So maybe for that reason they did not qualify for the National Register of Historic Places honor.

214. So what is this Mead name popping up? Well we and everyone else bought our land from the Mead family. According to a *History of the Town of Lewisboro* published by the South Salem Library Association, Enoch and Jeminma Mead came in from Greenwich Connecticut in 1776, the year the Revolutionary War started. Their beloved horse died near "Long Pond" so they decided to see if they could stay on there and buy the land. Much earlier, on June 17th 1697, a much too lucky chap named Stephan Van Cortlandt (1643-1700) by way of a royal

charter, became Lord of the Manor of Van Cortlandt. He was the first native-born mayor of New York City (1677-1678, and 1686-1688). In Westchester County alone he owned 86,213 acres (or 105,610,925 tsubo, a tsubo being 3.3 square meters or the size of two tatami mats. A decent fit for two Samurai to lie side by side). So 3,485,160,525 square meters. You can visit the Van Courtlandt House Museum, which is also called the Van Cortlandt House, built in 1748. It is the oldest building in the Bronx Borough of NYC. You can find it in the 1,146 acres (15,442,350 square meters) Van Cortlandt Park—the 4th largest park in NYC.

215. By 1730 Mr. Van Cortlandt was dividing his vast land holdings into lots of generally 150 or 240 acres (one acre is 1,225 tsubo or 4,040 sq. meters). These would be sold, or rented out to farmers, often on 99-year leases. There were also indentured servants who came from Europe to North America. Between 1630 and the Revolutionary War begun in 1776 (nothing to do with Enoch Mead's arrival in Waccabuc, and he wasn't dodging the draft), one-half to two-thirds of all the young white immigrants to America were indentured servants. A common service period was 7 years. Then they would be free, and 'free wage workers'. Unless they had had enough of that, and had just gone fishing, hunting, farming, or started their own business. There are parallels with Japan, and probably many countries. There were *Shugo Daimyo*, and later *Sengoku Daimyo*/powerful feudal rulers in Japan. Think in terms of about 200 of these Daimyo with the country carved up amongst them. Some of them had much, much larger holdings, and were much luckier than Stephan Van Cortlandt. Of course under English and other European royalty, the more feudal holdings of

the European lords was closer to the Japanese situation than any transient holdings/vestiges of royalty we had in North America.

216. Back to Enoch Mead (1756-1807). He built a house, called Elmdon in 1780. (This date is still marked on a stone in the chimney.) It still stands just across from the entrance to Schoolhouse Road (map by Carol Barrett and data supplied by Sally Marseilles—another name I used to hear when I lived there). As you come in on Route 35, and make the left on to Mead Street, immediately up on the left, but not visible from the street is the Mead Street Memorial Cemetery. Sure enough the oldest gravestone there is of Sally Mead, Enoch's daughter. The poor little lady died at 14 in 1794. Enoch bought more and more land from the Van Cortlandt estate.

217. During the Revolutionary War, Enoch was Adjutant on the staff of his brother general Ebenezer Mead (1748-1818). So a pretty young General at 28. But still 8 years older than little brother Enoch. In 1781 two brigades of French troops marched just in front of Enoch's Elmdon House. They were under General Comte Rochambeau and on their way to Bedford Village to spend the night. They met up with General George Washington and marched together to Yorktown, Virginia for the final battle of the war. The British surrendered on October 19 1981. This was largely due to Benjamin Franklin's tact, charm and his stay in Paris, where he got the French and their navy to blockade British General Cornwallis (1738-1805 death in India as the governor there) at the Battle of Yorktown. Tom Wilkinson played Cornwallis in Mel Gibson's 2000 film *The Patriot*.

*Waccabuc and other Local Boys Made History by
Capturing Major Andre, a Well-known Spy.
Andre was in Cahoots with the More Famous Spy,
Benedict Arnold. Andre Mucked Up and Blew his
and Arnold's Cover: You Paid with Your Life
and All Your Money if Loyal to the English King.*

218. The following details are compliments of Ms. Maureen
Koehl; Major John Andre (1750-1780), was one of
the most famous spies against America during our
Revolutionary War for independence against Britain.
Major Andre plotted with Benedict Arnold (much more
infamous!) to show the British how they could take the
fort at West Point, releasing the huge chain across the
Hudson. (Benedict Arnold was born in Connecticut and
was actually a very brave and successful leader. He won
against the British at the Battle of Fort Ticonderoga, and
the battle of Ridgefield, the nearest town to Waccabuc,
along with many other battles and feats of bravery. He
spent a lot of his own money on the Revolutionary War
effort. He felt he was passed over for higher military
rank promotions, became bitter, and did come to need
money.) So there it was. A spy was born.

219. He was not put to death like Major Andre, because the
British took him in and made him a brigadier general.
So he then went on and skillfully fought against the
American patriots. But net-net for him was that as kids
and adults in the USA, if a friend betrays you, everyone
may say, "You're a Benedict Arnold." Arnold died in the
UK in 1801 at age 60. There was an elaborate funeral
with coaches in the procession. Taking down the Hudson
River chain and handing over the strong West Point fort
to the British would allow the British fleet easier access

to Albany etc. in northern New York State. Then the British army could go up through the other colonies on to Boston more easily. So very strategic. West Point became the US army's military academy about 20 years later in 1801. Almost all the famous USA generals were educated there, including General MacArthur who kind of ran Japan during the Occupation from 1945 to 1952.

220. Few people know that some local boys had been drinking at Yerke's Tavern in North Salem. (According to a *New York Times* article by Eleanor Charles dated May 16, 1982, "Six months ago, Paul Newman and his wife, Joanne Woodward, bought a 54-acre/66,150-tsubo horse farm in North Salem with the idea of 'turning it into the best horse show and community educational facility in the Northeast'". There were 56 stalls for Mr. Newman's horses, and for other owners' horses that boarded on the Newman's farm. I had heard stories like this from our neighbors the Gullens.) Flashback—200 years. The boys left Yerke's Tavern in North Salem with Paul Newman and stopped by to pick up a buddy at his girlfriend's house on Long Pond—today Lake Waccabuc. The young man had been visiting her. You can be sure that this kid jumped off Castle Rock to show off to his girlfriend. The Rock was there to be jumped off.

221. They went together to Tarrytown. The boys met Major Andre on the road. Andre stuck his foot in his mouth. (Not really. It's a common English language expression.) They got in a conversation with Major John Andre. One lad's Hessian (German mercenaries who fought with the British) coat got Andre to assume the kid was not in favor of independence from Britain. Andre bubbled and bungled out the wrong question. Andre thought the boys were Tories, loyal to the King of England, and

asked to confirm that. The boys answered they were patriotic Americans. The boys didn't like the guy, and got suspicious. They checked his clothes including his boots and socks—putrid and funky I'm sure—further pissing the pissed (Yerke's Tavern) boys off. They found the 6 pages of wet and stinky letters and maps hidden in the rancid and reeking socks. They turned this major screw-up, Major Andre, into General Washington.

222. There were about 30,000 beer, sausage and sauerkraut-loving German Hessians fighting on the British side. This was about one quarter of all the soldiers the British sent to fight the American anti-England patriots during the Revolutionary War. We already established above how much the Bostonians despised the British foreign boots on Boston soil. German foreign Boots, with Kraut (named after sauerkraut) soldiers who can only shoot guns, swing swords, and scream in a weird language... Probably ten times more loathed and detested than the British. By the way, on the subject of sausage and beer, no cold beers today at Yerke's Tavern. Although you can easily find its foundations in North Salem, at the corner of two roads.

223. I have to add that the most common blood and roots of USA Americans come from Germany. Including half of me (mother's name was Gertrude Aname Schulter). Herbert Kohler Jr. up in Wisconsin built Waelderhaus, a faithful reproduction of an Austrian chalet. (Austrian's speak German, and most of the SS (*Schutz-Staffel*/ protection squadron officers during Hitler's Nazi days were Austrian.) All of us enjoy Mr. Kohler's company baths, toilets and sinks in hotels around the world. Kohler is the largest USA producer. Kohler was a good client, and the owner, Mr. Herbert Kohler Jr was one of the nicest gentleman I have ever met. He was the

grandson of the founder, and has been CEO from age 33, in 1972—the year I arrived in Japan! Mr. Kohler gave me a little time, and I thought I got him interested in buying property in Tokyo. Not sure if he did. ('The Silent Minority', February 7, 2015, Kohler, Wisconsin, *The Economist* (www.economist.com). Unlike say the Irish (my other half Irish), with their NYC Manhattan Saint Patrick's Day parade along Central Park, maybe we Germans plug along silently because of the above 30,000 Hessian mercenaries boots on our homeland, and Germany being the enemy during World War I and WWII. Not to mention Christopher Walken's vampire teeth and unworldly eyes as the spine-tingling and blood curdling Hessian headless horseman (later). But the Germans brought us Christmas Trees, Easter eggs and the Easter Bunny.

224. Being a loyalist to the British crown, and not supporting the patriots' cause for independence had a high price tag. Almost all of these Loyalist Tories' lands were confiscated. In New York, sure enough it was John Jay, the namesake of my high school, who drafted the Law of Attainment (euphemism for "Law of Rip-off/You're Hucked, loser, winner takes all"). We get the spoils of war. This law confiscated all the Tory Loyalist's wealth. You can visit John Jay's homestead not far from my high school of the same name. I finally first went to the Jay Homestead in 2007 or 2008. Strange. Even though our lives revolved around John Jay High School we never even had a school trip there. Never went there with my parents, or even knew it was there when I lived there. John Jay was federal secretary of foreign affairs for the new nation, the first Federal Chief Justice of the Supreme Court, and left the bench to be Governor of New York State. Nearby

rich, land wealthy New Yorkers such as Robert Morris and Frederick Philipse III, who had Van Cortland estate inheritance, lost their lands.

225. Philipse Manor House became Yonkers first City Hall. You can visit the very interesting museum today. There is also Philipsburg Manor, which was one of the family's working farms. It is located in Sleepy Hollow. You can go to nearby Sunnyside, Washington Irving's home. It is a 10-acre vine and ivy-covered house and tourist attraction in Tarrytown, where the boys left from Lake Waccabuc to grab Major Andre in Tarrytown, New York. Maybe you saw the Johnny Depp and Christina Ricci movie, the *Legend of Sleepy Hollow*, a Tim Burton 1999 movie set back in 1799. It was originally written by the above Washington Irving (1783-1859). Christopher Walken was the creepy, spooky, blood thirsty German Hessian 'Headless Horseman'. Once his head was returned to him he became a decent stand-up guy. I visited all these places in 2007 or 2008. Maybe as we get older we have more interest and appreciation for our roots and history. Tens of thousands of Loyalists were deported to Canada, to England, or to other colonies in the British Empire. The war and the new nation were largely funded from the sale of Loyalist's land. And the confiscation of their wealth.

226. Along an only somewhat similar line, I recently learned that in the USA some police departments have been overdoing it with civil forfeitures from innocent people. One couple lost an expensive house because their teenage son once sold $40-worth of grass (marijuana) from the front porch! Legitimate purpose cash, expensive cars etc. have been seized to the tune of a few billion dollars. What is going on with my beloved US of A? Luckily backlash

on these extremes has gotten many, including US Attorney General Eric Holder to announce in January, 2015, that misuse of the practice must end. (January 16, 2015, Christina Sterbenz, Erin Fuchs and Reuters, 'The Feds Just Restricted the Law that Lets Police Seize Stuff from Innocent People', www.businessinsider.com, and Wikipedia, 'Civil forfeiture in the United States'.) Some cities and states were especially bad.

227. So sometimes maybe we do need the Feds. When things get crazy, and authorities get heavy-handed like this, it is easy to understand why Americans need their 'right to keep and bear arms,' Second Amendment to the Constitution rights—even I guess including assault weapons! The crooks or brainwashed ISIL types will get their hands on them anyway. As we increasingly see around the world, if small groups or lone-wolf terrorists are gong to be popping up more at schools, museums, malls, airports, restaurants, movie theaters etc., I can see that gun-free zones are a bad idea—except airplanes.

228. We need some school teachers, and movie theater popcorn pushers down at the shooting range. Probably more plain clothes security personnel. Maybe fewer guards in uniform, as it makes them the first target. Japan can control gun possession and use. The USA can't. And the right to carry concealed weapons are a good idea. Even if we have no standing army, any foreign power that thinks they could invade the USA would get whooped, and run home with their tail between their legs. Same thing for little neutral Switzerland (every Swiss male is drafted, trained, and has a gun at home), and other countries. Unfortunately Iraq and Afghanistan are in this same category. Please, no more USA full-scale armies sent into foreign lands. Foreign boots are always

the most unwelcome. Our 'homeland security' is more secure without those strategic blunders. Let's mind our own business and stay at home.

The Start of the Waccabuc Country Club, One Room Schoolhouses, Lewisboro Elementary School, Petting the Cows, and Getting Chased by the Bulls on the Farm of the #2 Pacific and European WWII Leader.

229. In the early 1830's Mr. Martin R. Mead bought the land where the impressive Waccabuc Country Club house is located. In 1878 Robert Hoe bought it from Mr. Mead, enlarged it, built a carriage house, and stables for his racehorses. Mr. Hoe called it Indian Spring Farm. Hoe also bought the boat house, which would become the Club's waterfront facility. He also constructed the Waccabuc Post Office in 1880, which was always the smallest post office in the United States! In the 1950s and 60s I recall we got our mail from Mrs. Adams. I have read there was not even a lavatory there at that time. Maybe that's why Mrs. Adams was sometimes gritting her teeth, and mumbling. But I suppose she had a wide-mouth pickle jar, a pan, or took breaks and left the premises for a few minutes. She never chatted about that. Hoe also built a second school house on School House Road in 1894.

230. There were 7 one-room schoolhouses in Lewisboro, according to work done by Priscilla Luckow and the brilliant, hardworking town historian who has written many books, Maureen Koeh. About the only school that was below capacity was the Waccabuc schoolhouse. In

1939, there was 'a capacity of 25 students, even if the double benches' were trashed. But there were only 10 students enrolled. Other schools were old and overcrowded, so $150,000 was spent to build the Lewisboro Elementary School on 7 acres (28,300 sq. meters) of land. About 140 students started there from December 1940. The fact that it was closed in 2014 is a testament to there being fewer children in parts of the USA too. Not just a Japanese, European, and other regional phenomenon. I can only hope that the beautiful facilities like Lewisboro, and such schools in Japan, and probably in many countries, can be put to good use as childcare facilities, old age or nursing homes, or re-training facilities etc.

231. Another quick story about Lewisboro Elementary. When I went there between 1957 and 1962, adjacent to our playing fields and the two baseball diamonds, was a fetching timber fence. We could pet the cows. We were not supposed to climb over the fence. As some bulls would get jealous or angry. Not sure what that was. Alas. We were fleet of foot. When I went back with my son in 2007 he was 26. I was shocked. Over the fence was a forest. I mean a major forest with big, thick tall trees. We used to be able to see what I was told was Henry A. Wallace's farm. It was on the top of a hill not far away. I have learned that when President Truman asked Mr. Wallace to resign from secretary of commerce, Mr. Wallace bought the 115-acre/140,875 tsubo/464,888 sq. meters farm there in 1946. Truman asked him to step down because he criticized a speech by the Secretary of State.

232. I always thought the cows might belong to the former Vice President (under President Franklin Roosevelt from January 20, 1940 to January 20, 1945). That was what we

were told. The animals had a vice presidential air about them. It was at first confusing to me because I knew it was Vice President Truman who replaced President Roosevelt when President Roosevelt died in office before World War II ended. I found out Roosevelt died April 12th 1945. So Truman had only been V.P. for 2 months and 12 days. It was Henry Wallace who was the vice president during almost all of the Pacific War with Japan, and the war in Europe, and elsewhere against Germany and Italy. Vice President Wallace was my next-door neighbor at my elementary school. How little we know... So it seems I was petting the cows of the #2 USA Pacific War leader just 12 years after World War II ended.

The Gullen Brothers, Jack and George's Grandfather and Grand Uncle of Pretty much the Same Names, Came Over from Scotland and Put the Waccabuc Country Club's Golf Course on the Map.

233. In 1912 the Mead family bought back Robert Hoe's Indian Spring Farm, and the Waccabuc Country Club was established September 18, 1912. John S. "Jock" Gullen was engaged as the club professional. He held this position for 40 years until his death in 1952. Jock designed and laid out the first 9 holes. His brother, George Gullen was brought in from Scotland to supervise the construction of the back nine. This made for a beautiful, 18-hole regulation golf course. From 1925 the Alice Mead Neergaard house was also rented by the club. Finally, in 1960 the club members bought all facilities, the 200 acres, including the waterfront boathouse and docks for $200,000. My family had our place on Lake

Waccabuc, and Dad didn't play golf. So we never joined the country club. Sure enough, there were our almost-same-name buddies Jack (not Jock although he was a good jock) and George Gullen almost the same age as me and my brother. As I have written earlier, the Gullen boys were just two doors down from us also on the shores of Lake Waccabuc. Both Gullens were good students, and also great athletes and leaders at John Jay. They were our closest friends over all those and these years.

234. The Gullens 'stayed put' in the area, and had good reason to do so. Their father ran the Fifth Division Market in Cross River along with Ralph Felice above. They sold the market, but it is still there. Their dad, Mr. Waldie Gullen, turned 90 last year in 2014, and still plays golf, hunts, puts out fires, and plays cards at the local fire department with his many buddies. In May 2015, Waldie's wife Ms. Barbara Gullen also turned 90. I seem to recall that they were classmates at Katonah H. S. before John Jay H.S. was constructed in 1956. (I just looked at the 'John Jay High School (Cross River, New York)' Wikipedia profile. The school is stronger than ever in all those sports and other listed activities—New York State champions and even top nationwide achievements. Makes me proud. I'm glad I banned smoking, at least when I used that restroom back in Junior H.S. (above). I read somewhere else that John Jay was rated by *Newsweek* to be one of the top 200 high schools in the USA.) Just as Mr. Waldie Gullen's father and uncle were the golf pros, and could even custom make and repair golf clubs, so can 90-year-old Mr. Waldie Gullen—a big profile at the Waccabuc Country Club. Here's another quick story about our boyhood, high school, and continuing friendship with our Waccabuc lakeside friends Jack and George Gullen.

235. I was the youngest of the four of us. But there were only two years separating the lot of us. So not much younger. For a couple days in a row, the view was that it was time for our Castle Rock cliff jumping initiation. A couple idiots on the Lake about our age were already jumping. At least that is what they said. On the web, and even in a book, you sometimes see that Castle Rock is supposed to be 100 feet/30.38 meters high above the water. I think that is an exaggeration. Truthfully, I think it is more like 98 feet/29.8794 meters. The scary thing is you don't really know how deep the water is, or where the menacing underwater rocks might be. Actually the intermediate 50-or-so-foot-tall 'point' rock fell into the lake sometime during the last 30 or 40 years—ouch! I was in Japan, so it wasn't me who pushed it. Anyway, that day when it was time to do our cliff jumping induction, it was hot with the sun beating down. I wasn't even planning on jumping. For hours the older guys are just looking down like total wussys, trying to work up the courage to jump.

236. I fiddled around with myself back in the woods. But it was hot and boring. So I just walked out of the woods, kept walking, and then jumped as far out as I could. Never said a word. Within an hour or so the other older brothers had to jump. Again check Castle Rock out on YouTube. I guess I need to say that unlike times in the past there is no public access to the lake. And one reason they like to keep some of the roads unpaved, is to discourage too many people from coming by, and too slow the cars down. I don't think this book will sell enough copies to change that. After winter snowplowing, some of the roads are pretty rutted up, before the road scraping and oiling begins.

'What the Dickens' (Shakespeare, Merry Wives of Windsor) Happened to Dickens' Boathouse, and Mr. Dickens' Gold Teeth?

237. I know a few things about Dickens' Boathouse that maybe even Maureen Koehl, the town historian, doesn't know. From Mrs. Koehl I learned that in 1925 Samuel Dickens built a store by the Waccabuc Oscaleta channel bridge. God, I bumped my head on that bridge many times riding too high in my canoe. Mr. Dickens was selling soft drinks and snacks to passing boaters. Maybe someone complained about the traffic jams? Anyway in 1929 he moved to the northeast end of Lake Waccabuc. We always knew that to be Dickens' Boat house. It was very cool, built on wooden pilings with the water below and the boathouse about maybe 2 feet/60 centimeters above the water. Merwin, his son, took over in 1945 and ran it until 1960. At that point he converted it into his all-year-round residence. I know that in the summer of 2007 or 2008, our house that we sold in 1968 was up for sale again. That same summer when I was over at the Dickens' Boathouse, I noticed a 'For Sale' sign on that property as well. I forget the price. But I walked out there on the wharf to show the boathouse to my son.

238. Okay. Here is maybe something that only a few enterprising local kids knew. In probably 1955 Melvin and Mariana Ringstrom on Hook Road at the end of our Perch Bay Road, down by the Waccabuc River Waterfall, got us into catching crayfish and or mussels for Mr. Dickens' fishermen that came in from NYC and everywhere. A very thriving business. From 100 meters away, the Dickens' Boathouse smell of hamburgers and

hot dogs on the grill wafted and drifted above the lake water and the round floating lily pads, with their yellow bulbous flowers.

239. This was even before we knew the Gullen boys (one-door-down high school buddies, Castle Rock jumping courage story, and builders of the Waccabuc Country Club golf courses), because maybe the Gullen family had not built on the lake yet. M & M Ringstrom were our first lake friends. Twins that were maybe 2 years older. I was about 5 years old. I think we got 3 cents for the little crawfish or mussels, and 5 cents for the big ones. Mr. Dickens was selling them live as fish bait for I believe 10 cents to 25 cents each. He was usually out on the wharf, managing the visiting fishermen and the boats. So he had a deep, chestnut-brown tan, with bright greenish, hazel eyes that flashed all the more with the contrast. I recall he also had a couple of gold teeth, not run of the mill silver. The gold teeth sparkled and beamed under the bright sunshine that was reflecting off the crystal blue lake waters. We maybe only did this business one summer until Melvin went into the Boathouse snack bar/ restaurant to buy a Coke or something. Mel found out the retail price on our crayfish and mussels. Melvin was 7 years old. He was firmly against child exploitation. I didn't know what the huck he was talking about.

240. We made $11.63 if my photographic memory serves me; I know the $11 is accurate, and I'm pretty damn sure it was 63 cents. Like I said, I was probably 5, but sharp as a crawfish claw. It would have been 1955. My first job. If you take the average 4-cent price we got, the math is that we supplied 290 mostly crawfish. If you take the difference between our 4-cent income, and Mr. Dickens' average 18 cent-income; and if you multiply that 14-cent difference

times 290 critters, you get an inflated, despicable, exploitative profit of $40.60. I'll bet Mr. Dickens bought another gold tooth with that. Maybe we cleaned out all the crawfish, leading to the closure of the Dickens' Boathouse business in 1960… Or maybe not. These lake crawfish hid under rocks so the bass, pike, pickerel, perch, and big sunfish did not catch them before we did. And they only moved around in water too shallow for the fish to access. Every rock we turned over, we were careful to put back— always concerned with environmental issues.

241. I didn't hug him or anything, but after not seeing Melvin Ringstrom, our crawfish boss, who also had us all quit Dickens Boathouse because of its inherent worker exploitation, he came back into my life after 10 years. He had gone off to private school, but maybe punched an exploitive teacher or something. Anyway, for his senior year he was back with us at John Jay. As strong as a bull. Somewhere, somehow, he became best buddies with the Hawthorne brothers especially John, the older brother, who was Melvin's age. I don't know if Melvin Ringstrom's parents still had their lake-front property down on Hook Road, off my Perch Bay Road. Guys didn't ask about stuff like that. Maybe he was living with Nathaniel Hawthorne's progeny. I know that our star gymnasts, the Hawthorne brothers, yeah, the tree-skinning chimpanzees, brought him on to our gymnastics team. Melvin didn't have much background or flying hours in gymnastics so he just concentrated on the still rings along with me and a couple other guys. Melvin spent only one year at John Jay H.S., but graduated two years earlier than me in 1966. I asked a few girls to sign my yearbooks, but VERY few guys. Melvin was one *senpai*/senior who wanted to sign for me. He wrote, "Tom, what a team, heah? You wait

another couple years, you'll be another Greg Matthias. [A guy older than us who was a great still rings guy, and had been in my Lewisboro Scout Troop. Greg lived near the Fifth Division market in Cross River.] Keep up the work and good luck next year, and those to come, Mel."

242. Good stuff. I guess we are getting older when we look in the rear view mirror like this. As long as they are darting glances and we primarily keep our eyes on the road in front of us. My senior year at John Jay there were 11 gymnastic meets. I did three events: still rings, parallel bars, and floor exercise. I got 32 firsts. As described in the chapter titled 'Expectancy' in my *Know Your Own Bone* book, I visualized my messing up on the parallels just before I mounted. Sure enough we often get what we expect.

The King and Queen of the Waccabuc Country Club.
'As the World Turns' Playing and Working with the McCullough's at the Old Mead Cider Mill Property.

243. It seemed to me that the parents of one of my other close childhood friends, another Tommy, who lived on Schoolhouse Road, must have been the king and queen of the Waccabuc Country Club. Maybe I am totally wrong. Maybe an elderly club member is thinking, "No I was the queen, and my Freddy was the king." If so, my apologies. All I know is Tommy's mother, Priscilla, was gorgeous. I always had a huge crush on her. Totally and utterly unrequited love. She said she was part Native American. Not sure which part, but it was all good. She was a very sophisticated model out of New York City. Tommy

showed me her modeling pictures from magazines, and published glossy hard-cover photo collections. His father, Dan McCullough, was the WOR radio announcer, along with John Gambling—*Rambling with Gambling*, being its most popular show. Among other gigs, from 1956 to 1967 Mr. McCullough was the announcer for the opening of the soap drama, *As the World Turns*. This was the most popular daytime show on television for many years. They often flew off to Ireland even for a weekend. Maybe they put in plugs for the Emerald Island and its airline… got some free tickets.

244. Tina Kaupe was another country club girl. Also a consummate and unadulterated honey. I think she lived in one of the Mead-built colonial houses on Mead Street. Even though Tina (and Tommy McCullough) went off to private school, Tina is the one who saved, and organized our 40th John Jay H.S. reunion. Doug Owen, Senior Class President, and Westchester All-County star football tight end, had 'made his move' up to Vermont. Too far off site, he thought we would start out the 40th reunion meeting in the school parking lot—*American Graffiti*-style. Tina found out no parking was allowed during the summer. Thanks to Tina, I think about 80 or 90 out of 187 of us came to a well-organized reunion. See 'Doug's Trout for Dinner 1' on YouTube—still a good catch. Always had good hands. He does picture postcard—no; Christmas card perfect—Christmases in that permanent white beard, Santa Claus suit, and more robust frame than he carried back in high school on the American football field. Fits perfectly with his astonishingly decorated gingerbread-like huge log house. So nostalgically, partially buried in the pure white Vermont snow. Hallmark cards needs to

get that shot. His alluring hottie wife lived in Japan for a few years as a model. Doug met her on a ski slope in Vermont. Doug always did okay. 'Making his move' up to Vermont, and on her on the ski slope worked out great for Doug.

245. My 4th job after my toddler-catches-crayfish days, under the tutelage of Melvin Ringstrom, and the two summers with my Scoutmaster Dick Reilly working on the local houses he was building, was with Sam and Rube Moore. Remember the two gentlemen who built our fieldstone chimney on the summer cottage. About 10 years earlier, my brother and I had thought their abandoned jalopy needed gas. It was the above Mrs. Priscilla McCullough who either called my parents, or maybe Mrs. Gullen, to ask if I would work under Sam and Rube Moore to convert one of the McCullough's barns into a nice guest house. Actually, their main house, where I had often slept over with Tommy when we were 1 to 3 feet shorter, was the first building past the (Mead) Homestead. This Homestead was the 1820 National Register of Historic Places property on the corner of Mead Street and Schoolhouse road. The McCullough's house had been the Mead family Cider Mill, and there was a spacious apple orchard of several acres running back behind the house. So as long as I hung with Tommy, there were always plenty of apples to bring home for apple pie, apple cobbler, or just to bite into. Mostly we aimed and threw those apples at anything hard to watch for the best splish splash.

246. I kind of bit my lip when I heard I would be working with the Moores. Will they know and remember about their jalopy I disabled when I was 4 or 5 years old? (Above.) I got the job, and all summer Sam and

Rube never said anything about the old black jalopy we totaled 10 years earlier. I wondered if maybe they didn't know. They probably just drove off with a sputtering engine, and rocks clanging around in the gas tank. But maybe they knew. I worked with them for two summers, and about all they ever said during lunch breaks together, and other than my training/ demonstration or day's orders was, "Tom, you do good work, not much of it, but good work." And then the two old codgers would chuckle and chortle together for about a minute as if I wasn't there. And they were old. Older than some of the smooth, clean, gray glacial rock outcroppings.

247. But no retirement possible or wanted by these small-town craftsman. Fixtures of the community, and also probably living there for generations. Maybe I should have 'stayed put', or at least not 'made a move' as far as Japan... George and Jack Gullen's parents are 90 but look 57. George has all his hair in the right place, but both 'the boys' look about 40. Jack builds well and fast. George is more like your kitchen, and custom-made cabinet maker: slow perfection that used to drive big bro Jack crazy when they had jobs together. A new generation of craftsman who will always have great jobs in such custom built wealthy communities. Yes. The Gullen boys, like the Hawthorne brothers, with their tree service company, did just fine 'staying put'.

248. The second summer gig I had with Sam and Rube Moore was renovating an extra carriage house into extra living quarters. It was for the Dewitt's. It seems to me that that Dewitt property we were working on must have previously been either the Francis S. Mead 'Tradinoch' house built in 1914, or less likely the Elizabeth Mead

Cahoone house built in 1916. I can't jump on a plane right now to find out, but I knew my hood pretty well. And Sally Marseilles and Carol Barrett drafted a great map. Since the Dewitt house was so close to the road, dollars to donuts (whatever that really means), it was the house of Francis S. Mead. And she was the great lady that made the evocation or first commemoration speech when my Lewisboro elementary school was opened in December, 1940. I was not there. Not yet even a gleam in my father's eye.

Moving on to Cornell, Phi Gamma Delta Fraternity Brothers, and Working My Butt off at the 'Straight Desk'. More Great Senpai/Older Guys to Look up to and Mold Your Life Around.

249. No sports in college for me. But thanks go to my Phi Gamma Delta/FIJI fraternity brothers, Tony Biddle (many generations down from Nicholas 'Biddle of Philadelphia' who had a problem with President Andrew Jackson over where to bank) for having me join him and another Phi Gam brother, Tommy Inglis on the football cheerleading team. Tommy Inglis as of 2015 is still the general manager of the Cornell Club in Manhattan. He has been manager of that beautiful facility since 1991. This was the football team of my classmate Ed Marinaro. Ed was the runner up for the Heisman Trophy (top university American style football player), set 16 NCAA (National Collegiate Athletic Association) records, and was the first in history to have over 4,000 career rush yards. I never had a chance to see him in TV dramas such as *Hill Street Blues*, or *Blue Mountain State* because I have always been in Japan, I have never even seen *All in the Family* or *Saturday Night Live*!!!

I didn't know Ed, but he always said hi to me when I cashed him his (maximum limit) $25 check, or he bought something at the Straight Desk at Willard Straight Hall, the student union building at Cornell. Mr. Ed Marinaro's girlfriend, much shorter than Mr. Ed, but about my height, was the most beautiful blonde you can imagine. I would have given her free candy if Mr. Marinaro was not towering over us.

250. Another fraternity brother who was my 'big brother' and lived in the room next door was Craig Kammerer. I loved the Moody Blues, Crosby Stills and Nash and other great music always drifting from his door. I learned so much from Craig with his generosity, and intellect. He was always willing to offer a helping hand. Craig was also a 'Straight Deskman'. He went on to Stanford and got an MBA. Craig very quickly became vice president of Prudential in charge of huge real estate developments in Hawaii and northern California. On one of my trips back and forth I spent a few days with him in Hawaii. One of his projects was being in charge of the $500,000,000, 880-acre Kuilima/Turtle Bay resort on the north shore of Oahu. He was the kind of guy who could teach me and give me the confidence to gallop a horse over open, exposed, rock-strewn fields within about 10 minutes of getting on a horse for the first time.

251. Before that, back in 1972, when I drove my old white Volkswagen from Summit, New Jersey, to San Francisco, on my way to Japan for keeps, I stayed with Craig for a week or two in a shared house he had in Pacific Heights. I believe it was near the Buchanan and Union Street intersection. Craig, who was with Prudential, and I believe Kent Brooks with Arthur Anderson, were living with two ladies just as beautiful as Jennifer Aniston and

Courteney Cox. Except it was 22 years before the *Friends* TV show running from 1994 to 2004. On a short-stay road trip to see a Stanford football game, I had no choice but to sleep in the same bed with Courteney. Craig didn't believe me when I said nothing happened. Yeah. I was a good friend. Have regretted it every minute since. But I did learn some things. Craig cooked steaks right in his fireplace with something called Teriyaki sauce—the first time I even heard the word! And of course I learned the most from my own one-year-older real and actual blood brother Art, a New York and New Jersey attorney who has also had a Supreme Court Case.

252. The 'Greek System', fraternities and sororities may seem too traditional, too much for partying, or even lame to some students who never got into it. But out of what must have been over 3,000 kids in my graduating class at Cornell, I once counted that there were only 56 that I knew from the names and the senior individual yearbook pictures. About half were fraternity brothers, Straight Deskmen/women, fellow cheerleaders, a few sorority chicks, and the other half were kids from my ILR/Industrial and Labor Relations School. I remember there were 103 of us starting out in my ILR Class of '72. So unlike H.S. where I pretty much knew all 187 kids in my class, how do you get to know kids at a big university, where you have little in common, everyone is hassled and busy as hell? I saw thousands of faces because I worked about 40 hours a week at the student union desk from spring of my freshman year. I recognize a lot of faces, but I do not/did not know those names.

253. Fraternity life helps builds friendships, and comradery. After having been out of Cornell for about 15 years, one day at Nishimachi International School, I heard a

voice from behind, "Tom Nevins, what are you doing here today?" I turned and immediately remembered a brother who was one or two years younger. "I've been here since I left Cornell. You're the new guy." Chip Conradi had come in with a bank. I believe it was Chase Manhattan. Our kids were about the same age. This Nishimachi School was founded by Ambassador Edwin O. Reischauer's (1910–1990) wife's older sister, Tane Matsukata. Harvard Prof. Reischauer was President John Kennedy's appointment to ambassador to Japan. Nishimachi School had been the *honke*/main homestead land and house of Prince Matsukata, Masayoshi (1835–1924). He established the first Bank of Japan in 1882, served as finance minister in 7 of the first 9 cabinets!

254. Prince Matsukata was prime minister in 1891–92 after Yamagata Aritomo. He had this post again from 1896 to 1898 before Prime Minister Ito Hirobumi (October 16, 1841-October 26, 1909) got the position. Former Prime Minister Ito was assassinated in Harbin, China by the Korean patriotic independence activist and national hero An Jung-geun (July 16, 1879- March 26, 1910). So there are some complex political and historical relationships. Mr. Matsukata had 13 sons and 11 daughters. Unlike me, an early and highly skilled start. Knew what he was doing. A lot of kids. Is that why the house had to second as a school?

255. When Emperor Meiji asked Prince Matsukata, Masayoshi how many children he has, the Prince was not able to give an exact answer. A Japanese friend at Cornell, Otsuka, Kazuhiko was sent to Cornell by notorious MITI (Ministry of International Trade and Industry). Otsuka-san helped get me started in Japan. His wife was a great, great granddaughter of Prince Matsukata. Kimiko-san's father made my first

meishi/business card for me on that first short visit to Japan when I was 20 years old. Everyone laughed when they saw my meishi. I didn't know why. In Japanese I was given the girl's name 'Tom'oko'. Ko is the character for child, but it is only used at the end of girls' names. Must be an old Satsuma, down in Kagoshima, Kyushu, clan joke? Tease the dumb *gaijin*. Come to think of it, that clan was the only one to shoot cannons and make war on British battleships, declaring war on Britain from August 15 to 17, 1863. This was toward the end of the Tokugawa Shogunate.

256. Back to Chip Conradi and his kids, about the same age as my boys, at this Matsukata family founded Nishmachi School. I feel bad. Chip wanted our families to get together, and talked about it a few times. My family was not as functional—euphemism. My kids usually hungout with half indigenous-types like themselves. But at least I should have spent more time with Chip, and introduced him to more of my weird semi-native gaijin friends. A little regret I have. Chip is a great guy. He has been treasurer and vice president of tax at The Clorox Company (a Fortune 500 company) since March 2000. If you have stains you need removed, Chip's got the bleach – a good man to know.

257. One guy, in my freshman year dorm, Dave Ross, wanted to join another fraternity, Sigma Chi, but I and one of his high school buddies, Larry Nees, influenced him to join our Phi Gamma Delta house. Like me, Larry already had an older brother at Phi Gam. Dave was my best friend at 'the house'—fraternity. We were roommates sophomore year when we lived at the house. Dave was an architect, so had to do that 5-year program. He came and stayed with me in my shabby little Tokyo Minami-Asagaya suburban apartment when he wasn't traveling all-around Japan for the few weeks he was in Japan. His graduate thesis was

on Japanese architectural design, or something. So Dave, along with me, got to see the real Japan—*sento*/public bath and all. No shower or bath in the apartment where I lived those first 3 or 4 years.

258. Dave soon was one of the three founders of one of the most prominent architectural firms in the Pittsburgh area. He was key in designing the headquarters of such Pittsburgh firms as Alcoa Aluminum and Heinz Foods. When four classes got together for a Phi Gam reunion—'72 to '76 in the Boston area in 2007 or 2008, Dave picked me up at the airport. He outfitted me, and took me salt-water kayaking for my first time. He was a great, and very successful dear friend who died suddenly. That has already happened to too many. We have to be thankful for every day we are above ground, despite all our problems and challenges. The only people who have no problems are no longer with us. So maybe we should not fear death.

Tuxedos, House in the Rocks, Captivating and Matchless Beauties, and Wild Turkeys— I Thought Only the Bourbon was Left.

259. Funny, proximity does breed friendship. At least if you are all good guys. My sophomore year, other than the above Craig Kammerer, and Dave Ross, the only other guy in our mezzanine alcove of just our 3 rooms at the "The Oaks"—our fraternity building—was Charlie Hunt, one of my other best friends from Phi Gamma Delta fraternity at Cornell. He was a great wrestler at nearby Carmel H.S. In the same league as my John Jay in some sports. I think he wrestled at Cornell too. He and his wife do

an Ironman-type thing EVERY weekend—amazing. No knee pain or back pain or anything. I thought you could only be like that if you were like me eating a lot of sashimi, natto (stinky, sticky fermented soy beans), and seaweed, and climbing about 500 stairs per day. Charlie has been out to Japan a few times. We stayed over at their really cool house in Tuxedo Park around Christmas/New Year's 2007 before we had our family marriage party at the Cornell Club. Tuxedo Park is on the west side of the Hudson River in Orange County, New York. Almost at the same latitude as Waccabuc. Lakes and rock outcroppings over there too.

260. Yes. The Tuxedo is named after Tuxedo Park! A tobacco baron named Pierre Lorillard had property in town. He wanted to go to a formal party at the Tuxedo Club in something special. Lorillard designed it himself without the common, traditional tail in the back. Few American men would do this. This guy was French. He had his fashion statement debut wearing it at the October 1886 Tuxedo Club party. The town population is only about 120 people more than Waccabuc. Unlike Waccabuc, there are more turkeys. Wild Native American turkeys with feathers. The kind the Native Americans killed and brought to the Pilgrims for the Pilgrims' first Thanksgiving. Before the Indians got killed off by the Pilgrims. So turkeys are back in these areas. As are mountain lions, and black bear sightings. Charlie's house is built around a rock outcropping – it's actually in his living room. Very cool. Actually cool in summer and a warming effect in winter when the sun hits the rock all day. His house is surrounded by my beloved rocks. Some 10 meters high and 15 meters long. With our earthquakes in Japan, we might give that a second thought.

261. At Cornell, Charlie was more of "an assman" than me, as we used to say. Not that Charlie was a play boy. I was

basically a clueless late bloomer. I had not really discovered most men's greatest treasures yet. There was a gorgeous coed who for some reason must have really liked me. She invited me to a Sadie Hawkins dance. (These are dances where the girls get a chance to invite the guys, without the girls having to look too slutty.) I had not known this walking gem of a girl. I guess I sold her chocolate, or cashed her check at the Straight Desk and winked at her or something. On a scale of 10, in terms of also physical, full-body esthetics, she was an 11.74. Ursula Andress move over.

262. Ursula "Undress" Honey Ryder coming out of the water scene in the 1962 *Dr. No* movie. Remember? Holding a conch shell in each hand, while listening to the echo of the ocean surf. Sean Connery was watching from behind the bushes—not one of James Bond's finer moments. We've all done that. Peeping Tom—get it all the time. I didn't know what to do with this peerless naked princess. It was like when we give our blind doggie Lu-chan, a good-sized leather bone. Even when she could see, she gets so excited she runs around in circles. Should I hide it? Takes a while to settle down, cope and chew. Except in my case there was no bone. She must have thought I was gay. Or maybe that I didn't like her. Immediately after that, either intentionally or coincidently she dated Charlie for months right there in and out of our fraternity house alcove of just the three rooms. Charlie was a wrestler. He knew all the holds to put on her. I never said anything to Charlie. Just suffered in pitiful silence in a pool of regretful tears. She probably also said nothing. That's why Charlie seems not to be able to remember. Unless Charlie Hunt is a really good and considerate actor.

It Happened Again. Once in Tokyo the Dog Lost His Bone, and It Took too Long to Find It. And a couple More Reasonable, No, Cheap Restaurant Chains that will Make You Wonder Why it is written that Tokyo is an Expensive City. You Need to Know Where You Can Go. New York State Trooper's Divine Intervention—kept me a Virgin.

263. This excitement, leading me to lose my bone, happened once before with a similar perfect specimen of God's creation. Could not have been made by mere mortals. She was a half USA Caucasian and half Japanese lady without much spoken Japanese. Her name was Rose. A delightful and glorious Rose she was. Rose worked as a playboy bunny at The Esquire Club in Ginza, a knock-off of the Playboy Club—one of the WDI group's first businesses they brought in from abroad. Before WDI Group brought in Kenny Rogers fried Chicken (chickens didn't fly), Tony Romas, Hard Rock Café, Planet Hollywood, Outback Steakhouse etc.

264. WDI Group also helped a nearby Shibuya Italian chef who caught cancer. He had only a single Italian pasta restaurant. But it had those 100 or more people always lined up outside the restaurant. The WDI group bought his recipes, and helped him and his family financially until the end. That became Capricciosa. There are 138 Capricciosa restaurants in Japan, and in 7 other countries. The WDI group was founded by three friends who graduated from Keio University. Some of their kids went to Nishimachi International School with my kids. Back to my first encounter with Rose, my god-like Venus. At first not enough penis for my Venus, but Rose was very considerate and kind. She said, "Men often have that

reaction when they see me like this." It worked out fine a few times after that. Memories I cherish. I've come along way. Because I am married to one now. Gochisosama! As the Japanese would say, "Thank you for sharing that delicious meal/story with me."

265. Why was I such a lame slow starter? The hippy's head on the spike in Afghanistan? "Afghan girl, No!" Maybe an influence. It wasn't because of going to church every Sunday at St. Mary's Catholic Church in Ridgefield, Connecticut, or the church by the same name in Katonah, N. Y., or St. Patrick's church in Bedford Village, N. Y. It was not because of the time spent in dark, dusky and formidable confessional booths. It was mostly because of a New York State Trooper. In the States, you often spend a weekend at a university before you decide which university to go to. I went up to Cornell, and stayed at my brother Art's fraternity house, the one, of course, I was planning to pledge for/join. I slept over in the fraternity house, and saw/heard guys making whoopee with some very hot young ladies. But not nearly as nice as my own high school honey. This experience was a bad influence on the Eagle Scout. He thought he should finally find his wings and fly for it.

266. As I was driving home, I decided, *It's been 1.5 years. I really love her. If possible, maybe us too.* Just as I convinced myself of this—the moment I said, "YES!", a State Trooper jumped out on the highway about 150 meters in front of my sky blue speeding Comet. I stopped the streaking Comet on the shoulder of the 3 lane Interstate highway. The officer walked up to me. "Driver's license, please". I handed it over. "Thomas, you are a very fast driver, and a very bad boy." His exact words. He wrote up the ticket, and said, "You were going 81 miles/130.356864 kilometers an hour, and it should cost you about $40

bucks." Sure enough that is what came in the mail. I saw this as divine intervention. I remained a virgin, and late bloomer. On my 8-month trip driving and hitchhiking around the world, I didn't even think of doing anything but the scenery and historic landmarks. Kept my eyes off the goods, even though pimps often called me out in English. Then angry words in 29 other languages when I politely bowed away. This may have kept me alive. Recall what happened to the fellow European hippy traveler in Afghanistan.

267. A few paragraphs up, when I was checking on the web to see how many Italian restaurants Capricciosa has, I came across the Italian restaurant Saizeriya. It is a welcome sight when I am out on my long walks. You can find Saizeriya everywhere. Naturally, because I just learned there are over 750 of them in Japan! But here is the interesting story. If you look at their English Wikipedia profile, you can see that the chain was passed on to a new university graduate named Yasuhiko Shougaki. We used to eat all the time at that first Ichikawa Restaurant with the outside, metal circular staircase going up to the 2nd, or 3rd floor. My oldest son, when he was still one year old, grabbed one of the toothpicks on the table. He stuck it in his ear, and wailed out in pain. Like son like father. I also did that with a Q-Tip/*menbo*—just last year. Kept crying for quite a few minutes. We took him to a hospital emergency room. Not too much damage was done to his hearing. Our bad – should have been watching. I would say the older man who cooked us our steaks and pasta, was the man who passed it on to the young Mr. Shougaki. Multiple store openings only started from 1977. The rest is history as they say. So the Japanese market can be very good if you get the formula right.

*Making My Move Closer to Japan. Tremendous
Opportunities and Adventures in Alaska. They are still
there in Alaska, Japan, or Anywhere. Just 'Make a Move'
and discover them.*

268. The Straight Desk job at Cornell actually moves me
closer to Japan for a couple of reasons. I worked about 40
hours a week there, getting money to drive to Alaska after
freshman year I came back with Alaskan gold. I could
write a book about Alaska, so have to be careful here.
I've been there six times in all seasons. I was able to save
and come back with $5,000. The first night we arrived
at Cook Inlet camping ground, a nice half white and
half Athabascan Indian lady said we could stay for free
at her beautiful home in the upscale Turnagain area of
Anchorage. Then I got to work on the Snettisham Dam,
outside of Juneau. (By the way, until I was in Juneau
in 2014 — even though Juneau, not Anchorage, is the
state capital, where Sarah Palin spent some time — I had
forgotten that there are no roads into Juneau! You can
reach it only by ship, or airplane.) Doing manual labor on
the Snettisham Dam was camp life, with room and food
free. So no expenses. A civilian job with the Army Corp
of Engineers. But, before that, I got a job the first day in
Anchorage at the 4th Avenue Army Navy Surplus Store.

269. Established in 1947, and this great army navy surplus
store is still there! In 2007 or 2008 I popped in. The
owner's kids, my age, now running it, remembered
me. One reason was because I got beat up badly by four
Fort Richardson soldiers looking for a party and trouble.
The day I got back from the hospital, at the store in
Ray Williams', the manager, office, we watched those

astronauts walk on the moon live for the first time—July 20 1969. I got Indian friends out of jail a few times. In Alaska I learned to shoot a *Dirty Harry* 44 magnum. The lady of the house always packed/carried. I saved my neck from a grizzly bear because I learned that same morning over breakfast from an old Sourdough (experienced Alaskan) that you should run downhill, not uphill. Downhill we are more nimble and the bear will take a tumble.

270. The main thing that got me back to Alaska so much was Mike Smith, alias "Tree". Mike had all kinds of big jobs in Alaska such as chief of habitat, working on Indian land claims, oil rights, and all kinds of environmental impact responsibilities. And these days consulting on such stuff. "Tree" was 12 years older and also a Phi Gam at Cornell. He came back to Cornell as the in-house resident advisor after my trip to Alaska, the summer after my freshman year. Mike got his masters at the University of Fairbanks, spent a year with penguins—seriously—in Antarctica, and was finishing up his PhD at Cornell. He was in Ken Blanchard's class, the famous author of *One Minute Manager*. He also knew Tom Peters who was a couple years younger, and later on wrote *In Search of Excellence* (Harper Business) and so much more. Mr. Blanchard and Mr. Peters were also Cornell Phi Gams. They are Mike's good friends. They both visit Mike in Alaska, and they also meet up in the lower 48.

271. Last time I saw Mike Smith and his family in maybe 2008, he took me out to look at Anchorage from a surrounding hill top. He heard the clashing of antlers. Mike knew where to look with the binoculars he ALWAYS carries. It was two huge male moose fighting over a female. She was hiding behind a nearby bush, and trembling. Couldn't

see the trembling, but if I had antlers you would be trembling. I guess she has to wait to see who wins. No Sadie Hawkins dance for her this time. Ken said I brought him good luck; because out of his over 45 or so years in Alaska, even though he is walking, skiing, or paddling in the wilds several months each year, it was only the second moose fight he had seen. Yet we see moose all the time up there in Alaska.

272. Ken Blanchard and Tom Peters got in touch with me not knowing about the Cornell Phi Gam connection. I never met Tom, but he had me write something for his newsletter a bit before 1990. The article is in my *Taking Charge in Japan* book (Japan Times, 1990). Ken saw me in Tokyo, and had me visit with his group in San Diego. He was the inspiration for one of my books, *Know Your Own Bone* (nothing to do with the overly excited dog, and losing one's bone—maybe just a subliminal triggered association). I went with some of Ken Blanchard's people south of the border. Tequila shots had me on my hotel bed remembering only the beginning of my first time in Tijuana. The only other time I got plastered like that was in Jamaica during spring break freshman year at Cornell. I was down there with my brother Art, Craig Kammerer (above, who taught me Teriyaki sauce in San Francisco and horseback riding in Hawaii) and two other fraternity brothers. We all ended up with the blistering, searing Jamaican sunrise on us as we slept in the sand on a beach. None of us had any idea how we got there, or where we came from. Did remember entering a local bar. This time it was a rum punch. No money missing — had no money to miss. Lucky all our kidneys and other organs stayed with us. We just drank too much, I guess.

My Job at the Straight Desk at Willard Straight Hall was a Huge Part of My Life at Cornell. I was on Duty the April 18, 1969 Day Leading to Cornell Making the Cover of Newsweek and Myriad Newspapers when Some Gun-Toting Black Students Took Over the Straight Building on Parents' Weekend.

273. Kept working at 'the desk' so I could take that trip around the world, driving from London to Katmandu and then about 3 more months hitchhiking in Thailand, Malaysia, flying into Saigon, Vietnam in the middle of the war, walking Hong Kong, and hitchhiking in Taiwan and Korea. And last stop Japan. That was during the summer and first semester of my junior year. Freshman year I was pledge class president at my Phi Gam Fraternity. Easy peasy because I was at all 'the smokers' 'rushing' for the house as if I was already a brother. A classmate and fellow 'deskman' at Willard Straight Hall, Pete McCarthy, became Phi Gam president our senior year. During a shift at 'the desk' our senior year, Pete surprised me by saying, "Tom, who knows, you'll probably spend your life in Japan." He knew I had been there, and was studying Japanese. I thought he was very thoughtful and creative, if not nuts. He saw that life-in-Japan possibility before I did. Pete went on and was in Japan himself running his foreign bank's Asian branch. Later on he got a President George Bush Jr. political appointment and became assistant secretary for management and CFO at the U.S. Department of Treasury.

274. When you pick up colleagues' student union desk shifts for them, and work 40 hours a week, interesting things can happen. I was assigned to the desk on that Homecoming Parents' Weekend Day, when the Black students took

over Willard Straight Hall. We had to get the parents out of the hotel section of Willard Straight Hall. The rifles and bandoliers of bullets worn by the black students standing and guarding the entrance to Cornell's Willard Straight Hall was powerful imagery for the Newsweek cover and other front page newspapers photos.

275. Maybe it was about this time that the Willard Straight Hall Deskmen had to sleep over and guard the Andrew Dickson White House, right in the middle of the campus. Mr. White was the co-founder of Cornell along with Mr. Ezra Cornell. The house was built in 1871 as White's residence, and as the residence for future university presidents. Now, and, back in my years at Cornell, it is a museum with a second more private office for the university president. It was a little exciting, but it seems like that gig should have gone to the karate club guys, or the wrestlers, rather than we straight deskmen! And they were always 'men' at that job. Until I also helped push for female deskpersons my senior year. My sophomore year, when I was a cheerleader, was also the first year there were female cheerleaders—believe it or not. Cornell with its large 'Greek' (fraternity and sorority presence) was a very diverse place. But some archaic traditions remained. There were many 'independents' too, but as I recall there were 53 fraternities and over 20 sororities. More details about getting to Japan, and getting started in Japan appear later on in the book.

276. I should mention a couple other guys. Out of the 500 who applied for the highest paying campus job—this job at the Straight Desk in the USA's first dedicated student union building, Cornell's Willard Straight Hall. As I recall, only 12 kids out of the 500 students who apply make the cut. Craig Kammerer, mentioned several times above, was already a

deskman. He says I got it, because a very senior deskman named Chris Snell (different fraternity, Phi Delta Theta, I think) "was screaming for you". Just because Chris liked my wisecracks. Chris Snell had girl friends. It was just my wisecracks he liked. Thanks, Chris! I used your name as a banker in one of my books. Then we 'compet'/compete in a probationary status, actually working and being watched by senior deskmen, for a month, I think. Then only 6 or 8 out of the 12 who passed the interviews survive the on-the-job probation.

277. A guy named Tom Hughes got in that first freshman wave of deskmen with me. Tom, and his high school honey Sally were also cheerleaders with me our sophomore year. Tom grew up in Ithaca, or at least went to Ithaca High School. Tom also got the American Legion Boy's State honor selected by his high school. As did I. When I met Tom at Cornell I had remembered seeing him duke it out at Boys State with the other ambitious guys who were running for 'state office'. I think Tom made New York State Boys State Governor. That's my memory. When I complimented him, he just smiled. That is what President Bill Clinton was able to do in Arkansas when he was in high school.

278. As an American Legion student state governor you get to go to the White House. That is when a handshake with President Kennedy, resulted in Mr. Clinton being inspired and pretty committed to becoming President of the United States himself, so I have read. Tom Hughes didn't bother with that. He had spent so much time in freezing, small-town Ithaca, I guess he wanted to 'make a move' off to exotic foreign lands. As a Cornell Hotelier he opted to work almost exclusively in foreign countries. At Boys State I guess I saw my limitations, or anyway

couldn't get into it. Mostly I shot baskets in the back. When my dad heard this story, he said, "Your brother would have done more than that." That is probably true. Being told things like that never bothered me much—or maybe… As Dirty Harry said, 'A man has to know his limitations', or at least what he wants. But I knew I had to try and do something with my life on my own and away from my brother. I ended up 'making this move' to Japan.

Doing Something on the Path Less Traveled.
Anyway, Stepping Out and Doing Something Exciting
for You, Can Lead to Good Things such as a Cornell
White House Summer Internship for Me. I suppose
the Wrong Path could also Screw Someone up Big Time.
Donald Rumsfeld Really Impressed Us.

279. Because of me 'making a move' up to Alaska after freshman year, I came back with the $5,000 in savings. I wanted my real blood brother Art to come with us to Alaska. There was lots of room in the 1953 Desoto. I was going up with a kid from another fraternity I met only once before. We took off from Ithaca in his car. My brother said he had to definitely work that summer and could not take the risk of taking off to Alaska. It was then my trip to Katmandu and ultimately Japan, after the summer of my sophomore year that won me Cornell University's nomination for a White House Summer Internship. It sure as hell wasn't my grades.

280. I had also gone into Vietnam in 1970 (2 years after the Tet Offensive, and 5 years before the Americans had to escape by helicopter from our USA Embassy roof).

I went in to Vietnam to meet with another two-year-older Waccabuc buddy Dick Duffy. He was a lieutenant. I was also meeting Leo Reinsmith's dad. Leo was a fellow straight deskman from another fraternity house. His Dad was a full air force colonel. I had lost friends in Vietnam, and wanted to pay respects, and at least partially put my own ass on the line. Maybe for these reasons I got assigned to the Office of Cambodian Affairs at the State Department. This is a stone's throw from the Watergate Complex. Where my H.S. two-year-younger Student Council President Election Campaign Manager, Roger Stone, would start throwing stones at the Democrats, with his involvement in the June 1972 Watergate break in. (Above.)

281. With my Eagle Scout, and other credentials, I was trusted not to leak about the illegal secret carpet bombing of Cambodia. I was wined and dined by famous folks— mostly the staff of famous politicians. A couple of their famous politician masters did walk over in the Senate dining room, or whatever, to shake my hand and say hi. I never have and never will mention their names. Not even to my wives or my dog. I would not, and did not leak any state secrets, or embarrassing telex cables.

282. By the way, a very young and good-looking Donald Rumsfeld, was chosen to make the speech to all of us "White House Summer Interns". Even though most of us don't work at the White House! We were all brought together to listen to Mr. Rumsfeld. He was 39 years old then. At the time, from 1969 to 1973, he was counsellor to the president for President Nixon. Later on he would be White House chief of staff, and secretary of defense. Mr. Rumsfeld was very impressive. He told us he was basically against the Vietnam War, and talked of the

difficulties of a victory there. A good German client of mine, Dr. Klaus Kran had been president of Bayer Japan. After that he was president of G. D. Searle in Japan. Of course Klaus would have contact with Mr. Rumsfeld at meetings and such, as Mr. Rumsfeld was CEO and chairman of G.D. Searle from 1977 to 1985. Dr. Kran had good things to say about Mr. Rumsfeld as a leader, and as a man.

283. Since I was in Washington that summer of 1971, I took the initiative to walk over to the Department of Labor. After all, I was a labor guy not an international relations guy. The go-to person about internships was a very attractive, and nice young lady named Gaele Fanning. She was two years older. So Ms. Fanning had that important job at age 23. I was 21. Thanks to Gaele getting the process started, I got an internship at the Bureau of International Labor Affairs at the Department of Labor. When you are an intern you get to meet with so many senior people, although briefly. I remember, meeting very impressive deputy secretaries, and having lunch or dinner with really cool people like Mr. Lawrence Schultz, the head of the Federal Mediation and Conciliation Service. Of course my immediate boss, a Chinese American lady named Beecee Laval, was a dynamo.

Action is the Key. One Good Thing Can Lead to Another. I Lined up an Internship at the Department of Labor for the Summer Before I came to Japan—a Great and Lucky Start with Fine and Powerful Friends There. Should I have 'Stayed Put' as a 'Supergrade' at the Department of Labor?

284. I suppose I at least shook hands with President Nixon's political appointee to Secretary of Labor, Mr. James D. Hodgson (1915-2012). Mr. Hodgson passed away at 96 years old in Malibu, California. Yes. I remember something. I first came out into the Tokyo international community when I joined the American Chamber of Commerce in 1976—a full 4 years after living the native, local beat. At a big party or a function, I was surprised to meet Mr. Hodgson again, and learned that he was at the time serving as the Ambassador to Japan (1974-1977). So Mr. Hodgson followed me out to Japan—hah! Before he passed away in 2012, he had been the longest surviving USA former cabinet officer.

285. Gaele's father was John H. Fanning (1916-1990), a legendary member and board chairman of the NLRB, the National Labor Relations Board. (Similar to Churoi, the Central Labor Relations Commission in Japan. The past chairman of Churoi, Nakayama, Ichiro, was technically my first visa sponsor in Japan, even though I did not know him well at all. This was in Professor Nakayama's capacity of being chairman of my research institute, The Japan Institute of Labour. This was the research organ for the Ministry of Labor. Dr. Nakayama has also been president of the University of Tokyo.) In 1957, Mr. John Fanning was appointed by President Dwight Eisenhower to be one of the only five members of the National Labor Relations Board (NLRB). His daughter Gaele became quite a good friend that summer. Her father is the first member of the NLRB to serve for so long. He was reappointed for the 5-year terms by Presidents Eisenhower, John F. Kennedy, Lyndon B. Johnson, Richard Nixon, and Jimmy Carter. Mr. Fanning's reappointment to the NLRB by President

Nixon in 1972, for a fourth five-year term set a record. He was appointed chair of the NLRB by President Jimmy Carter in April 1977.

286. Mr. John Fanning stepped down as NLRB chair on August 14, 1981, a record-long service at the NLRB of 25 years. His youngest daughter Gaele strongly encouraged me to stay on at the Department of Labor. She told me, "You are 'supergrade' material. You can start in that category. People here like you." That meant the very top non-political appointed federal career bureaucrat positions. And Gaele had a very big role in the supergrade section of the Department of Labor Personnel Department. So was I a fool to stick with my plan to go to Japan to build on my one year of Japanese study at Cornell, just prior to working that summer at the Department of Labor with Gaele? And all those other fascinating, powerful people who would have probably given me a nice fast start at the Department of Labor. Should I have 'stayed put' in Washington DC? Should I have had Laura, my high school girlfriend, go to university with me at Cornell almost four years earlier?

287. I guess we can only daydream, or wonder about such things. The serendipitous twists and turns of our lives. One thing helps me all the time. Whether it is big stuff like this, or tiny things we do or say wrong, and the little mistakes we make each day. We have to stop 'shoulding' (or *hitting) all over ourselves. Because at the time the conditions were there to make the decision we made. To say we should not have done or said something is wasteful. Nothing can be done about that. So here we are. Here we go. Do better. Do the best we can from here.

*Moving on to Omotesando, and Leaving My old Mostly
New York and Stateside Friends Where They are.
Underground Rivers, 827 American Houses in U.S.
Washington Heights Military Base becomes Yoyogi Park.
Johnny Kitagawa of Johnny's Jimusho (Talent Agency—
SMAP, Arashi etc.) gets Inspired, Discovers, and Recruits
his First Boy Band in Our Hood.*

288. Omotesando is the name of the subway station, and the wide avenue that goes down from Aoyama Dori/street, crosses Meiji Dori, and goes up to the entrance to Meiji Shrine, and Harajuku Station. It is often termed Tokyo's Champs-Elysees, and along with the Ginza has the most luxury brand stores. But also so much more to the left and right, where you have Aoyama, Jingumae and Harajuku. Before Christmas and for New Year's they fasten LED lights right up to the very thin branches of the Zelkova trees, lining both sides of the boulevard. This was the first street in Tokyo where this was done to that extent. From the Meiji Dori entrance up to in front of Harajuku Station (built in 1906) is Takeshita Dori/Street. This is a center of young people's 'cool Japan', and the center of eclectic and mesmerizing fashion and items of all kinds. For reference, Google key words such as the English Wikipedia entry for Kogal (abbreviation for high school gal). It's not just Takeshita Street, with one entrance point on the left side of Meiji Dori (about 100 meters after making a right at the corner of Omotesando Avenue and Meiji Dori), there are also tens of small streets with boutiques and stores, many of which are antenna shops to test run a new look or product. Many stores are run out of older residences or small apartment buildings. Of course lots of outdoor cafes, and places to eat as well.

289. As you go down the Omotesando Avenue slope from Aoyama Dori, on the left side, past the Oriental Bazaar specializing in souvenirs for foreign tourists, and the toy store Kiddy Land, there is a continuation of Cat Street, also part of this Ura- (in the back) Harajuku. This is at the lowest point of Omotesando Avenue, before the slope starts up toward Meiji Dori and Meiji Shrine. As you look to the left, and walk down the Cat Street pedestrian pathway that leads to Shibuya station, it is easier to see that it once was a river, and now the river runs below your feet, out of sight. In front of the beautiful white retro classic Ralph Lauren store on Omotesando Avenue, you can still see the two stone supports of what was the bridge over this river. You can also see similar stone bridge posts across the avenue at the entrance to Cat Street. The main tributary of the river is the Onden River, which starts in Sendagaya. It flows under Cat Street, merges with the Uda River in central Shibuya, forming the Shibuya River, which is 2.6 kilometers long. It then merges with the Furu River near Hiroo, and flows into Tokyo Bay near Shiba Koen. Actually, it flows under Shibuya Station, and under the Tokyu Department Store. In the next few years as they rebuild Shibuya station, including a 46-storey building, with shops, condos, and I'll bet a hotel on a few upper floors, there is a plan to expose parts of the Shibuya River and attractively landscape it. There will also be pedestrian access to the river banks.

290. Along a 250-meter stretch of Omotesando Avenue, there is a long, thin building—Omotesando Hills (built 2005) with its 130 shops, restaurants, and 38 apartments above the shops and restaurants. Replacing the Dojunkai Aoyama Apartments built in 1927 , it was a bit controversial. After

the 1923 Great Kanto earthquake and fire, the Home Ministry decided that such reinforced concrete, more fireproof buildings must be built. Between 1926 and 1934, 15 such apartment complexes were built. The last remaining one was demolished in 2013.

291. On the subject of vanishing landscapes. Yoyogi Park, adjacent to Meiji Shrine, used to be a military training and parade ground for the Japanese Imperial Army. After that, during the US Occupation from 1946 to 1952, and continuing until 1964, it became 'Washington Heights'. This was an American Army and Air force base with 827 American-style homes with grass lawns and all. It covered an area of 924,000 square meters, or 228 acres. There were also churches, shops, theatres, schools, and officers' clubs. Surrounded by fences, Japanese and all non-military personnel were not allowed access. This came back under Japanese control in 1964 and was used to house the 1964 Olympic athletes and for the athletes' village etc. After the Olympics, the houses were torn down except for one which was used by the Dutch Olympic team. That still stands within current day Yoyogi Park.

292. In 1962, Johnny Kitagawa of Johnny's Jimusho/talent agency created his first boy band from youths he found playing in Washington Heights. Johnny was born in Los Angeles in 1931, but came back to Japan with his family in 1933. His father had been the buddhist priest at Koyasan Buddhist Temple in Little Tokyo, L.A., California, from 1924 to 1933. Johnny went to live in the States from 1949 to the early 1950s. At that point he came back to work at the United States Embassy in Tokyo. Mr. Kitagawa still actively manages the agency now in 2015 at 83 years old. After a big success with Four Leaves, he went on and pretty much monopolizes this boy band idea, getting

many of them into films, and TV shows etc. His agency's groups also include Shonentai, SMAP (huge, with the 4 guys seen everywhere), NEWS, V6, Arashi, Tackey and Tsubasa, KAT-TUN, Kinki Kids, Tokio, Kanjani8, Hey! Say!, Jump, NYC, Kis-My-Ft2, Sexy Zone, ABC-Z etc. 'Johnny's' has open try-outs, and company-run dormitories and training schools in singing, dancing, and acting. Sure enough the only Johnny's Shop in Tokyo is off the Omotesando exit of Harajuku station.

Hattori Hanzo and His Ninja are in Harajuku and Omotesando History, not Just Imperial Palace Hanzomon Gate and Environs History. Good Things happen if you loyally save the Life of the Future First Tokugawa Shogun, Tokugawa Ieyasu. Meiji Shrine Gets about 3,500,000 Visitors Every Year! —Japan's most, during just the First 3 Days of New Years!

293. Maybe time for some history. Harajuku was a small inn and post town on the Kamakura Highway. During the Gosannen War fought in the late 1080s, a Minamoto no Yoshiie gathered his army on a hill called Seizoroi-saka, currently at Jingumae 2 chomes. Looks like not much else happened for 500 years. On June 21, 1582, a samurai general, Akechi Mitsuhide (1528-1582) who served the very famous Oda Nobunaga (June 23, 1534- June 21, 1582), decided to betray Nobunaga when Nobunaga was staying at Honno-ji temple in Kyoto without his army. Oda Nobunaga was surrounded by Akechi's army, so he committed suicide and had the temple burned down. He wanted to burn himself up so Akechi could not parade his head on a spike around town.

294. Tokugawa, Ieyasu (1543-1616), the first Edo-era Tokugawa Shogun, probably would have met a similar fate. However, his retainer and loyal ninja leader Hattori Hanzo (1542-1596) came to his aid. They fled through several provinces, crossed the mountains of Iga (current Mie Prefecture) the strongest ninja-controlled backwater area, and made their escape to the shore of Ise, returning to safety by sea. Because Hattori Hanzo and his ninjas also helped rescue Ieyasu's captured family members, as a reward, in 1590, the nearby Ondenmura/village, and Harajuku-mura were given to Hattori Hanzo.

295. Of course Hanzo's gate to the Imperial Palace, and current Wakaba between the Palace and Yotsuya were also bestowed on Hattori. Up until the 1943 name change, today's Wakaba, was called Iga-cho. Named after the Iga province, the part of Japan from which Hattori came. Hattori Hanzo's ninjas based in Harajuku and Omotesando, and up on the high ground of Aoyama, had the job of protecting the Tokugawa Shogun and the Imperial Palace from enemies coming from that direction. Today's Hanzomon subway line and station are also named after this most famous ninja of all time.

296. Meiji Shrine was established in 1919 to honor Emperor Meiji (1852-1912). The forest around Meiji Shrine is 700,000 square meters, about 175 acres. It has 120,000 trees of 365 species donated from governments and people all over Japan. Before the forest, there was an iris garden, and it must have been mostly farmland. President George Bush Jr. viewed Yabusame Archery there in November 2001, just after making war on Afghanistan. It was one of the first places Hillary Clinton visited as Barack Obama's secretary of state. The German Foreign

Minister Guido Westerwelle also visited there in January, 2010. Most Japanese try and do Hatsumode shrine visits the first three days of the New Year. Meiji Shrine gets the most visitors of any shrine in Japan. It gets about 3,500,000 visitors during just those 3 days! Several other shrines also get over 2,000,000 visitors: Narita-san 2,980,000, Kawasaki Daishi 2,960,000, Fushimi Inari Taisha 2,700,000, and Sumiyoshi Taisha 2,600,000.

Three Larger than Life Japanese Leaders from the Same Kagoshima, Kyushu Neighborhood. The Main Two Characters Colliding in the Watanabe, Ken and Tom Cruise's Last Samurai *movie, had been Boyhood Friends. The Larger than life Admiral Togo, 'Horatio Nelson of the East', was from the Same Neighborhood, but about 20 Years Younger.*

297. In 1940 Togo Shrine was built and consecrated in honor of Imperial Japanese Navy Marshal-Admiral Marquis Togo Heihachiro (1848-1934). The shrine is located near the entranceway to Takeshita Dori, off Meiji Dori. It basically goes back to near Harajuku station spilling out into that hip, eccentric and funky part of town. — Pretty cool place for a proper and stuffy shrine of such a dignified, and properly British-educated gentleman. Mr. Togo was termed by Western journalists as "the Horatio Nelson (1758-1805) of the East". He was from the same Kagoshima, Kyushu (Southernmost main island) samurai housing district that also gave birth to Saigo Takamori (1828-1877) and Okubo Toshimichi 1830-1878). In the *Last Samurai* movie (2003) Watanabe Ken played a character modeled on Saigo Takamori carrying out the

Satsuma Rebellion of 1877 along with Tom Cruise. Saigo had to go against his neighborhood friend, schoolmate and former ally, Okubo Toshimichi. Okubo was the home minister—the round-faced guy in the western business suit with the weird mustache. In the movie he was portrayed to be a major cornhole. In real life he was very competent. Mr. Okubo did a great job, and was respected by both sides of most issues.

298. As Home Minister, Okubo led the army and squashed the rebellion on September 24, 1877 at the Battle of Shiroyama overlooking Kagoshima city. This *Last Samurai* movie battle scene was based on history to quite an extent. At the real conflict, within 5 or 6 weeks, the rebels were cut down from a force of 20,000 to only 500 remaining on the Shiroyama hill. And then, as in the movie, only 40 remained for the final desperate charge. All of them were killed except Tom Cruise. Only 8 months later on May 14 1878, Okubo was assassinated by 7 disgruntled, still rebelling, pissed-off Samurai. They wanted to keep their swords, their long hair, the privileges of their class, and their way of life. Also revenge for putting down the Satsuma rebellion a few months earlier.

299. The place of Home Minister Okubo's murder is marked with a big stone marker in the park between the Imperial Palace and in front of the back of the New Otani Hotel. The entrance to the New Otani near the Akasaka Mitsuke subway lines. Not the 'Osato Chemical' side where James Bond drives through in *You Only Live Twice* (1967). Mr. Okubo came down the elevator from the 4th floor after having polished off a couple Mai Tai drinks at Trader Vic's. He was feeling no pain as he weaved his way toward the Imperial Palace. Then he was bushwhacked. Out of the bushes jumped those whacking seven Samurai swordsman.

300. In contrast, Admiral Togo from that same Kagoshima neighborhood lived to be 86. Mr. Togo learned much by 'closely watching' on Google satellite the Sino-French War (1884-1885). He captained the Naniwa in the Sino-Japanese War (1894-1895), and did well at sea. His big victory, which stunned the world, was the annihilation of the Russian fleet at the Battle of Tsushima in the Russo-Japanese War (1904-1905). From 1914 until 1924 Admiral Togo was put in charge of the education of Crown Prince Hirohito, the future Showa Emperor. As I recall, there was a display in the Tokyo American Club (TAC) lobby, before they tore that club down, to replace it with the beautiful facility we have today. I remember for sure that Hirohito lived and was educated in a house on those same grounds before TAC ever moved there. So I suppose Admiral Togo lived there or spent quite a lot of time on current day TAC grounds. When Mr. Togo died in 1934 he was provided a state funeral. The navies of the USA, UK, Netherlands, France, China, and Italy all sent navy ships to join a navy parade in Tokyo Bay in honor of Admiral Togo. I guess still a little too sensitive for Russia to participate in that event.

A Statue Erected for Hachiko at Nearby Shibuya Station during Hachi's Life. For Dog Lovers, but Also became a Symbol of Loyalty to the Emperor and the Nation. The Hachi/8th Pup in the Litter makes it Big Time.

301. Let's switch over to a more heartwarming topic. Especially for us dog lovers. I have met 223 people in front of the Shibuya station Hachiko (November 10, 1923-March 8, 1935) statue during these 43 years in Tokyo. Few were

clients, because we meet at each other's offices. They were new and old friends I met in Japan, or from around the world. Yes. Most of them had shoulder length, or longer hair. Shibuya, a 15-minute walk from here, is the best place in Tokyo to have fun. I'm always on time, or early. So enough time to give this solid bronze statue of the dog Hachi a light pet for good luck, without my friends thinking I'm in to heavy metal. Hachi means 8 and Hachi was the 8th puppy to come out with his siblings in that litter. If you saw the movie *Hachi* (2009) with Richard Gere, you probably know there was a Japanese Professor at Tokyo University, who suddenly died from a cerebral hemorrhage. Surprisingly, the professor's death, and permanent parting with Hachi was only about a year after getting together. The professor and Hachi had a routine of walking to Shibuya station together each morning. Unfortunately this relationship only lasted for this single year.

302. Then Hachi would come after the professor's work day, the same time each day when the train was due. So Hachiko was smarter than I thought. I thought Hachiko was a dumb as paint dog that waited in the same place day and night. Truthfully, I assumed Hachiko was a girl, because names ending in ko usually mean girls. Except, I realize this dog Hachiko's ko means 'public' or open. I guess I preferred the idea of petting a girl in private, more than in public. Think about it. This boy dog was not on a short leash. In fact, although it is illegal now, maybe then, there was no leash. This well-endowed king-sized pooch was free to walk Center *Gai*/street, Dogenzaka, and donkey punch at will in Maruyama-cho, the huge nearby love hotel district. Hachi would not even have to check into the hotels.

303. When Hachiko was done messing around with bustling Shibuya all to himself, Hachi would often go to the home of Mr. Kikuzaburo Kobayashi, the former gardener of Hachiko's master Professor Hidesaburo Ueno. Actually, Hachi did wait at the same place at the station, but only at the appointed hour. Somewhere in Shibuya station there are bronze paw prints marking the place Hachi always waited. I will get our Luna-Tuna, our mini-dachshund, to try and find those paw prints. She's blind but her nose works even better now.

304. The station personnel and other people were always trying to seduce this doggie with all kinds of treats, food, ramen, and yakitori etc. When Hachi was given an autopsy, four yakitori skewers were found in his stomach—so dog not so smart after all. But it was determined the four sharp yakitori sticks did Hachi no harm—tough dog. Rather the cause of death was terminal cancer and a filarial infection. Despite being so wined and dined, and despite becoming famous especially after an October 4, 1932 *Asahi Shimbun/* newspaper article, Hachi let none of this go to his head. Until Hachi's death on March 8 1935, he continued to go to meet his old master the professor at the same time every day. I suppose Hachiko could tell the time from the positioning of outdoor clock hands, or from the pattern of the trains, and the sounds they made. Even in those days I am sure the trains always ran on schedule. I was thinking, either for the benefit of his beloved dog, or because Professor Ueno had an easy schedule he could control, it is quite something that the prof. could take the same train home every day. Just like my dad coming down the driveway at our Lake Waccabuc house at 6:15 every evening. And like Hachiko, we all

would run down the back stairs, bark out greetings, and properly meet our dad after his day of toil.

305. Hachi was loyal until the end, even with the fame. Especially after the *Asahi Shimbun* article, and then for years after Hachi's death, Hachi was a national sensation. Teachers and parents used Hachi as a symbol of family loyalty. This also got shifted and aimed to nurture faithfulness and loyalty to the person and the institution of Emperor Hirohito. One of Professor Ueno's students, Mr. Hirokichi Saito, was really into Akita dogs. If you think my labor consulting is abnormal and off-beat, think about this kid. He worked hard at it and determined that there were only 30 purebred Akita dogs in all of Japan, including his prof.'s Hachi—hello? Sounds like a good story, but sounds like the professor's student Saito was pinching the loaf a bit.

306. With all the mountains, valley, caves, barns, islands—6,852 islands making up Japan—in this very long Japan archipelago, how did this dog-crazed student know there were only 30 purebred Akita dogs? I would like some research done on all the half-breed Akita dogs that the unleashed and fancy-free Hachi must have surely sired in the parks, alleys, and in front of the love hotels, watering holes and drinking and eating establishments of Shibuya. They would be gone by now, but surely their descendants live on. Anyway, at least the kid had a good line in his research paper, and some minor articles he wrote about Hachiko's loyalty got the attention of *Asahi Shimbun*. Hachiko's stuffed and mounted remains are kept at the National Science Museum of Japan in Ueno, Tokyo. The doggie's cemetery monument is alongside Professor Hidesaburo Ueno at Aoyama Cemetery.

307. Hachiko himself was in attendance at the unveiling of his first bronze statue at Shibuya Station in April, 1934. How many people get a statue erected of them while they are still alive? Hachiko's statue was melted down for the war effort during WWII. The son of the original Hachiko sculpture followed his father into sculpting, and made a second statue of Hachiko in 1948. Richard Gere's *Hachi: A Dog's Tale* was filmed in Woonsocket, Rhode Island. The local tourism commission and the Japanese Consulate in the US unveiled an identical statue of Hachiko in front of the Woonsocket Depot Square train station. A 3-D printer? In the movie the station was called Bedridge. Richard Gere has a hotel/inn in Bedford. He probably came up with the name plucking the ridge from nearby Ridgefield and the Bed from Bedford. Both towns my old haunts too. On Sunday March 8 2015, at the University of Tokyo ('Todai') in celebration of the 80th anniversary of the dog's death, a life-size statue was erected of Hachi standing, and trying to lick his standing Professor's face. My constantly supervised mini-dachs, yes. Shibuya free-roaming slobbering big dog Hachi? Hmm… this Professor Hidesaburo Ueno, is also considered the father of Japan's agricultural engineering studies (same *Japan Times* article.) Maybe Hachi is worth a visit at Todai too—Japan's best and most famous university. The date of Hachi's birthday is on record. Usually births are celebrated with statues. Not deaths—weird.

Hachiko and Master are buried at Nearby Aoyama Cemetery. A Nice Place to Walk Among the Graves of the Two Conflicted Characters in the Last Samurai *Movie. General Nogi, Prime Minister Yoshida Shigeru, and a Taxi Cab-Hopping Ghost of a Lady.*

308. Let's swing over to Aoyama Cemetery where Hachiko and her professor's ashes, and at least Hachiko's spirit are interred. It is about a 15-minute walk to the cemetery from our TMT Building in Omotesando, Shibuya. Our address is a Shibuya address but even taxi drivers often think we are wrong and that it is in Minami Aoyama. Actually our building is the 5th building from Minami Aoyama in Minato-ku. The road where we met the Biohazard pony (details above) separates Minato-ku from Shibuya-ku. We are also about 5 buildings up from Roppongi Dori, so you can easily hop a cab. It is minimum taxi fare to Shibuya station and to Roppongi crossroads.

309. Walking in cemeteries may seem strange in some cultures, and sometimes our dog and my wife get some kind of supernatural, paranormal, goosebumpy reaction. The dog barks, and digs in her heels to go no further. Chika, my wife, doesn't bark, but sometimes also wants to get the hell out of the graveyard. However, for an edgeless, opaque and duly obtuse bloke like me, I just enjoy the fresh air, breezes, and calm and tranquil scenery including the stunning cherry blossoms and other greenery in their season. The cemetery has an area of 263,564 square meters, or 65 acres. On a hill, there is good distant scenery as well. Maybe the taxi driver was pulling a young *gaijin's* chain. About 35 years ago I hailed a cab while walking on one of Aoyama Cemetery's drive-through roads. The driver told me I had guts to walk through the cemetery so late at night. He said he once picked up a woman close to the same spot. Closed the cab door. In Japan the doors are controlled by the taxi driver. He swears the doors were locked as usual. The woman said nothing. When he turned on the cab light and turned around to ask her where she wanted to go, the back seat was empty. Actually, I'm tearing up a bit, and

getting goosebumps just remembering this. Another taxi driver told me the same story years later.

310. This 65 acres, 79,625 tsubo/262,763 square meters of Aoyama Cemetery all belonged to the Aoyama family of the Gujo clan (now Gujo, Gifu Prefecture) in the province of Mino (now Gifu). This is Japan's first public cemetery. It was taken over by Tokyo Prefecture from September 1, 1874. It is the largest public cemetery out of all the public cemeteries in the 23 wards of metropolitan Tokyo. Okubo, Toshimichi, the Kagoshima-born Home Minister who put an end to his schoolmate and neighborhood friend Saigo Takamori, and had Tom Cruise wounded at the final battle of the Satsuma Rebellion, was buried at Aoyama Cemetery after he was assassinated near the New Otani Hotel on his way to the Imperial Palace (details above).

311. Yoshida Shigeru (1878-1967), a famous prime minister from October 1948 until December, 1954, is also buried in Aoyama Cemetery. As is the very famous General Maresuke Nogi who did on land what Admiral Togo did on the seas. Except, Nogi Taisho/General committed ritual *seppuku*/hara-kiri suicide in his very small brick house with some bleached out natural wood clapboard in the front. It's very close to, and visible from the street adjacent, or very near to Nogi Shrine. It's on the left side of the street as you go from Aoyama 1-chome toward Roppongi. Nogi did this upon the Meiji Emperor's death. Nothing in particular to be sad or ashamed about; just wanted to follow his master. Even at that time many were shocked with that brand of loyalty. After the professor's death, even loyal canine Hachiko never tried to run in front of the train the professor had always taken—the train that took Hachiko's master away for keeps.

*No Story about Tokyo and Japan Can be Complete
without Mention of the Incredible Train, Subway,
and their Station Infrastructure. We have Three Iconic Train
and Subway Stations in Our Neighborhood.
The 3 lines of Omotesando Subway Station is Close by,
and then Shibuya, and Harajuku Stations are about
the Same 15-minute Walking Distance.*

312. Talking about trains and Hachiko, let's go back to Shibuya station. Rather than change at Shibuya station on to the Ginza line or Hanzomon subway, and go one stop, most of our staff would walk to this TMT building from Shibuya station. The walk is basically a bit uphill in the morning, but downhill after work. I would hear numbers varying between 10 and 17 minutes, depending on walking styles, length of legs, on two feet or four feet etc. Shibuya station first opened in 1885, and has 9 different train lines, with the most recent one constructed in 2008, the Fukutoshin subway line.

313. There were a total of 2,765,727 passengers using the station on an average day based on 2013 statistics. The Yamanote line had 378,530 passengers (boarding passengers only, so maybe twice that many?); the Keio Line was used by 336,957 passengers, Ginza subway by 212,136; Hanzomon and Fukutoshin subway together was 731,184; Tokyu Toyoko Line 441,266; Den-en-toshi Line 665,645 daily passengers.

314. Omotesando Station is 6 or 7 minutes on normal foot from our place. Could be 2 minutes by fast foot. Maybe 40 seconds by Usain Bolt after a big meal of sushi. It opened in 1938 with the Ginza line, Japan's first subway which made its first shorter run in 1927. The Chiyoda

Line platform opened on October 20 1972, the same autumn that I came to Japan. The Hanzomon Platform opened on August 1, 1978 along with the birth of my first son, Tommy. Not a railroad man. Pure coincidence. There is same-direction cross-platform interchange between the Ginza and Hanzomon lines. The Ginza line comes more frequently, and the train is much shorter than many newer subway line trains. They can't lengthen the trains because some of the original Ginza line station platforms are also short.

315. Many people who want to change on to the Yamanote line or Keio Inokashira Line at Shibuya station can save Shibuya station walking time if they change to the Ginza Line at Omotesando by simply crossing the platform. People who want to have shorter walks at Shibuya station, and want to take the Tokyu Toyoko Line, the Fukutoshin subway, or the Tokyu Den-en toshi Line will change at Omotesando from the Ginza line to the Hanzomon Line by simply walking across the platform. I didn't know any of this crossover stuff before I decided to write this book just weeks ago. Now I know what all that fuss is about—why so many outsiders like my station, and run across my platform. I thought they were like me, and had screwed up and gotten on the wrong train.

316. I read that our Omotesando subway station is the only station in Tokyo, or maybe all of Japan that has had three different names! For the old bottom burpers out there, you will recall that your mothers carried you to Aoyama 6-chome Station when the station opened on November 18, 1938. The day I arrived in Japan 34 years later. On September 16, 1939 it became Jingumae Station, so you got lost on the way home. But it wasn't too hot. Wasn't

too cold. When the Chiyoda Line platforms opened up on October 20 1972 it became Omotesando Station. Hopefully the name does not change before this book gets printed.

317. Tokyo train and subway stations are much more than that. They are constantly getting better and better with more chic and sophisticated classy underground and nearby shops, restaurants, boutiques etc. There is almost as much action, great things to do, and to buy underground in Tokyo as there is above the ground. Also great improvements with the building and renovation of surface, above-ground station buildings. This is especially since the Japan National Railway/JNR became privatized since 1987. This stimulated all the many private railroad lines to further spruce up their stations.

318. Usually, when my wife and I are in foreign cities, we don't take the subways or trains. Not so much about taking taxis; mostly doing long walks following north, south and east, west magnetic compass bearings. Then if enough days, further slicing to 45-degree bearings. Yes. My wife may leave me for this and other reasons. I wonder if I could be missing as much as you will miss in Tokyo if you never go down those staircases and escalators. Especially, when it is raining, colder than a witches' Subway sandwich, or hotter than her turbocharged broomstick, it is good to know that you can do the same walk of sometimes even several kilometers all underground. With a lot of resting places, delicious restaurants, and restrooms. No matter how clean the bowls look, please don't drink the eau d' toilette from the bowl the way my junior high school buddy The Hood did (above).

319. Above ground, Yoyogi Park deserves a little more comment. It is 54.1 hectors/ 134 acres/164,150 tsubo. It is about a 15-minute walk from here. You can go down the main wide beautiful Omotesando Avenue or take some of the back streets of Ura-Harajuku, known internationally as the center of Japanese youth culture and fashion. As I earlier wrote, current day Yoyogi Park was an army parade and training ground before it was the Washington Heights USA army and air force base from 1946 to 1964. Sure enough it was Captain Yoshitoshi Tokugawa (1884-1963), the grandnephew of the last Shogun, Tokugawa, Yoshinobu (1827-1913), who was the first one to go out and buy an airplane and ship it back to Japan. They didn't fly very far in those days.

320. On December 19 1910, he made the first successful powered aircraft flight in Japan, taking off and landing in what is now Yoyogi Park. He also piloted the inaugural flight at Japan's first permanent airfield in Tokorozawa, Saitama Prefecture. This Mr. Tokugawa helped establish the first Japanese air force, and was commander of the Army Aviation Corps three times through the 1920s and 1930s. I'll bet Commander Tokugawa could land a crippled vintage airplane on a golf course as well as Harrison Ford did in early March 2015—even without Han Solo's training in his *Star Wars* Millennium Falcon ship. Han Solo, the grandfather, and *Star Wars* are coming again soon to a theater near you! Mr. Tokugawa, "The Grandfather of Flight" in Japan, got off to his flying start in what is current day Yoyogi Park. As did lots of rock bands, musicians and dancers exercise their skills and pursue their dreams in the park. They still do. It is the most popular gathering place for Japanese performers and music fans. The area was/is also a major center for

the 1964 and 2020 Olympics. Yoyogi Park has beautiful cherry blossoms, lots of room, and beautiful landscaped picnic areas, bike paths, cycle rentals, and public sports courts.

Omotesando is Particularly Flooded with Foreigners during Christmas and New Year's Holidays, When it is Easier for many around the World to take some Time off. Apple's Only-In-Japan, Fukubukuro/Lucky Bag Sale.

321. The day I write this section is January 2 2015 at 10:45 am. Yesterday, New Year's Day, I took Luna-Tuna, our mini-dachshund, along Koto Dori, a right on Aoyama Dori, and a left at the first light on the main Omotesando Avenue. When I can walk her, I take this route because the streets and sidewalks are so wide. Especially Omotesando Avenue, sloping down to Meiji Dori, and then going up the slope toward Meiji Jingu/ shrine and Harajuku station, which can, of course, be teaming with people. But Lu-Tu has come to love this. Especially during the Christmas/New Year's season it seems about 30 to 40% of those walking are foreigners from all over the world. They love our sausage dog. And so do so many Japanese, who want to pet her. And Lu loves it. Each time it gives her *genki*/pep to walk the next 200 meters.

322. I decided months ago to stop telling people our dog is totally blind. Her eye color is pretty normal, so why bother. Sausage's eyes don't look weird like Zatoichi the blind swordsman, and masseur played by Shintaro Katsu's (1931-1997) very popular TV series from 1974

to 1979. There were also 26 films from 1962 to 1989. All based on a fictional character created by novelist Kan Shimozawa. The 2003 film directed by and starring the incredibly talented and boundless Beat Takeshi/Kitano, Takeshi, won an award at the Venice Film Festival. If only our Luna-chan could be such an enduring character. Many do notice and say she moves in funny ways. As Luna try's to feel out where and what the foreign tourists are, speaking all the strange languages they speak. Omotesando is an avenue of long lines. Ben & Jerry's has 4 stores in Tokyo, and the lines there got dwarfed by a nearby chocolate, and even a popcorn store. Always at least 100, often 200 people happily lined up for chocolate or popcorn!

323. Yesterday, New Year's! January 1, 2015, at about 1:30 in the afternoon, there was another very long line of people about 3 meters wide, and 120 meters long. They were camped out for the night, still half a day away, with sleeping bags stretched out, and really bundled up warm. A guardsman told me it was for the Apple store's annual New Year's fukubukuro/lucky bag sale. Japan is the only country where Apple does this. The store was closed, so all those people waiting would be spending the night. It was cold for Tokyo, and the temperature was to go down to -2 degrees centigrade—below freezing. I was especially intrigued, as I assumed the lucky bags would be free. (But now on second thought I realized that the fukubukuro/lucky bags of department stores and other stores are never free.) The next day, I happened to wake up early at about 7 am. I decided to check out that Apple store, to see if any of the mostly crazy kids were still breathing. Or would there be a path of frozen lumps? This store opened June 13 2014, and is the newest one

of the 3 Apple stores in Tokyo. It's huge. Glass on 3 sides. Difficult to figure out how it stands firm with our earthquakes. There is off-street access and a basement. There is nothing above the sales floor roof, and that steel roof that juts out must be very expertly stabilizing the glass walls below.

324. The next day, I arrived at the Apple store at about 9:15am. Sleeping bags were rolled up, and all were standing. I found out from a young European Apple staff, whose job was to oversee the end of the waiting line that the store opened at 8am, earlier than usual. This chap was in an orange Apple fleece that did not look so warm. Maybe he was Norwegian or Finnish. But there were other Apple staff at an outside station only in an Apple T-shirt. One guy looked like a Samoan who didn't make it high enough in Sumo wrestling. But not all had such natural insulation. The Finn said that when he arrived at 6am, the campers went all the way up to Aoyama Doori, and curved around to the left going another 100 meters up Aoyama Dori toward Gaienmae station. He added that since he guarded the end of the line from 6am, only about 10 or 20 people added themselves on to the line for the two hours between 6 and 8am. This means that about 400 meters of overnight campers spent the night on cold stone in below freezing temperatures!

325. It looked like there were about 100 Apple staff manning the store and the scene inside, mostly in red Apple T-shirts. Whenever about 12 waiting customers in one cluster were let into the store, all the Apple staff clapped and cheered. During the time the customers let into the stores waited in about 4 lines to get their *fukubukuro*, they could play with all the Apple gear on the long product display tables that are always there. The bags were all

nice sturdy canvas, gray-colored shoulder knapsacks, about the size of a large school bag sized knapsack. I checked to see if the bags had an Apple logo. She must have been Chinese or something. At first she must have thought I was trying to steal her lucky bag. No logo. A Japanese staffer told me that he, and most staff did not know what was in the bags. He told me about 20% of Apple's staff are foreigners. He said he thought most of the people camping all night were Japanese. Now you understand all the patience, perseverance and toughness, waiting on those long lines to get food etc. after the March 11 2011 magnitude-9 earthquake and tsunami (later). No roof tonight, it's cold as hell, but we're okay.

Kua'aina Hawaiian Hamburger Shop—another Success Story in Japan. So Many More Stores in Japan than in Any Other Country. This Chain is founded by a Caucasian Guy in Hawaii, and is now operated by Four Seasons Corporation (not the Hotel Chain).

326. On my way to the Apple store, I noticed that the Hawaiian Hamburger shop, KUA'AINA would be opening from 10 am that day to greet the New Year. Many restaurants are closed 3 or 4 days during New Year's in Japan. But KUA'AINA only 2 days. (This year's calendar had pretty much all businesses except such restaurants, and retail stores closed from Saturday December 27 2014, to Sunday January 4 2015. Nine days off for everyone, yet including only one public/national holiday—January 1—yeah! for 'the hardworking Japanese'! (As with this effort, I have decided to write several of my books, when

such long Japanese holidays pop up.) This Hawaiian hamburger and sandwich shop is an interesting success story about how great the Japanese market can be. The KUA'AINA chain was started by a *Haole*, a white dude, who lives in Hawaii. Globally, there are 2 stores in Hawaii, 2 in London, and all the rest are in Japan—9 in Tokyo, 3 in Kanagawa, 3 in Chiba, 3 in Saitama, 1 in Tochigi, 1 in Shiga, and finally 2 in Osaka. This chain has very special burgers and food. When I'm not with clients or friends for lunch, I get their Hawaiian Cobb Salad and minestrone soup. We get burgers, roast beef etc. sandwiches, or very wicked, nasty pancakes sometimes on weekends—special treat! Today was the first time I went into the restroom. They had about 20 little clear cups of sealed mouthwash, with tiny paper cups to pour the mouthwash in. The food is so good, I don't know who would want to wash out their mouth. Eat your heart out McDonalds! Haole makes good in Honolulu and hooks up with the right partner in Japan!

327. Back to the Apple store—almost... As I had hoped, walking into KUA'AINA at 10:02 am, I was their first *okyaku-san*/customer of 2015. It doesn't give me any lucky hamburgers. Just something to write home about. By the way, since KUA'AINA opens from 10am, I had some time to kill. Even after almost 4 years in Omotesando, I never completely took the time to grasp the subway station with its 3 subway lines. The Hanzomon line becomes the Tokyu Denen Toshi line. The Ginza line is the oldest subway with construction beginning in 1925. It also hits a lot of great destinations between the traditional *shitamachi*/old down town area popular tourist spot Asakusa, and Ueno etc. to Shibuya. Shibuya is about a 15-minute walk from our building. It is probably the

most filmed and talked about station along with Tokyo station.

328. Then there is the Chiyoda line. Like the Hanzomon subway, it is a very long line becoming the Joban line to the north and the Odakyu line to the southwest. I knew this, but had not walked the whole subway underground area. I had a couple questions for a couple subway officials in their office with their window counter facing the subway wickets/entrance gates. They said the station opened at 5am that morning, and the first train came through just a couple minutes later. So there was no access to the two big subway toilets until 5am. I was worried about the freezing Apples sleeping on the street above all night. When I asked about that, the older official snapped back, "Our restrooms are for the use of our subway passengers."

329. I quickly nodded full agreement. And realized that is why all the nearby *konbini*/convenience stores like 7-Eleven are in fact so convenient. With all their prepared foods and free toilets. And many of the Japanese Apple Lucky Bag campers probably brought *bentos*/boxed food made at home. There also is an always-open very nice public toilet at the outside edge of the upscale Omotesando Hills, near the single rebuilt retro Dojunkai Apartment structure. I use it all the time when walking the doggie. Luna is so friendly and cute she would be dognapped within a minute if I left her in front of a convenience store while I took a wiss. When I hit a deadend farthest away from the subway exit we use to our place, sure enough I came out directly in front of, guess what? This morning's topic: the Apple store.

The Craziest Thing about Camping Out All Night on the Hard Omotesando Stone Tile Sidewalk in Below Freezing Weather is that it was Not Necessary! Everyone had a Numbered Tag with a Lucky Bag Waiting for Their Morning Pick-up. Japanese People Love these Omatsuri/ Festival Events. Anyway Make the Scene! Apple would not have Been Responsible for the Frozen Bodies.

330. The second customers at KUA'AINA were a cute young Japanese couple. On the way to the restroom, I noticed they had the gray Apple lucky bags. I nodded with respect to the bags, and the guy. He smiled and tweeted out a bow. A chance to learn a bit more. I found out his Apple lucky bag number ticket was 392. He picked up this ticket the night before at 11:30 pm. So a staff member was outside the store to do that for him? It was their first year to do the Apple lucky bag. His lady friend said, "I got dragged along with him." He said he was satisfied with the contents, "Worth doing it" he said. Their contents were the same. But that is not always the case, apparently. They said that in the store it seemed like about 30% of the people were babbling along in foreign languages, mostly some form of Chinese or Korean we supposed. He said Japanese people are, "Crazy, *deshoo*/right?"

331. But here is the craziest part. He says none of those people had to spend the night camping out like that, unless some of the foreigners were clueless about the rules. Like him, if you got your number you could simply show up at the Apple store the next morning like this cute couple had done. I said, "Many Japanese also slept out in the below-freezing temperatures, right?" His answer: "Japanese like *omatsuri*/festival-like events. Some other foreigners

probably didn't know about train schedules etc." So even some Japanese end up scratching their heads in awe of their fellow countrymen.

332. Back in my office, I was a little disappointed, or even more surprised that people camped out all night like that even though the web says last year's Apple Lucky Bag price was 36,000 yen, say $360. People always get at least that much value in products. And the lucky ones might get as much as 80,000 yen or even 150,000 yen worth of mostly Apple gear. But the biggest news last year from Apple was from Mr. Tim Cook, Apple's CEO. If as we read in various media, about 5% of the population is primarily gay, it is about time the biggest CEO on the planet makes his and many others' life a bit easier.

Especially After the Economic Sanctions on Russia, Since the Ukraine Crisis, it is Particularly Uncomfortable to Meet Russian Tourists up Close and Personal on Omotesando Avenue. They, like Us, Have nothing to do With the Crisis. They Just Want to Live the Best and Happiest They Can be.

333. Especially when I walk my little eye-ball-driven, attracting sausage dog, a lot of Japanese and even more foreigners on Omotesando Avenue say hello, and pay her a visit. Our silver dapple mini-dachshund does attract attention. Many foreigners and some Japanese have asked what kind of a dog it is. When she was looking through the net of a carry-on bag on a train, one maybe-Japanese guy asked me in English, "What you have in there, a squirrel?" Pretty insulting for a big-boned 7 kilogram/11.2 pound dog. Solid muscle like her master. One of the only times

Luna-Tuna ever barked at a person. Our doggie's face is unusually symmetrically perfect and balanced for these silver dapple dogs of black, silver/gray, and orange/brown color. Lu has black rings around her eyes and a black stripe completely down her otherwise orange/brown face. Looks a bit like a mask and has startled a few toddlers when they are taken by surprise. *Oya baka*/'parent dumb' as the Japanese say. I guess we love our dogs and cats in every country. So much so, some end up on the menu— not in Japan.

334. Since late 2014 and now in early 2015, it is awkward and uncomfortable to meet Russian tourists. More so now than when we would meet so many in Europe over the last few years. When they ask me where I'm from, I try and dodge it with, "in Tokyo 43 years." If further pursued I'll say New York. USA Civil War Confederate General Robert E. Lee was a Virginian first, and a federal citizen second… These nice tourists probably don't have anything to do with Ukraine or the Crimean Peninsula. And that is a complex and nuanced history and situation to begin with. Most are from Moscow, or Saint Petersburg etc. But sanctions are a hot stove that burn all who touch it. And with the Russian ruble down about 50% in its value the last few months, Omotesando shopping is not as much fun. Our Japanese next-door neighbor is married to a Ukrainian lady. As you may recall, at their wedding, it looked to me like I was the only non-Ukrainian, non-Russian white dude. If only the world could be one big happy wedding.

335. I had a business meeting in Saint Petersburg, Russia. It was late March 2007. I went alone, without my wife, on this trip. I tied the meetings in with my long compass bearing walks and with some touring. Vladimir Putin is

a son of Saint Petersburg, born in 1952. After 16 years with the KGB, he entered politics in Saint Petersburg from 1990 to 1996. Mr. Putin made it up to first deputy chairman of the government of Saint Petersburg. He also founded the branch of the pro-government "Our Home is Russia" political party, and led its Saint Petersburg branch. I had no problems walking everywhere, and late at night as well. There were a lot of mostly black Mercedes jeeps, black Land Rovers, and convertibles with a lot of blaring music, and young guys on mics and waving flags. I was clueless. But it was pretty impressive. Kind of like in that 1997 movie, *The Saint* with Val Kilmer and Elizabeth Shue. As my wife knows, another one of my favorites. Elizabeth not Val. Nothing against Ice Man (*Top Gun*—1986)—he just leaves me colder than Lizzy.

I was Lucky to Tie-in with a Renowned Simultaneous Interpreter who had translated for People like Presidents Jimmy Carter, Bill Clinton, Vladimir Putin, and Prince Charles. Went to the Top Saint Petersburg Restaurants Where they had dined. How about Joining Mr. Putin on October 7 for His Birthday Party of Bear Meat at the Same Big Log Cabin?

336. I was really lucky to be able to get some special insights into Mr. Putin, and the Saint Petersburg scene. At the famous Hermitage Museum, a Ms. Galina Formina of www.galinatravel.com thought I was Swedish and asked if I wanted some special private tours. Her English was obviously superb. She told me she had interpreted for Mr. Putin, and Presidents Jimmy Carter, and Bill Clinton. She mentioned a few other huge names. If you

check her above website, there are such pictures. You can see she and her company are the real deal. She took me to a couple of Saint Petersburg restaurants where those dignitaries had dined. My last day with her, and my last day in Russia, she picked me up early in the morning in her white Mercedes. I got a private showing—just the two of us, and security, at the Chinese Palace. She had done the same thing for Prince Charles, and I think she said Bill Clinton. Then she wanted me to try bear meat at the restaurant where Mr. Putin always, or whenever he can, celebrates his birthday party with his old Saint Petersburg buddies.

337. When I was 19 years old, I was almost eaten by a bear outside the camp garbage dump at the Snettisham Dam outside of Juneau, Alaska. So I thought it was right that I eat some Russian Bear—the national symbol too. The restaurant is a big multi-floored log cabin, about 30 kilometers south of Saint Petersburg. Ms. Galina arranged for me to shake hands with the owner, Mr. Serguey E. Gutsait. Mr. Gutsait has also developed an amusement park modeled on an old-fashioned Russian village, with craftsman and real people living there in the old fashioned way. Verkhniye Mandrogi is surrounded by woods and water about 300 kilometers northeast of St. Petersburg on the banks of the Svir River. You can land by tourist river cruise ship. The river goes between Lake Ladoga and Lake Onega, northern Russia's two largest lakes. I can't type those Russian letters for this log cabin restaurant much closer to Saint Petersburg—not on my keyboard. But the website is www.podvorye.ru It was a really fun time. If you go there on October 7, unless it is *kashikiri*/closed-out party, maybe you can meet Mr. Vladimir Putin.

338. Since this book is named after a lake, and a lake of only 2 miles/3.2 kilometers in length—and that's 'a country mile', which means Waccabuc may not be that long—and because no one names a book about a small body of water except Henry David Thoreau (*Walden Pond*), we should talk more about lakes. Got your interest? This is going to be sexier than *Fifty Shades of Grey* (Cornerstone). The above Lake Ladoga is the 14th largest lake in the world by volume of water, and coincidently also ranked 14th in terms of surface area. The river cruise ship will take you over to Lake Onega. This lake comes in 20th in terms of water volume, and 17th in surface area. Which means it's a deeper than average lake—dah... Russian Lake Ladoga is the largest lake in all of Europe. Ladoga is 93.1% the surface area of #13 Lake Ontario shared by Canada and the USA. Russia's No. 17 Onega is 21.5% larger than the next largest lake, #18 Lake Titicaca shared by Peru and Bolivia.

Russia has the Largest Lake in the World by Water Volume, Lake Baikal—about 20% of all the Fresh Water on Earth!—more Water than all the USA Great Lakes Combined. Lake Baikal is the Deepest, the Oldest (25,000,000 Years), and One of the Clearest Lakes in the World. Just a Little North of the Mongolian and Chinese Desert. Armies of the Han Dynasty defeated the Xiongnu Forces from the Second Century BC to the First Century AD (Long Battle!) along the Shores of this Monster Lake.

339. If you examine the world from Google satellite, cruising all around the globe in the same setting at the same altitude, you can see that post-Soviet Russian is quite

a consistent green. Russia is greener than many of the western areas of the Midwest, and greener than most of the USA-west accept parts of Colorado, California and of course Washington and Oregon. Take a look at China. Not just the Mongolian Desert, but so much of China is close in color to most of the Mideast and to northern African deserts. China is verdant and green only in the Southeast regions. While some of the primary Lake Baikal inflow rivers such as the Selenga, Barguzin, and Upper Angara Rivers flow in from parts of Mongolia, this huge lake's only outflow is the Angara River. It flows up north through Russia. Lake Baikal is pretty much surrounded by mountains. That is why it is the deepest lake in the world at a maximum depth of 1,642 meters or 5,387 feet deep. The water surface is at an elevation of 455.5 meters/1,494 feet, so I suppose it lends itself pretty well to a water supply pipe line taking advantage of gravity. Water may become more valuable than oil. By that time hopefully desalination technology should be further advanced. If, as is written 60%, of China's ground water is too polluted to be potable, China's attempts to clean itself up are a pressing priority.

340. As with Christopher Columbus, Henry Hudson, or the Pilgrims at Plymouth Rock, Russian history of Lake Baikal starts with Mr. Kurbat Ivanov who was the first Russian explorer to reach the lake in 1643. Even though the Chinese Han Dynasty had fought the above battles there 1,500 years before that. This was part of the first Russian efforts at exploration and conquest of Siberia. The Trans-Siberian Railway was built between 1896 and 1902. Construction of this scenic railway around the southwestern end of Lake Baikal required 33 tunnels and 200 bridges to be built. Reminds us of the more Anglo east-coast American

expansion west 100 to 200 years after the above Mr. Ivanov 'discovered' Lake Baikal in 1643. Even though the Spanish were already in the American west and on the west coast in small numbers along with Native Americans. Although the Ainu were in Hokkaido for 20,000 years, it was not until about the time of the Meiji Restoration in the mid and later 1800s that Japanese mainlanders took more interest in getting up to, and settling that colder region.

341. You can check the Wikipedia write-up on these lakes. There seems to be something uniquely isolated about this Lake Baikal, the world's largest lake. Other than the sheep, cattle, camels and goats raised by the Buryat tribes residing on the eastern side of the lake, there are more than 1,000 known species of plants, and 2,500 known species of animals based on still incomplete current research. But here is the unique thing. I suppose because of the surrounding mountains, tundra, and desert especially to the south, and because it's damn cold to chilly (average winter temperature -19 Centigrade/ -2 F, and summer maximum 14 C and 57 F) over 80% of these species are found only on or in Lake Baikal—all huddled or swimming together for warmth. It's scary to think what all these some 2,000 unique species of animals might be. I hope they tend to be small, with dull teeth. I hope they are happy with themselves and not angry at the world.

More on Lakes and Dams. By Surface Area, The USA has 60 Lakes that are as large, or larger than the Largest 15 Russian Lakes. About Half or 27 of those USA Lakes are Man Made. 55 Out of the USA's 101 Largest Lakes are Man Made. A Whooping 75,000 Dams in the USA (many of them small? Maybe built by beavers?) About 500 Dams are in Japan. This explains why we have all these Unatural Lakes and Reservoirs.

342. About 17% of USA rivers have been dammed. In Japan, it looks like Nagano Prefecture has the most dams at about 50. Other prefectures each have more like 5 to 15 dams. Tokyo has two dams, Lake Okutama Dam and Shiromaru Dam. The surface of Japan is 12.07% fresh water, the USA is 2.23% water surface, and Russia is only .46% water. Of the 101 USA lakes by surface area, the bottom 3 smallest on the list are Lake George in New York State at #99, man-made Beaver Lake in Arkansas at #100, and Great Sacandaga Lake also in New York at #101. The largest 5 lakes by surface area in the USA are the Great Lakes of Superior, Huron, Michigan, Erie and Ontario in that descending order. Lake Michigan is the only one that does not also border Canada. The deepest lake in the USA is the 9th deepest lake in the world— Crater Lake in Oregon. It is 594 meters/1,949 feet deep. Just deeper than that is #8 Great Slave Lake in Canada, the deepest lake in North America at 614 meters/2,015 feet deep. Other than that there are top 10 deepest lakes well distributed around the globe in of course Russia, #1 Lake Baikal, #2 Lake Tanganyika in central Africa, #4 Lake Vostok one of 400 known subglacial lakes in Antarctica, #5 Lake O'Higgins-San Martin in Chile and Argentina, #6 Lake Malawi bordering Mozambique, Tanzania, and Malawi, #7 Issyk Kul in Kyrgyzstan, and #10 Matano in Indonesia.

343. You may have noticed that #3 is missing. This is because it is the Caspian Sea, and is questionable as a lake. It is

totally landlocked from outflows. The only outflow is evaporation. Over 130 rivers flow into the Caspian Sea, but its primary inflows are the largest river in Europe, the Volga River, and the Ural, Kura and Terek Rivers. Russia's mighty Volga River drains 20% of European land area, and the Volga is the source of 20% of the Caspian's water inflow. The Caspian Sea was part of the ocean, but became landlocked about 5,500,000 years ago. It is by far the largest landlocked body of water in terms of surface area, and water volume. But the water is about 1.2% salt, which is about one-third as salty as the worlds' oceans.

344. It is also a low rider, with its surface elevation, varying at times, basically at 28 meters or 92 feet below sea level. Thus outflow rivers are not possible. The Caspian's surface level fell 3 meters/9.84 feet between 1929 and 1977, but then rose by the same height between 1977 and 1995. Since then it has not oscillated very much. Maybe this is because Russia has built so many dams and reservoirs along the Volga River. So river volume and flow can be more controlled than if the great Volga River had its own way. This monster sea/lake has 3.5 times the volume of all 5 North American Great Lakes. The Caspian is bordered by Azerbaijan, Iran, Kazakhstan, Russia, and Turkmenistan. It is 4.5 times larger in area than the next largest Lake Superior, and 3.3 times more water volume than the next most voluptuous (unholy Bible reference) Lake Baikal. But, again, the Caspian is 1.2% salt. That's a lot of contact lens solution. But I guess easier and cheaper for desalination plants.

345. That reminds me. Do you want to hear something sexy about the Japanese and Chinese…lakes? In terms of voluptuousness, they don't make the list of the top 35. In terms of body size there is one Chinese lake that

comes in at #34, Qinghai Lake, or Kokonor. She has two names. And then there is a half Chinese and half Russian named Khanka. She comes in last on this list of 37 of the world's largest lakes in terms of surface area. Focusing on Japanese and USA lakes, Lake Biwa in Shiga Prefecture is 4 times larger than the next largest Japanese lake, which is Kasumigaura in Ibaraki Prefecture, not far from Tokyo. It is near the ocean, and when I first went there I thought it must be a bay. There are 22 USA lakes larger than Lake Biwa, and 77 USA lakes larger than this second largest Japanese lake, Kasumigaura. Twenty out of the 29 largest Japanese lakes are fresh water. The other 9 are for your contact lenses. Many Japanese and foreigners reading this will have visited, or definitely should visit Lake Chuzenji in Nikko, Tochigi Prefecture. It can be a day trip from Tokyo. Out of these 29 largest Japanese lakes, Lake Chuzenji comes in at #25 in surface area. But one of the reasons Lake Chuzenji, Nikko, with its rows of huge trees, and its beautiful, famous and impressive Tosho-gu Shinto Shrine, are so special and popular is that this is by far the highest altitude large lake in Japan. At 1,269 meters/4,163 feet, considerably cooler than the world below.

346. For all you Lake dwellers and lovers that will not be able to get to Lake Waccabuc, here is the global summary you have been waiting for. Out of the 37 largest Wikipedia listed lakes by area, 16 are in North America; 11 are in Eurasia, including 1 each in Iran, Sweden, and Finland; 6 are in Africa; 2 are in South America, 1 in Peru/Bolivia, the other in Nicaragua; and 1 in Antarctica that you can't see—either dried up, or submerged under the ice. My list is missing one lake. Sorry. Yeah. Must have dried up.

Enough of this Lake Water, Contact Lens Water, Dams, and Weird Isolated Animal Species. How about a Russian Beer, a 99-Year-Old Gorgeous Prima Ballerina Mistress, and an Aeroflot Flight Home?

347. I had a few Russian beers, with my bear meat, was not watching the clock, and was fully depending on Galina to get me to my Aeroflot flight back to Tokyo, the Big Mikan/Tangerine on time. We arrived very late at the airport, about 10 minutes before the flight was to take off. The check-in counter, the luggage belt, and even the gate were closed. Galina and I talked with a nice Aeroflot lady. She brought over a manager who was the size of Peter the Great, who built Saint Petersburg from scratch—actually had been a desolate, usually frozen swamp. (And Peter was great. He died at 53 years old from catching pneumonia within days after diving into the freezing sea to save one of the sailors who was on the ship Peter happened to be on. No one else was moving to save the sailor.) Well the Aeroflot manager said, "Okay, I will help you. Follow me." The luggage doors on the plane were already closed. He brought my bag up the airplane stairs for me, and got it and me into the main passenger cabin. I was flying business class, but on any other airline, or in any other country, I don't think this could have happened. I told this story back at the company. One of our consultants from Uzbekistan said, "I'll bet that cost you a lot of money. Russians don't move unless there is money". All I could say was, "Not a ruble, and I never thought the Aeroflot manager expected it or would have taken money from me." All I had were great experiences in Russia. I hope things get better for Russians, Ukrainians, and all of us.

348. If you get to Russia, please do check out a place where I spent a full day reading about Russian history, Communism, an honest refutation and documented disproof of Communism—fascinating and illuminating stuff that most of us know so little about. Also original documents from Catherine the Great, Napoleon, on up to Mikhail Gorbachev. It is called the Museum of Political History, the former Museum of the Revolution established in 1957. All day I was surrounded by Russian school children in their uniforms. I believe it was mostly Amherst College Russian majors or specialists who provided the adequate translated versions of the exhibits. This was before I met up with Ms. Galina Formina.

349. This impressive structure used to be the Kschessinska Mansion built for Mathilde Kschessinska (1872-1971)—died at 99 years old! She was the most famous ballerina in Russia before the revolution. A very beautiful woman who was Nicholas II's mistress before he became the czar. The ballerina's large home was seized by the Bolsheviks in 1917. The Russian Revolution was launched in Saint Petersburg, not in Moscow. When Vladimir Lenin returned from Finland he came to this ballerina's mansion, his new headquarters, kicked out the prima ballerina, and announced and declared the Russian Revolution in a speech from the balcony of her main bedroom. This is why until 1991, the city was named Leningrad. I believe the ballerina's mansion, now this museum, was next to a very large Islamic Mosque. I went in and prayed at the Mosque too. Even though a lot of people standing and sitting around outside the mosque starred at me, and must have thought I was on drugs and was having a bad trip to the mosque. I'll wish for the luck and help any God can give us.

Alright. We had better get back to Shibuya, Omotesando, and Aoyama Area. I Thought Shibuya was the Name of the 'Bitter Valley', but There Actually was a Shibuya Family with a Castle. The Chicken or the Egg?

350. Yes. There was actually a Shibuya family that lived in a castle from the eleventh century through the Edo period. The village of Shibuya was incorporated in 1889 through the merger of the villages of Kami (upper)-Shibuya, Naka (middle)-Shibuya, and Shimo (lower)-Shibuya. This village covered the area of modern-day Shibuya station as well as the Hiroo, Daikanyama, Aoyama, and Ebisu areas. The town of Shibuya merged with the nearby Sendagaya (including today's Sendagaya, Harajuku, and Jingumae, as well as Yoyohata, which included today's Yoyogi and Hatagaya.) This became Shibuya ward of Tokyo in 1932.

351. The Tokyu Toyoko Line opened in 1932. This resulted in Shibuya becoming a key terminal between Tokyo and Yokohama. A year later in 1933, the forerunner of the Keio Inokashira Line was open. Ginza subway opened in 1938. During the late 1990s Shibuya also became known as the center of Japan's IT industry. It was often called 'Bit Valley', an association with Silicon Valley, and a pun on Bitter Valley, the literal translation of Shibuya which means 'bitter valley'. The pun also worked well with 'bit'. The techie term for 'binary digits.'

352. Shibuya Crossing deserves some special mention. It is located right beside the statue of Hachiko, Tokyo's cupid and matchmaker extraordinaire. The busiest Starbucks in the world is in view, just across this scramble intersection. The traffic from all sides stops at once, allowing all the pedestrians to periodically

scramble. On average 3,000 people scramble with each light change—500,000 per day. This intersection's heavy traffic, and flood of huge *Blade Runner* type (1982) TV, digital color screens on nearby buildings, have resulted in it being compared to the Times Square intersection on Manhattan in New York City. Shibuya Crossing is often featured in films and television shows that have their setting in Tokyo. Some of the examples are *The Fast and the Furious: Tokyo Drift, Resident Evil: Afterlife and Retribution*, Bill Murray's *Lost in Translation* (the walking dinosaur scene.) It is also probably the most common setting for domestic television shows showing the temperature, the rain, the wind, or the snow. Or for street interviews on all kinds of topics.

The Rest of this Beautiful Country Deserves a Few Kind Words!

353. Shibuya, Omotesando, Aoyama and Harajuku are great places for sure, but I need to say there are other wonderful places in this huge city. Another great strength of this country is its beautiful countryside of very varied coastal and mountain scenery. Great surfing, snow skiing, hiking, mountain climbing, fishing, paragliding, biking etc. And, of course, the onsen hot spring resorts—*konyoku*, naked mixed bathing or not. Land in the countryside is very reasonable. Yamanashi, where we have the traditional house with views of Mount Fuji and surrounded by the snow capped Japan Alps, is surprisingly convenient to Tokyo, even by car, if you know how to deal with weekend, and the very frequent 3-day weekend traffic. This Koshu area, its name before it became Yamanashi Prefecture, is

the center of wine vineyards in Japan. It could make an interesting move for a winemaker from abroad. Dairy farming on these gentle mountain slopes was introduced to Japan by an American, Paul Rusch (1897-1979) before and after the war. His Kiyosato Educational Experiment Project (KEEP) is still going and is one or two stations up the Yatsugatake slope from us on the Koumi Line, which goes from Kobuchizawa on the Chuo Train line to Nagano. Mr. Rusch also brought American style football to Japan. There are many days of sunny blue sky, and not the deep snow that drops on the side of Japan facing China, Russia, and Korea. Also less rain than many areas of Japan. Well suited for vineyards, and Japan needs more serious winemakers and farmers of all types. The farming population is down in numbers and getting a bit long in the tooth!

354. Some foreigners and Japanese find getting out of Tokyo, to popular tourist areas by car crowded, a bit tedious, and expensive. When booking at traditional inns, the meal times and menus are quite fixed etc. It is not cheap, and requires advanced reservations. One formula I worked out was leaving Tokyo at even 10 or 11pm on a Friday night. NO BOOZE for the driver on these trips until after hotel check in. The police and law is very tough on drinking alcohol and driving. There are those 40,000 very reasonable, spic and span, brightly lit and gaudy love hotels very visible from big expressways or Kokudo/ national trunk toll-free roads. The rooms, and beds, and baths are much larger and more upscale than most hotels. These Kokudo trunk roads are older and go through the countryside, cities and towns with lots of drive in restaurants and things to see. Think of USA Route 66, as opposed to US Interstate 10, or the German Autobahn.

355. If you time your Tokyo departure like this, you can quickly get yourself well outside the metropolis or even into the more rural area you want to explore. If you don't want to be charged for extra hours above your fixed stay-over price at the love hotel, you get yourself out by 10am. No breakfast available, but lots of restaurants and convenience stores. Or bring a little something. You don't need a word of Japanese for check-in, or check-out, and often there is no face contact—a curtain or opaque bank cashier-type window. Just pick the room and theme of your choice, nicely pictured, and press the button. The shortstay, and overnight (starting from usually 10pm) price is written on this full-color, brightly lit-up wall display. Even overnight stays are usually around 8 to 10,000 yen. Going in alone or with more than 2 people of any number of sexes does not raise eyebrows that you can't see anyway. And no extra charge.

356. You then have all of Saturday to explore the rural area. Car navigation screens in Japan, are large and excellent, often 3D imaging of the countryside, as well as flat map presentations. The screens are not like the little screens on stems of rent-a-cars in the States and elsewhere. English and probably other language car navigation is available. Your car should not be too big. That way you have confidence to follow your car navigation and to go anywhere it is leading you. Or just drive along as you see yourself moving like a bug on your car navigation map. Explore the regional city at night, and enjoy the great food, and excellent Japanese soft drinks if you have driving left. When you leave the outlying area Saturday night, you can cover even 200 or 300 kilometers, 125 or 187.5 miles, easily and quickly back to Tokyo. Since it is dark, and maybe you already saw the sites on the

way to your destination, you can take the much faster expressways back. Then just sleep in at home on Sunday until noon or so.

357. Often it was not until we got in the car Friday night that we picked a destination. Or we just started driving off in a given direction. It can be that extemporaneous if you like that style. Less spontaneous travel getting tied into more confining and expensive reservations etc. seem to be what most people do and know about. That is also great fun. And no worries about being out on dark roads at night in the middle of nowhere. In a pinch you can also catch a few hours stretched out in the car in a convenience store parking lot. Everything except a full bath is right there!

358. When I started out in Japan for keeps from November 18 1972, I had the grammar books and tapes used at advanced Japanese courses from Cornell. I was lucky to have had the star Japanese teacher in the States, as my classroom teacher for that one year of senior class study at Cornell. Eleanor Harz Jorden had started Japanese programs at many universities while she also chaired the Foreign Language Program at Cornell. My government labor research institute suggested that I quickly learn Japanese early on so that I would not need to pay for interpreters. Therefore between self-studying Japanese intensively with my tapes and grammar books, I followed my institute's advice. "Go out to the countryside, where no one will try and speak English at you." So during the first 1.5 years I lived in Japan, after intensive self-studying a few months, I would hit the road, hitchhiking and sometimes taking trains on 3 different 6-week trips to all parts of the country.

359. I achieved fluency on my limited subject matter during my first trip. The good thing was that you could keep trying to repeat the same boring content, but to constantly changing people. If it was the same person they would have strangled me, Samurai-sworded me, or deliberately aimed and sped their car screaming at the top of their lungs into the base of a tunnel, bridge or rock outcropping. My budget was just 40,000 yen to last each of the three 6-week trips. That is all the money I brought with me! No credit card for me in those days. The Leatherman (above) with a little change in his pocket. I visited every prefecture in Japan. There are 43 prefectures/*ken*: Osaka and Kyoto are *Fu*/urban prefectures, Hokkaido is a *Do* or territory, and Tokyo is a *To* or metropolis—so 47 jurisdictions or administrative districts in total. I made sure I went from the northernmost tip of Wakkanai, Hokkaido, to the (almost) southernmost Ibuski, Kagoshima; and easternmost Shiretoko and Nemuro peninsulas also of Hokkaido, to the westernmost spots like Wajima Ishikawa-ken, Matsue Shimane-ken, and Sasebo Nagasaki-ken. Those 3 towns are along the coast facing Korea, Russia and China. I circled all around Shikoku too. Incredible scenes to behold, and experiences to be had!

'Make a Move' to Omotesando, or Get a Beachhead in Tokyo too. It is the Safe, Pollution Free, Stable, and Enjoyable Stepping Stone to Asia—the Largest Regional Market in the World.

360. When I wrote the Old Testament, I hadn't yet realized how much more of a contribution I could make if I could pass on my labor consulting experience and

know-how to some larger corporate players. Actually at my age, and after doing much on my own, it was time to come up with this new vision. Working on a larger and different scale we can help so many more companies, their employees, and do something about the inflexibilities of the Japanese labor market. A major aim of the Old Testament, the second part of this book, was to bring my more effective practices to owner-controlled, mostly Japanese companies who would welcome the approaches. I was also hoping to be able to get more companies to realize that they can and should keep their manufacturing plants in Japan. For the benefit of Japanese workers, and the Japanese economy.

361. When I wrote the material below, I was thinking about selling my building, independent of transitioning the business. And that may very well be what happens. Most M & A experts, and real estate people tell me it would be hard to transition the business, and have the new building owner be a key party in the new TMT operation. Or conversely stated, difficult to have the main business transition party, perhaps licensing our know-how to others, also buy the building. Maybe so. However, I began to realize that it would not be easy to move our over 35 years of client files, thousands of copies of book inventory and promotional business publications, and our fully operational office with all its equipment etc. It would be an expensive and wasteful exercise as well. If there are multiple new parties, different companies and brands, working out of just one of the party's offices would be a bit strange, and have its own challenges. The work we do is sensitive. It may be wiser to put more emphasis on the TMT brand, rather than performing the consulting engagements under these even more

known and prestigious brands. And without using the very content rich TMT website, and taking advantage of our history and reputation in this field, why would a company not known for this type of consulting have credibility in this new area of activity?

362. I also realized it would be easier on my own self-esteem. At least for the years that I teach, train, and pass on the skills; working out of this TMT building would not be a bad idea. Separating selling of the building, from transitioning the business would also be quite a logistical nightmare. There would be no synchronization on timing of moves. Clearing ourselves out of the residential floors, but me staying on in my third floor office, and fully committing to the transition, sounds like an easier and smarter way to go—for all parties involved. It takes about an hour to show and explain about this building to a potential buyer! Tough to do when living here and working here. And that blind little doggie gets so excited, happy, but noisy whenever people come by. For these reasons we made a quite detailed You Tube video of each floor—so 5 English videos, and 5 videos with me narrating in Japanese. They all pretty much pop up together. The English videos titling format is in the format of Omotesando 5Flrs yonkai/4th The Japanese video titling is Omotesando 5Flrs J – 1F. The building cannot be left vacant, and must be maintained. We are hoping for as few property showings as possible! These videos should help on that score. Also we can email, as an attachment, a bilingual version of the detailed document below. We also have digital pictures we can email to potential buyers.

Some Insight on Buying and Selling Real Estate, or getting Started in Japan. Surprisingly Few Wealthy Foreigners have a Stake Here. Bill Gates of Microsoft, and Larry Ellison of Oracle have 'Made a Move' Here.

363. Therefore we have left this below detailed presentation aimed at selling the building pretty much intact. For these reasons, this is basically a private sale. We have not, and at least for now, do not want to list this property on the Japan website REINS (Real Estate Information Network System). Doing this gives open, public, access to all Japanese real estate agents. I believe answering those calls, visits, or turning agents down would not be good for any of us. <u>I think the only place we are listed is with Sotheby's Real Estate. I think the English version of our property will pop right up if you Goggle 'TMT Building Japan Sotheby's'.</u> The price below, and the one on the Sotheby's website is more than I need. One comment was 'better to keep the price higher, because Chinese and others have a tendency to low ball, and want to negotiate'. One reason I chose Sotheby's is that they were so helpful in selling a penthouse we had. They put it in some very slick hard-copy English international and Japanese language publications as well. And of course Sotheby's can deal in all languages, and in all countries.

364. By the way, in Japan, the seller and the buyer both pay the typical and maximum of a 3% real estate commission. In some countries such as the USA, the seller pays a maximum commission of 6%, but in reality they average out to 5.1%. (A percentage of that amount will go to the buyer's agent.) I suppose if a customer does not use an agent, or for example, told Sotheby's, TMT is the only

property I need to see, there would be no buyer side fee, or it could be negotiated down. Then again, if somebody from the famous '1%' is buying this building, having Sotheby's and me, and my wife Chika, wholeheartedly helping the buyer understand the property, dealing with SECOM security, or our ORIX cleaning/maintenance company, the appliances and their manuals, where and how to procure/replace light bulbs, understanding Japan, the local schools, the neighborhood, introducing things to do, organizations to join, or strategic and fun friends etc. etc. becomes important too. Especially if it is a foreigner new to Japan, and without Japanese language ability.

365. And as you will see below, I was hoping that more famous, wealthy people, maybe especially Westerners, would come and live here. I knew of none. They might have a place in Paris, London, Rome, New York, Palm Springs, or San Francisco, but not Tokyo. That bothered me because Tokyo and the Japanese countryside, with English or some other language car navigation, is a heaven in so many ways, and for so many reasons. It was only recently that I learned that apparently Bill Gates of Microsoft has built/is building a huge place in the Karuizawa countryside. Also Larry Ellison of Oracle has a beautiful Japanese-style place and huge garden in Kyoto. By the way, I/TMT did Microsoft's first 'Rules of Employment' (ROE) and sent the invoice for it on February 25, 1986, when the company first broke off from their distributor in Japan. I also did Oracle's first ROE with the invoice dated February 26, 1990. I hope many more of my old clients decide to also hedge their bets with a beachhead in Japan. And more specifically discover how great it is to live in the 'Big Mikan'/tangerine Tokyo!

366. When I read about the droughts and water shortage in the USA West Coast, southwest, and in Australia, or the

flooding elsewhere, it gets me really worried. There is so much wealth at stake. Problems there can impact the whole world. In California, the South and Mid-west, underground water tables are going down to the extent that there are some little earthquakes over there too. In Japan, we do indeed know about earthquakes. Shortage of water is one thing I doubt we have to worry about in Japan.

It can be Very Easy to Get Started with a Multiple Reentry 'Investor/Business Manager' Visa in Japan. Japan is Tolerant of All Religions and Will Make Sure Japan Stays Free of Religious and Racial Turmoil. Being an Island, with Rough Surrounding Seas, and Far from Shore, Greatly Helps.

367. <u>As you will see below, undoubtedly from your country, no visa is required for you to visit Japan. Anyone who bought my building would already have a residence and an office. An additional investment of just 5,000,000 yen/ US$50,000 in your own business activity here of deal making or whatever, would provide you with a multiple entry 'Investor/Business Manager' visa. Even if you hired no Japanese staff. That is all it would take.</u> With the growing religious conflicts and violence in Europe, and elsewhere, we have been reading that Jewish people no longer feel safe enough. They are leaving Europe for Israel and elsewhere. Japan being an island, and distanced from such turmoil, and without much of a colonial past, with less of a mix of people in conflict with each other, has a distinct and lucky advantage in this area. It also has a beautiful Jewish Community Center club, a minimum taxi fee from our building, largely rebuilt by

the philanthropic donation of an old friend, Fred Harris, who designed my first big office for me in 1982. There is also an art gallery named after Mr. Harris at the Tokyo American Club/TAC.

368. My vice president of Business Development, Ms. Angelina Angeles (nickname "Boots") was general manager of the Jewish Community Center for 18 years, before coming to TMT in 2004. Jewish people cannot work on the Shabbat, so such GM's tend to be non-Jewish. She is a very trilingual and extremely capable Filipina. Her younger brother was a very famous Filipino in Japan, Rex Angeles. He was in Japanese dramas, movies, and was a popular singer who has written some great songs. Rex has a very impressive web presence. Also very smart. Believe it or not the TMT Rubik Cube video at the top of our website, and shown every day on CNN and sometimes BBC here in Japan for years, is Rex's voice. Big sister Boots made the video. Rex also did a lot of voice work in English and Japanese for Nissan under Carlos Ghosn, and for many other major companies. Even though Rex is a native of the Philippines and his Japanese is that good too. At age 50 he suddenly died in February, 2014. His big sister Boots is still getting over it (definitely not a suicide). My executive assistant and I were the first on the scene. Rex and Boots were very close. Although she loves Japan, being with family in Manila is helpful. If anyone has a good career opportunity for Boots, much appreciated! Her spelling and writing in English is better than mine—yeah, I know—doesn't say much. Her Japanese is also excellent.

369. In addition to the Jewish Community Center, the recently rebuilt Tokyo American Club/TAC would have to be one of the most impressive such facilities in the world. There are many other international clubs such as The Foreign

Correspondents Club, International House—so many other organizations, and foreign chambers of commerce that make living in Tokyo very comfortable and stimulating for foreigners new to Japan. And for long-term residents of Japan too! As a long-term member of the Foreign Correspondents Club, I have at least heard talks by, and sometimes been able to question, an incredible array of famous Japanese and foreigners. I think this would not be possible in most major cities. People always got/get to Tokyo. And Tokyo is the equivalent of 10 of the largest USA cities combined, in terms of a single cities pulling power, or exposure to foreign visitors.

370. Japan does not appreciate religious extremism of any nature. But especially with the decreasing population, Japan, and the Japanese government will welcome any hard-working foreigners who make a contribution to Japan, and her economy. The Japanese are very spiritual, are mildly superstitious, and there are many huge Shinto shrines and Buddhist temples. There are also many small and even tiny neighborhood Shinto shrines tucked into nooks and crannies everywhere. A surprising number of Christian churches too. The Christian churches are probably supported by holding weddings as much as by the more limited numbers of Sunday worshippers. In Japan another's faith is never criticized. But if one of the hundreds of religious cults runs amok, this will not last long. The Japanese people basically believe one's religion, or one's God, cannot be better than another. The typical pattern is to be blessed when born at a Shinto shrine, get married in a Christian church, or hotel or wedding hall's Christian-looking chapel, and be buried by way of a Buddhist temple. New homes, business ventures, factories or even major

capital investments are often met with a visit of a Shinto *kannushi*/priest's offerings. This is for good luck and prosperity, more than thinking about the myriad of Shinto deities found in nature and life.

As Much as I Loved Lake Waccabuc, My Family, Friends and Life in the States, I will be burying my Burnt Bones in Japan. Tokyo is a Great Place to Stay Young, Maintain a Healthy Lifestyle, and with Excellent Reasonable Universal Health Care for Newcomers Too. So Also a Good Place to Grow Old.

371. I loved Waccabuc, and New York. But I guess I love it over here in Japan, and even more in this glittering, exhilarating, scintillating, and bustling great Tokyo metropolis. I miss my Waccabuc forest floor, rock outcroppings, my secret swamp/ponds and other spots, the curving drives along beautiful roads covered in a canopy of green, hikes in the woods and up the hills, the beautiful lake's activities, the pure white snow and winter iced-over lake, and most of all my family and friends. But, I guess, not as much as I love the excitement, yet complete safety of this city, and all my close friends here. And especially this spot. I like a lot of people around me. And it is very easy to meet foreign/ *gaijin* residents or travelers from all over the world just a few minutes' walk from this quiet block. I do especially love being in Omotesando, and more particularly in this property, surrounded by these magnificent and palatial homes. We have spectacular rooftop terrace scenery of a few of Tokyo's iconic lit up skyscrapers. It is also satisfying to wake up to the rising sun. And to pop up to

the 5th floor with drink in hand to watch the sunset over the Shibuya station buildings. There is also the largest, roundest, bushiest tree top I have ever seen nearby!

372. I have lost a few friends living in different countries. As they got older, and retired, maybe life was not as exciting. Maybe they just needed a change. Maybe they are widowed, and have lost their wives. Well, Tokyo is a city that will make an old man young—especially Omotesando, Harajuku, and nearby Shibuya! You may have read about the 'herbivore'-type Japanese guys that are growing in number. They are more interested in their gadgets than in their girls. The birthrate is down because of lack of activity in that area. This is also a result of not getting or holding down a high enough paying job to support a family. And more women are working. They watched the way their mothers were treated by their fathers, not helping out much at home with family and home chores. Not always having a ball together. Let's leave it at this. There is room here for a few good foreign men, and of course women. I regret that I did not get a couple of my burned-out buddies from abroad over here, to start a new, fun and productive life. Unfortunately, I did not know they needed help.

373. Local governments are putting up money and sponsoring events to get couples together, and hopefully married, to stop the population decrease. According to Eleanor Warnock in a January 28 2015 *Wall Street Journal* article, this effort at 'marriage hunting', or Konkatsu, a name first coined by Masahiro Yamada, a Chuo University Professor, is taking new forms in terms of apartment designs and construction. For example, a Mr. Rintaro Kikuchi is designing and building units where there is a stripper pole in the middle of the living room.

His and others apartments can also have clear, non-clouded glass-surrounded showers and baths that are right in the middle of the living room. And open, airy kitchens facing all this. When we went to buy this, our current building, we saw living room baths with see through glass in a couple upmarket, large luxury homes. Actually, we designed our current bath with a clear, unclouded glass door. Locking wooden doors to the double sink changing/entrance room is possible. Our last upscale condo also had such a set-up, similar to upscale hotel rooms. There is room for lots of stripper poles in our place! A Konkatsu business/club with small, intimate meeting rooms, and spacious areas to socialize and mingle for large groups at this ideal Omotesando location could fly well around the stripper poles. Too bad I'm stuck with my labor consulting ☹. My first *Japan Times* book was titled *Labor Pains and the Gaijin Boss*. Quite a few pregnant expat, or trailing spouse wives bought that book for themselves or their husbands. Japan today needs better labor conditions for many, but also a lot more labor pains!

A Bad Japanese Habit of Knocking Down Perfectly Good Buildings Much Too Soon. This TMT Building was Built by a Celebrated 5-Star, Top-Quality Construction Firm. In 2011 it was Totally Renovated by Another First Class Firm.

374. For Japan, a building whose initial construction was completed in November 1973 can seem a bit old—believe it or not! This place was built like a castle, with heavy steel beams, and thick steel reinforced poured concrete walls. And now everything is brand new, and state of

the art technology as of 2011. Funny. One of the most expensive, and exclusive NYC condominiums is The Dakota on Manhattan. It was built and opened October 27th 1884 as a home of Mr. Singer, of Singer Sewing Machine fame. Poor John Lennon lived there, and was shot and murdered at the entranceway. The outside was extensively filmed in the film *Rosemary's Baby* (1968, Mia Farrow). Many famous people live and have lived there. I have seen luxury condo ads in the *New York Times* for condos that were first built in about 1950—not old at all by global standards.

375. I saw a November 7, 2014 article from the *New York Times* supplement in the *Japan Times* newspaper. A home on Lord North Street in London, not far from the Houses of Parliament, built in 1725 was on the market for 5.9 million pounds, or US$9.44 million. This would now be 1,113,920,000 yen. It is 3 stories above ground, 333 square meters/3,587 square feet, with original staircases, woodworking, and no elevator. Whether you use our Omotesando 427.95 square meters/4,606.4 square feet, or our 524.47 square meter/5,645.3 square feet, we are quite a lot larger. We also have a 4-person capacity elevator. (The reason for the discrepancy in these two square meter numbers, is that since the original construction, the third floor balcony has been added, and the first floor was converted from a very large garage to living space. The 524.47 figure came from the renovation company as to the area renovated in 2011.) But maybe better to use the 427.95 square meter/4,606.4 square feet figure!

376. The renovation company that we used in 2011 is famous for building large, new luxury houses and sometimes houses with clinics, businesses or museums attached. They are earnest-home.jp — not to be confused with

www.earnesthome.com This website is also in building but has a cartoon, manga-type look. (I didn't know you could have a website without the www. in front. But our Earnest contractor's website pops up without the www.) The original contractor that built this basic structure in 1973, now has over 100 years of history. Like Earnest, they are also famous for doing high-class, high-quality, and expensive work too! Their website is www.mizusawa-inc.co.jp This K.K. Mizusawa Komuten (construction) is currently (as of January 2015) still working on a very large impressive Japanese style structure within about a 3 or 4 minute walk from our building. It looks like a temple or shrine built hundreds of years ago. My wife told me it is an Otera/Buddhist Temple.

So here is a document that we can email as a bilingual attachment. Some parts of it are interesting. Most readers not interested in 'making a move' to Tokyo, will want to skip details on building design/details of layout etc. But we can pass it on to a friend who can test the life-in-Tokyo-waters for you! Maybe you will someday 'make a move' too…

Tokyo Castle—Omotesando/ Shibuya/Aoyama 5 Story, 524.47 sq. meters/5,645.3 sq. feet/158.65 tsubo Property—a Rare Option to Combine Full time or Occasional Tokyo Visit Residence with Business/Executive Head Office, Showroom/ Gallery, School, nearby Aoyama U. Coed Club Dorm, or Your Overseas Guest House/ Networking/Party Facility on a Quiet, Secluded, Serene Street, yet just tens of meters from the Center of Tokyo's most Trendy and Fashionable District. Special lucky feature is having the scenery of two of Tokyo's largest and most beautiful residences next door to our side and in the back.

For residential and visiting guest entertainment use: 9 bedrooms; 9 toilets; 11 sinks and wash basins including kitchen and two kitchenettes with vanity/cabinet and 8 with large mirrors; a Japanese style-bath taking up to 4 people at once; a unit shower with seat fitting two or three people; a good-sized living/dining room with open kitchen; a large open-space wood-paneled to the belt line room on the second-floor, reachable from outside front stairs with large balcony that can take over 100 event or reception guests or 60 to 70 in seminar format, and 5 storage rooms of varying size, also useable redwood third-floor balcony, and fifth-floor wrap-around roof terrace, large wine cellar. The outside façade of brick tile does not streak or show dirt.

So much is happening and will continue to happen in Asia, yet **Japan,** along with Taiwan (but what if Taiwan is absorbed by mainland China where no one can own land), **is basically the only Country in the Whole Region that Allows Foreigners to Own Land and Buildings without even having a Visa or ever living, or ever even visiting the Property!! The Owners address in his/her home country can be the Formal Address of the Owner on the Japanese Land and building.** Korea and Hong Kong are easier than most countries in Asia, except Taiwan, but only with ownership of condominiums. Even in Hong Kong permanent land ownership is not possible. In Korea, conditions and rules make it virtually impossible to buy land, such as the requirements of not owning more than one property, and having to live in a special economic zone etc. And Japan has no extra charges or taxes applying only to foreigners like Korea, Hong Kong etc. Even Singapore allows foreigners to own land only in one special development. In the long run, assuming a change in Taiwan as it occurred in Hong Kong, except for Japan, throughout the region buying land is impossible, and the extra charges and hurdles even on condominiums are considerable. Even when buying with cash! Buying with cash is easier in Japan too. For both foreign individuals and companies, buying land in Japan has been possible for tens of years, and perhaps always was—not sure from when it became possible.

As the population is decreasing in Japan as a whole (but the population keeps growing in Tokyo!!), and because Japan has unusually always been open to foreign land freehold owning, there has never been even mention of restricting land purchase by foreigners, except if near a sensitive military installation, or perhaps if certain countries are buying up too much cheap rural land in anticipation of gaining from the resources within the land. But so far only fringe talk at the most even in that sensitive area.

Castle-like 4.5 Story, Hideaway with Roof Terrace for a Jet Setting Foreigner, or Japanese Who Wants His/Her Piece of the Largest, Cleanest, Safest and Most Exciting City on the Planet. (And the Current Owner is a Foreigner from New York!!) If you are a well-known name or face who needs to Come and Go and do Confidential Deals with Privacy and Anonymity this property is perfect. For such Meetings, Entertainment, Networking Events, or for Spur of the Moment Trips to Tokyo for You and Your Friends, there is a Flexibility and Spontaneity of Space and Use that Typical Luxury Homes, Hotel Suites and Condominium Penthouses Cannot Provide.

Land:

157.12 sq. meters/1,691.20 sq. feet/47.6 tsubo—Freehold, direct ownership by foreigners has always been possible and easy in Japan—details above. In China and many other countries only long term leases are possible.

Newly 2011 fully renovated/rebuilt living and office, event or large guest house for your Tokyo visitors. Renovation on 524.47 sq. meters/5,645.3 sq. feet/158.65 tsubo (not counting the outside staircase, third-floor balcony, the path to, and the smaller East side of the fifth-floor roof terrace.)

1973 – November initially constructed

1991 – Reconstructed, enlarged steel structure with reinforced concrete, and 4 person elevator up to 4th floor. Outside walls were redone with current brick surface.

2011 – Entrance way and interior completely redesigned, gutted out, and all electric wiring, water pipes, all equipment, air conditioning, all floors, walls and ceilings rebuilt brand new during a 6-month renovation period.

Brief Layout summary of the current floor plan:

3 good-sized shared-use toilets with 3 male wall-type urinals, and 3 sit-down toilets on 1st, 2nd & 3rd floors (2nd and 3rd floor sit-down toilets have fully enclosed and separated lockable stalls so toilet entrance door can be left open for efficient shared use). Separate residential apartment with sit-down toilet and good-sized shower unit with built-in molded bench to sit on third floor. 2 kitchenettes on second and third floors, main

fourth and fifth floor residence with 2 bedrooms, good-sized open kitchen/dining/living room, 2 sit-down toilets and large Japanese-style bath and double sink separate room. One large open room on 2nd floor, and 3 more rooms on 1st floor that could be used for meeting rooms, offices, bedrooms, and 2 more good-sized rooms on the 3rd floor that could also work as bedrooms or dining or living rooms. Also lots of storage space throughout the building including large wine cellar.

Price: 1,338,877,000 yen (about US$13,300,000)

Overview

A one-of-a-kind 524.47 sq. meter (158.65 tsubo/5,645.3 sq. feet) all recently completely redesigned and renovated (Oct. 1 2010 to March 31 2011) luxury residence or residence combined with business, clinic, artist/sculpture/jewelry gallery, music studio, showroom, entertainment/event space, professional services firm, or school etc. on lower floors. Could make an ideal embassy with offices and meeting rooms on the 1st floor, a large open reception room with balcony accommodating 100 guests or more on the 2nd floor, the ambassador's office and residential apartment with utility unit shower, toilet, and sink on the 3rd floor, and main ambassador residence on the 4th and 5th floors. The open space big room on the 2nd floor could also accommodate 60 to 70 people in seminar format, or quite a number of office work stations.

For the jet-setting foreigner who is tired of packing and who wants something handy in Tokyo, this property could work well for a movie producer or director, and actor, or actress. For such film industry celebrities this property is the minimum-fare taxi ride to Roppongi Hills, where most film previews, with the actors making an appearance, take place. The property could also work for a well-known painter/sculptor/photographer desiring a permanent showroom/gallery in the prime location for fashion and galleries in Tokyo, and closer to the Chinese and other Asian markets—while still able to breathe clean air and drink and eat anything in this vast Tokyo metropolis. A change of pace for a famous writer, public figure or well-known CEO or professional athlete sick of getting their picture taken and getting ogled at in hotel lobbies. Investment bankers, venture capitalist, financial hedge-fund-types or property developers who want to keep their deals and the parties they are dealing with confidential would find that all parties involved are more comfortable entering the building from this quiet street. It has virtually no car or even pedestrian traffic. This property would be a good secluded spot to work things out secretly and only at the top with a potential JV partner, or whether selling or buying at divesting or acquisition time.

Tokyo offers a globally unique anonymous and safe lifestyle for famous people with recognizable names and/or faces.

For example, tens of thousands of normal Japanese housewives (and perhaps famous Japanese faces) wear those full-face-covering sun visors or face shields worn by V. Stiviano that created such a stir outside Japan when the Los Angeles Clippers owner Donald Sterling made his comments about race. For many outside Japan, Donald Sterling's girlfriend's use of the full face visor seemed unique and strange. Not here in Japan. Also it is common for men and women to wear large white surgical face masks when they catch cold, or want to cut down on air pollen or the possibility of catching colds from others. So even with its 40,000,000 greater Tokyo area population, if they want it, it is much easier for famous people with famous faces to freely walk about town, get in and out of taxis, and even take the fantastic train and subway system. <u>There are few if not any active, aggressive paparazzi in Tokyo, and even at restaurants etc., when such masks are removed, the Japanese people leave famous people alone, and try not to even look in their direction. So if you are a famous face, and if you long for a normal life where you can walk where you want</u>, and even walk anywhere late at night — whether you are famous or not — how about setting up your own private digs in Tokyo? The New Yorker who owns this property was an Eagle Scout and still will often walk 10 to 25 kilometers on a Saturday without looking at maps but simply taking a train out to a randomly selected station. Then with a regular non-digital (no battery recharge challenge) magnetic compass (usually made in by Suunto in Finland—seriously!), you do a dead reckoning north or south to stay out of the sun, and keep the sun out of the eyes (with or without that face visor). No need to look at any maps but maybe carry one. When tired, you will recognize a station nearby from the concentration of taller buildings a few hundred meters away. Then just jump on the train back to Omotesando/Shibuya/Aoyama, your new digs. It is amazing what the compass will guide you to, and what you will see and experience. And this safe, interesting, convenient, metropolitan to suburban area is so vast that you could do a different little adventure walk hundreds of days, and never take the same route or see the same scenery!

Why jog over the same boring terrain, or walk on a moving belt? At night, for extra safety from traffic on narrower streets, all you need are brighter clothes, maybe a couple reflectors or a head band cave/mining light around your leg when walking at night. Vending machines for drinks, little parks and more than 15,000 convenience stores (just in Tokyo) for take-out food, or anything you need, along with the store's free toilets are abundant, and you will come across one as needed. Charming little restaurants can be tucked away in surprising places. Just in time you always come across an exciting, often very bright *shotengai*/shopping street feeding into one of the over 1,000 train and subway stations on over 130 (and growing) different train and subway lines in the Tokyo area.

In preparation for the 2020 Olympics, Tokyo maps, stations, signs and restaurant menus will have even more English/ romanization of names than they have now. English and roman lettering is already abundant enough, and it was always easy in Japan to go out to many restaurants' display windows and point to the beautiful colorful wax recreation of the dish you want.

Try Googling "50 reasons Tokyo is the world's greatest city". This was prepared by CNN Travel at http://travel.cnn.com/ tokyo/visit/best-japan/worlds-greatest-city-50-reasons-why-tokyo-no-1-903662. The #4 reason is about Shibuya station, "the busiest station in the world", and only 15 to 20 minutes' walk from your quiet, secluded street. #5 talks about your Shibuya/Omotesando/Aoyama address, and, with nearby Harajuku and Jingumae, the article states that this is the largest fashion district with the most boutiques and major brands in the world. #8 quotes from the Michelin guide which has given Tokyo restaurants by far the most Michelin Stars. It's written that there are 160,000 restaurants in Tokyo, more than 10 times the number in Paris. According to *USA Today* there are 4,200 restaurants in all 5 boroughs of New York City—about

3,500 on Manhattan, about 800 in Brooklyn, and only about 100 in Queens/Staten Island/the Bronx according to "New York Restaurants"—maybe this does not include fast food joints?! So the Japanese people must be pretty active at night, and there are lots of cheap and great places to eat. In Tokyo you can find any food your heart desires, and many of these restaurants are owned and run by non-Japanese foreigners who came here and fell in love with the city—probably now just as many more Europeans, Africans, Middle-East, North and South American, other Asian, and down-under Aussie/ New Zealand types, as the more traditional Chinese and Koreans who have been here much longer—think Chinatown in adjacent Yokohama, from when the port opened up. They all love it and all the foreigners toe the line, because they love Japan the safe and clean way it is. Plus the Japanese allow such foreign entrepreneurs to earn a good living. They don't get jealous or upset about that. You will love it here, just like the rest of us.

If you are a foreigner not confident enough to pull off buying and managing a property in Japan, the current fellow foreigner owner from New York is happy to give special help and orientation. The current owner is a long-term Tokyo resident born and raised in New York. He has a charming, international and cosmopolitan Japanese wife. They are both totally bilingual in Japanese and English. They, along with of course our bilingual and bicultural staff and real estate agents, will be happy to make buying this property as easy as you would buy in Paris, New York, London, or Zurich. They and we will help you get a handle on all the tax, utility payment, use of facility, and cleaning and maintenance issues etc. The current owners have used a trustworthy, English-speaking Filipino female home helper once a week for many years. She is still quite young and already has a sponsor in Japan. This well-known Tokyo couple will also help show you the ropes in Tokyo, and make sure you get an idea of all that Tokyo has to offer. The current owners will continue to live nearby in Tokyo, after scaling down a bit. If Tokyo is an off-and-on residence and business destination for you, one thought the current owners had would be to hire, or line up someone you know—a bilingual Japanese Man Friday, or Lady Friday living in the third-floor apartment with unit shower to take care of such property issues, and your furnishings and things, help with appointments, your business, and setting up any parties or catered events that you throw. Or such a responsible live-in assistant can be easily found. You would be paying them some salary, and better not to charge them rent. Maybe could be fun and helpful. Again the current owners are happy to give advice, and get such things started for you. Including on how to use that Boy Scout compass and do your anonymous Tokyo/Yokohama city walking adventures—optional! But seriously, the exotic, and perhaps seemingly too difficult additional dream of having your own residential-and-whatever building in Tokyo is right here. For the non-Japanese outsider woman or man who has everything, or really does want a lot more of Tokyo and Japan—this property and new life experience will be something very different but very reachable.

The fifth floor is smaller and has a wraparound redwood (*actually a resin/plastic composite that is more expensive than wood, and unlike wood will last forever and needs no maintenance) roof terrace with sunrises to the East, and views of a garden with a lawn and trees below, beautiful large neighborhood homes, trees, and Roppongi Hills and Tokyo Midtown in sight beyond that. These were the two tallest — and pretty much still are the tallest — and two of the best known building complexes in the whole city. Off the spacious roof terrace facing west, you will have beautiful sunsets and the Shibuya skyline including Shibuya Hikarie (also famous and new), Cerulean Tower Hotel and the colorfully lit up AO Kinokuniya Aoyama Bldg. on nearby Aoyama Dori. The fifth-floor roof terrace has a good-sized sink and counter with hot water for roof parties. Easily accessible large matching redwood* veranda balconies are off the second and third floors. There is enough space to get tables and chairs out on those balconies.

For exercise and convenience you can use the attractive outside spiral staircase up to the 4th floor. There is also a 4-person capacity elevator also going up to the 4th floor. <u>After extensively searching all of central Tokyo, major Japanese TV stations have reported that this was/is the best property, and the one building that worked perfectly as the home of a wealthy family on the upper floors, combined with a successful cosmetic surgery clinic on the lower floors, as portrayed in this particular daily drama that went on for 3 months.</u> It was a popular drama, and based on a book that sold 1,800,000 copies. It was a bit of fun for the owner, but the owner has since turned down other offers for the property to be the setting for dramas and movies. (There were only two mornings, and one evening of film shoots, but the owner felt too many production people and vehicles disturbed this secluded, quiet street, and might be bothering the neighbors who had become their friends.)

From the 2nd floor up, the building's northside windows face onto the neighbor's inner garden of the courtyard of their beautiful European Renaissance style house. Luckily our seller's property is not the nicest residential neighboring building! Indeed it is a gem of a quiet neighborhood, yet so close to one of the most visited and busiest fashionable districts of Tokyo—fun, sophisticated, with more outdoor cafes, restaurants, and more trendy and popular among the younger set than Ginza.

The 157.12 sq. meter (47.6 tsubo/1,691.20 sq. feet) plot of land is on a gentle slope. There is also a gentle slope down to the street, so no chance of flooding from even the heaviest multiple days of continuing rain. According to Japan flood maps, the building is somewhere between 30 and 40 meters above sea level, probably about 35 meters above Tokyo Bay. With Tokyo Bay's rather narrow entrance between Chiba and Miura Peninsulas, Tokyo is actually quite safe from Tsunamis.

The inside of the building was stripped down. Every floor, ceiling, wall, toilet, sink, and air conditioning facility and system were completely changed and rebuilt in 2011. Not to mention that all telephone, internet, electric wiring and all water pipes and related equipment was completely changed and renovated in 2011. Before most of the ceilings and walls facing the outside were rebuilt, they were sprayed with additional insulations. Visitor's assumed and question if it is a newly constructed building. Although the outside brick tile walls constructed in 1991 are fine and in great shape, all other outside walls and roof were recoated with waterproofing materials in 2011 to be ready for the many more years that this building will serve and please its owners. The elevator was put in when the building was extensively renovated in 1991. And the elevator has also been renovated, and the hydraulics and machinery will soon be (in 2015) completely replaced. For many years the current owner is only the 2nd one to own this property. One wealthy family had owned this land and had their first home on this property since 1973. It is possible to discuss with the current foreign English- speaking owners about leaving furnishings, curtains, utensils, pretty much anything behind if this is a convenient turnkey approach. This could especially be helpful if this new owner is from outside Japan, and visiting here on and off.

A Little about Land Prices and Investment Potential

The former owners were able to borrow 2,800,000,000 yen (about $28,000,000) using this property for collateral, but indeed that was representative of the more bubbly times here in Japan, and especially in Tokyo. With the 2020 Olympics, and still more hotels etc. to be built in time for the Olympics on the drawing boards, land and building prices are going up, and it is generally thought that this will continue. Other factors contributing to this are the rise of wages, growing shortage of labor, and increase in labor disputes, and other unrest in China and other regional countries. It is felt that social instability along ethnic, socioeconomic, and even religious lines will also increase in other Asian and many other countries. Because of the continuing political, ethnic, and class frictions in places like Thailand and Vietnam, factories, and operations there as well as in China and other countries are in fact coming back to Japan. Japan is also in better shape to handle the effects of climate change than many countries that are more affected by hurricanes, flooding, and droughts. Even extremes of heat and cold are less in Japan due to the moderating effects of the surrounding oceans. Japanese, Western and other expatriate executives and their families are more and more aware of the dangers coming from pollution, sanitation, and personal safety issues in most other Asian countries and on the Indian etc. subcontinent. Yes. In terms of these health and life-determining considerations, Japan really is a safe haven, and local long-term expats often refer to Japan, and of course, more specifically, Tokyo as a heavenly paradise compared to so much they must deal with off these shores.

This particular Omotesando, Aoyama, Harajuku, and Shibuya area is scheduled for more nice developments, and nearby Shibuya station is being almost completely redone, and will become even cooler over the next few years.

As an island with virtually no guns; peaceful, calm, and stoic people; and people and a government that take care of each other. Should there be civil instability, class and religious disturbances and chaos in many countries around the world, as feared by Survivalists and some of those with much to lose, a beachhead in Tokyo is another good option and hedge.

Used mostly as a guest house for more spontaneous trips to Tokyo/Japan with friends or business associates. As of July 2013, an increasing number of 66 countries require no visa of visitors for your stipulated 15, 30 or 90 days visit in Japan. No visa needed for tourists, but also no visa needed "for commerce, a conference, visit to relatives/acquaintances etc." — the Ministry of Foreign Affairs website www.mofa.go.jp Beyond such temporary visits, that can be easily repeated, there also will be no problem in you procuring permission for long-term periods of stay.

Without doing any redesign or renovation, it is possible to have 3, two of them good-sized, bedrooms on the 1st floor, 3 more bedrooms, two good-sized and one large on the 3rd floor, and

2 more bedrooms on the 4th and 5th floor. <u>This is a total of 8 or 9 bedrooms</u>, if also counting a possible smaller bedroom on the 2nd floor that faces into the neighbor's garden. *With many of these rooms able to take twin, double, or bunk beds it becomes possible to sleep even 20 to 30 people*, having a blast also at Tokyo Disneyland or all over this great city. For example, this could be enough for the Stones, or any rock group or entertainment team, and their entourage to use the property as a stepping off base for doing their gigs throughout Asia, Russian and "down under" Australia etc. There still would be enough room on the open space second floor to practice with equipment and technicians, or even record tracks in this quiet neighborhood in-between concerts! In addition to the main, good-sized living/dining/open kitchen on the 4th floor, this second floor open-space room can also work for cocktail parties and events with more than 100 attendees. This building could work well for any large group of entertainers, or even scary corporate auditing teams, or teams of lawyers working on business deals. A lot cheaper, flexible and a more fun experience than having to book hotels.

There is room for tables and chairs, places to eat, in most of those bedrooms, and even if the 2 kitchenettes, and one full kitchen are not used much, almost every day in Tokyo, different take-out menus are stuffed in mailboxes. And we are not talking about just pizza; Chinese, sushi, burgers, sandwiches, noodles, Indian, but many more order-out options.

<u>Okay, but what about toilets?</u> They are on all floors—3 men's wall urinals, and 6 sit-down toilets for a <u>total of 9 toilets — more than enough for an army of guests or touring visitors.</u>

What about bathing and showering? There is the one <u>unit</u> <u>shower</u> with a built in molded sitting bench on the 3rd floor — <u>Two or three people can fit in that</u>. And maybe the best part and fun part is the Japanese-style bath on the 4th floor with a large window that can be opened for a great view of the outside, but really not easy to see inside your bath. And <u>this Japanese-style bath can take up to 4 people—in Japan at certain *onsen*/hot springs there are men and women who are even complete strangers bathing together at the same time in Konyoku-style</u>★. We don't have a Jacuzzi but can be dressed like in a Jacuzzi. Two can stretch out in a long deep bathtub. And 2 or 3 can be outside on the floor stools with the shower, two full-length mirrors, and bowls to scoop water if needed from the clean bath water. In Japan, you first wash thoroughly with soap outside the bath tub, completely rinse off, and then go into the bath water. And the water automatically keeps getting replenished to the temperature and water depth that you desire. There is a soundproof studio door between the bathing and double sink vanity area and the bedroom on the 4th floor. Anyone can get access to this bathing area directly from the entrance hallway. Of course there is a door with a lock there for privacy if and when needed.

★*Konyoku*/women and men bathing together naked: After tens of years in Japan, the current owner from New York must have kept himself too busy! When he was 23 or 24 he did go into the *Konyoku*/mixed-sex "Jungle Bath" once on a trip to Ibusuki in Kagoshima. If your little Tokyo castle, which can sleep and take care of 20 to 30 friends or associates, has one weakness it could be the lack of a lot of separate shower and bath areas. But then again, this is Japan, and it was not until Admiral Perry's Black Ships first came to Japan in 1854, and the Meiji Emperor Restoration in 1867 with Japan forced to open up to the world, that there was any separation between men and women bathing naked at the city, town and country public baths, and of course at the more private *onsen* hot spring baths at *ryokan*/inns. When the current building owner first arrived in Japan he was a researcher from Cornell U. in New York, and lived in a small apartment that did not have its own bath. So the *sento*/public baths had a fixed price (48 yen per daily use) in those days. The *bandai* or the husband or the wife who owned and ran the bath would sit up high, right in between the two changing and bathing sections to collect money from both separate sexes entering from separate doors right next to each other. Let's just say the *bandais* and anyone entering and paying that was only somewhat tall could keep an eye on everything. That alone was worth the 48 yen, even if you got excited and forgot to take your bath. <u>My Executive Assistant wants me to emphasize that readers should not believe that Japanese family members or friends, in their normal, daily lives, are always doing *konyoku*/mixed-sex bathing together.</u>

Well the New Yorker recently found a website htttp:www.secret-japan.com/onsen/location/japan.php. There is a detailed list of 129 *onsen* hot springs, 82 of which are *konyoku*/mixed bathing. And at most of these baths wearing bathing suits is not allowed—bringing in that small white towel, yes. And if you Google a few articles such as (5th April 2008) "First *Konyoku* Experience: Floating Mammary Glands of The *Bijin*", (beautiful lady), you will find that the old myth that only old women do *konyoku* is absolutely not true. It is interesting to note that out of those 82 Konyoku/mixed baths, there were none in the Kansai (Osaka, Kyoto, Kobe area), there were 3 in metropolitan Tokyo but out on islands in the sea, but there were 34 within the (distant) Kanto (Tokyo) area mostly in Gunma and Tochigi Prefectures.

But why go that far if you have an open-window partially outdoor bath that will take up to 4 or 5 people at once right on your own fourth floor? Out of necessity with too many people staying over and waking up at the same time sometimes we "had to do it". Sounds like it could be fun and a way to build "skinship" as the *sento*/public bath buddies used to tell the current New York-born and raised property owner during his first 3 or 4 years in Japan. Actually it was etiquette to offer to wash the bath mate's back, even if you barely knew each other, but happened to be sitting side by side. (Of course separate alternating bathing hours can be worked out as well.)

Another dimension to this is that the Japanese are more inclined to bathe at night than in the morning. Of course sometimes mornings too. If at night, or in warmer weather, if you still want the fourth floor bath big window open, you would have the lights in the bath off anyway. It is possible to have hot water in the bathtub all day long, if going in shifts. The tub can be covered to keep the water warmer. <u>This fourth floor Japanese-style bath, taking up to 5 people, has its own heating and air conditioning system on the ceiling</u>. Also fast for hanging and drying laundry, although the maximum size washer and dryer of course comes with the property.

What about wash basins and sinks? Currently there are 3 good-sized sinks and vanity counters with mirrors and only cold water (can add hot water if wanted), and 4 wash basins and vanities with mirrors and hot water. And then there are 3 kitchens with hot water and still another sink with hot water on the roof terrace. This makes for a total 11 sinks/wash basins to tend to such matters. Again, this is an unusual property that can quite well accommodate a very large group of visitors, friends or co-workers.

It is getting much easier and convenient to fly your own private business jet in and out of Narita, or Haneda airport, which is much closer to central Tokyo.

Even more slots and such business private jet airport facilities are on the way. Same day, spontaneous landing and take-off reservations have become possible. And helicopter services in from the more distant Narita airport are up and running. From Haneda airport it is a fairly short and reasonable taxi ride. The number of days the aircraft can be parked has also increased meeting most anyone's needs.

More details by floor

1<u>st</u> <u>floor</u> is now an easy in and out parking area, with covered roof, large for a large car, a little tight for two cars, but possible. (It is the width of a standard two-car parking space in Japan— the Japanese are good at parking!!) The quiet, peaceful street has virtually no passing traffic, which is a real convenience and pleasure when moving the car in and out. There are 3 good-sized meeting rooms (could also be bedrooms!) with internet, TV, and phone connections, two types of lighting. There are both business bright white lighting, and warmer amber mood drop lights. Pretty much throughout the building these two types of lights can be used together or separately. There is a good-sized sit-down toilet, urinal and sink, a guest waiting bench in the hallway, a large computer server and storage room in the back (can get air conditioner down to 18 degrees centigrade so can double as a large wine cellar), a utility closet with large deep sink for the cleaning/maintenance company also toward the end of the hallway so out of view, and a good-sized storage area for large garbage cans etc. in the closed off elevator room at the front of the building.

2nd floor is a large open space with attractive curved split-level design, so the front of the room facing the large balcony has higher ceilings. Toward the back northside, there is a small room with a soundproof studio door with a large window facing the neighbor's courtyard garden with its trees right there. This room facing the garden could be a storage room, little office, or another bedroom, or whatever. There is a toilet set-up, again of both male and female types as on the first floor, and also quite a large entry hallway, and kitchenette with hot water, built in cabinets, refrigerator etc. And finally there is also a storage closet at the end of the hallway. Adequate internet, phone, TV, and electric outlets are spaced around half-height wood-panel walls (in a few places wood grain veneer where wood had been removed—but this difference is not very noticeable), so if used as an office probably best to have the desks along the walls, with the middle of the room looking quite large and open. Currently there are 10 very large work stations. (It is also possible to leave much office furnishings and technical server and PC equipment, an excellent phone system integrated throughout the building, and including the current outside contracted part-time IT pro—offering the buyer such a turnkey start if this is desirable.) If used as an event, or cocktail reception, party room, over 100 people can easily be accommodated not including the large outside mostly rain free covered balcony. The beautiful staircase to the second-floor big open room is visible from outside the building, so most people can be directed to go up the short flight of stairs.

3<u>rd</u> <u>floor</u> has the same hallway as one leaves the elevator or comes up the outside stairs. Same design double toilet and sink set-up off the hallway. There is a residential apartment with unit shower, sink and fancy, full-feature sit-down toilet on the northside facing the neighbor's courtyard garden and trees. Then there are two large rooms with a large walk-in closet/ storage facility between them. And there are PC, internet, TV, printer and telephone connections. The large front room opens up to the redwood balcony. The slightly smaller backroom has a kitchenette with built in cabinets, and hot water. It is on the Southside, in the right-hand corner and not visible from the hallway. These large rooms could be a younger generation of the family living/dining room, large bedroom, study, office, set up for guests, or whatever. As one leaves the elevator, in front of you is a clear glass door niche with a display ceiling light. If something valuable is in there, the door only opens from inside the room on the other side of the wall. The glass hallway display window cannot be opened from the hallway.

Throughout the building the owner planned it to be ready to flexibly meet the next owner's needs. So there are brighter office lights but also nice atmosphere lower ambience lights and several light systems with brightness adjusting and dimming capability. Motion sensors turn on some of the hallway lights. They are currently set to stay on for 6 minutes.

4<u>th</u> <u>floor:</u> Only on this floor is there one more residence entrance door beyond the glass doors off the outside spiral staircase. The inner *genkan*/area for shoes is curved, with a beautiful wooden and rod iron spiral staircase going up to the smaller 5th floor and roof terrace. There is a toilet to the left of the hallway, and a view possible all the way through a good-sized double sink vanity cabinet washing/changing room, on to a large and very well designed bath. This bath used to be a bedroom over the garden and facing the beautiful huge white house in the back. It was easy enough to cover the windows with opaque white film that does let in a lot of light. And it can make for your own semi-outdoor bath if you open the large window and keep the lights off at night! Actually no one is close by for a good view inside the bath. Anyway, the bathing is a pleasure. <u>This bath can accommodate up to 5 people together at once if used Japanese-style</u>. There is a fair-sized storage area hidden under the curved staircase. The entire 4th floor, except the bedroom, is white stone tile; the ceiling has a very interesting triple curved design. The owners wanted to have the same upscale kitchen and cabinet custom design firm make a beautiful almost 2-meter bar with interesting lighting, glass sides, glass and wooden doors and mirrors; a custom designed beautiful all white open kitchen with everything hidden, and other cabinets and a "PC corner" work area. Lots of storage space throughout this building. Again, there are soundproof studio doors between the large living/dining/open kitchen and a good-sized bedroom. Only this bedroom and the living dining have gas water heated flooring. There is another soundproof door between this 4th floor bedroom and the large double sink, changing and bath area. The current owners used a famous, very well-known renovation company, specializing in luxury residence construction and renovation. Together they tried to think of everything, and anticipate the needs of a future owner.

<u>5ᵗʰ floor</u> is now used as a good-sized bedroom that is soundproof from the rest of the house. Thick steel reinforced concrete floors between floors and unusually thick concrete walls keep things quiet, warm in the winter, and cool in the summer throughout the building. This fifth-floor room has sliding double UV glass door easy access to the wrap around roof terrace. Since stairs have to be used to get to this fifth floor, having a nice toilet/powder room on this same fifth floor was more important than having another bath. So where there used to be a bath, there is now a toilet with a good-sized built-in cabinet and sink. This is quite an attractive powder room for the guests at those roof top parties.

Location:

Just as good as the building, is the location. For taxis, although Koto Dori to Aoyama Dori also works, the building is about 120 meters from Roppongi Dori. Yet perhaps also because of the curving street, not a sound is heard from Roppongi Doori and other nearby busier streets. As for the subway, it is 6 or 7 minutes' walk to Omotesando station, (3 different subway lines) and about 15 to 20 minutes' walk to Shibuya station. Shibuya is the busiest and biggest station catering more for the fashionable younger set. And it will keep the older of us young! Those familiar with the area know it to be pretty much unsurpassed for fashion, restaurants, outdoor restaurants/cafes, walking, and the atmosphere offered of everything from the United Nations University Headquarters' weekend outdoor Farmers' Market, to the Omotesando Boulevard, and on to Harajuku, Cat Street, and all the other excitement and fun of the Aoyama, Jingumae, Meiji Shrine, Togo Shrine, Shibuya and Yoyogi Park area. It is also within a 15-minute walk to the main 2020 Olympic venue building, and Aoyama Cemetery with all its paths, cherry blossoms, greenery, and attractive views from the top of that hill. Other popular international districts of Roppongi, Hiroo, Daikanyama, and Ebisu are just short cab rides away. The most film premiers take place at Roppongi Hills, with the actors and directors appearing and commenting on the film. Roppongi Hills is a minimum fare taxi ride away. <u>And taxis stream by on Roppongi Dori, which is just about 100 or some meters down your quiet, curving, sloping street.</u>

<u>Aoyama University with Elementary, Junior High, Senior High School and University all on the same campus and all about a 5 to 10-minute walk from this property.</u> Aoyama University is ranked as the 5th most popular university in Tokyo. It is ranked #8 in Japan in terms of the number who have passed the National CPA (Certified Public Accountant) exam, #13 in terms of the number of directors on the Board of Directors of stock exchange listed companies in Japan, and 15th in terms of the numbers of alumni who have been elected members of the Japanese National Diet (Parliament or Congress). Perhaps especially for families from other Asian, Russian or nearby countries, that would like a foothold in Japan, note that <u>the Aoyama school system's policy is that virtually all students who graduate from a lower level school, may secure a place at the next highest level. The vast majority of students who start at the elementary school, or even as late as the high school, will go on and graduate from the university. These Aoyama schools are more international, and have more courses taught in English than most other Japanese lower-grade school systems and universities.</u>

Security—Police Box 150 meters away across Roppongi Dori, and across the street from Coca Cola head office building, first-floor video intercom, access to the building, and SECOM security company: Each floor can be called from the outside ground-level video intercom (with digital images stored until deleted), and the lock to the ground-floor front door can be released at the intercom video station on each floor. In addition to a traditional metal key lock, which staff, visitors and even most family members do not need, from the outside staircase there is a digital touch screen combination lock on first, second, and third floor. It is possible to set a different number combination on each floor. For weekends and at night there is also an aluminum mesh door that can be locked from the inside, and opened from the outside only with a key. There is a matching attractive aluminum mesh cage designed in to block access to the staircase. This combined with an excellent security system set up by SECOM (the industry leader in Japan) makes for a very secure and safe property. SECOM guard personnel arrive within 1 to 3 minutes.

Current land tax, and optional Elevator maintenance, SECOM Security, and daily building cleaning and maintenance costs: (about 102-104 yen/US$, or 141-143 yen/Euro)

- Land and Building Tax in 2013 can be paid quarterly and for the full year totaled 822,700 yen, about US$8,000. If more of the building were declared to be used as residence, this amount would be less.

- Elevator maintenance (optional) is 34,650 yen/month including the consumption tax. Every other month might be possible?

- SECOM security system totals 23,760 yen/month, even when the resident's mistakes lead to false alarms, and the Guards arrival.

- Daily Mon. to Fri. (non-holiday) cleaning and maintenance is 71,734 yen/month. And twice a year, an all-day full-scale cleaning of everything by a professional team with special equipment (more complete steam cleaning of parking area, front terrace, stairs, balconies, roof, and inside and outside windows, and more thorough cleaning of floors etc.) is 54,000 yen both including consumption tax—once every 6 months. If the building is not being used every day by many people, and/or if the building is left largely unoccupied for periods of time, probably the 71,734 yen for daily weekday service can be greatly reduced. The twice-a-year complete team cleaning, coordinated when someone is resident in the building, would be recommendable.

- All prices include the higher consumption tax increased from April 1, 2014.

- CURRENT PHONE SYSTEM can be left behind (also newly installed in 2011). There is a phone in every room and now 10 in the second-floor big open room. As used now, there are separate numbers for the company on the first, second and third floors, and for the fourth and fifth floor resident portion. However, intercom calling for free is possible between all the rooms, including the residence portion of the building.

As mentioned earlier, the current owners will scale down but stay nearby in this part of Tokyo. They can help with these kinds of issues.

Earthquakes and Structural Integrity, choosing a condo or this property: This building was rebuilt and reinforced in 1991 well beyond the 1982 revision of earthquake resistance building codes. Even when initially constructed in 1973, as with so many Tokyo buildings, it was built beyond the 1982 code requirements. As a couple examples, the very famous Kasumigaseki Building, 36 stories, was Tokyo's first skyscraper opened from April, 1968. Also the World Trade Center building, 40 stories, at Hamamatsucho station, from which the monorail to Haneda airport departs, was opened from March, 1970. As with our building they were already built to exceed the 1982 revision of the earthquake resistance building code. The current owner's 2011 complete renovation, taking 6 months, was scheduled to finish the end of March 2011. The wallpaper had already been completed when the big earthquake and tsunami struck on the afternoon of March 11, 2011. There was only one small slit in one place on the wallpaper. Since trains, phones and elevators were down for a couple days, many of the renovation workman stayed overnight in this property. And this hydraulic elevator worked fine, just as before and with no downtime.

In most condos, and even in those luxury hotels, it took 1 to 3 days to get the elevators working. People in high-rise condos were greatly troubled. Downtime was shorter in most hotels. Should even the very worst imaginable earthquake hit Tokyo, at least there is the land, and as a single owner necessary repairs and, worst case, rebuilding or selling the land is possible. This is not possible with a condominium. All owners will not be able to handle the burden. There are large luxury condos in Tokyo, but they are not nearly the size of this building. Yet they can cost about the same. And they do not have anywhere near the flexibility of use that this property aims to provide. <u>With its particularly thick concrete walls, if the windows are closed, and with single-owner use, there is much more freedom to party, jive, have a band practice, or make the open space 2nd floor a large recording studio. It is possible to make much more noise than in a condominium, hotel suite, normal house, or shared building</u>.

Luxury condominium maintenance and owner association fees are significant and increase soon after a new development is sold. There are parking fees. Why have to deal with the fickleness, factional frictions, rules and pressures from a condo association? Why live in a luxurious condominium penthouse half the size of this Omotesando building, but at a similar price? And why not have the stars and moon of a clear, pollution-free Tokyo sky above you, rather than the irritating sounds of a young lady's piano lesson in progress? Throughout the region, Tokyo's clean air can be enjoyed only in Japan. Australia and New Zealand have clean air but are a bit down under! Personal safety and freedom of movement and business dealings is unsurpassed in Japan.

Buying, maintaining, and enjoying a new dimension to your life, at your own little Castle in Tokyo can be made surprisingly easy and fun for you. Why not 'make a move' here?

"Tokyo voted 'Best Experience' for Tourists" by over 54,000 travelers surveyed on TripAdvisor, beating New York, Barcelona, Paris, Prague and all the other cities. http:// blogs.wsj.com/japanrealtime/2014/05/21/tokyo-voted-best-experience-for-tourists/

Tokyo land, building prices rising—"Mitsui Fudosan plans big share issue on Olympics"—Plans to raise as much as 324.6 billion yen (about $3.246 billion), the largest share issue by a property company in 43 years. http://www. japantimes.co.jp/news/2014/05/28/business/corporate-business/mitsui-fudosan

"Foreign Buyers Have a Yen for Tokyo Real Estate" At the end of the article it states Mori Building Co., is offering 172 units on the top 10 floors of Toranomon Hills (nice new building but non-descript neighborhood—no Omotesando/ Aoyama/Shibuya) "for up to $3,606 per square foot—a price that hasn't been seen since Japan's property bubble burst in the early 1990's". http://online.wsj.com/news/ articles/SB1000142405270230470450457943312307 6 516890. *At that $3,606 price your Tokyo castle would cost about $20.4 million.*

"Shibuya's next big screen to rival basketball court" 5/23/2014 *Japan Times.* At this Shibuya scramble crossing, some 15 to 20 minutes' walk from your castle, about 3,000 people often cross in all directions at once. The article goes on: "Around 500,000 people use it (the scramble intersection) every day". This is the scene of Tokyo that all the movie directors and documentaries show the most. The new screen is 17.3 meters tall and 24.3 meters wide, and will be the largest one in this nation of large screens.

Nearby International Schools:

According to the US Embassy (www.japan.usembassy.gov) there are 7 colleges or universities with an international division within Tokyo. I will just mention the above Aoyama Gakuin University because it is a 5 minute walk from here.

There are almost 20 international lower-level schools, including a few within walking distance, or short, no transfer subway rides. From preschool to Grade 3, the British School of Tokyo is a good example, and is about a 15-minute walk from here. Just 2 (express) or 3 Hanzomon Subway stops away at Sangenjaya your child can continue at the British School from Grade 4 to Grade 13.

Reconfirmed Tokyo is the safest city in the world, out of the 50 cities that were evaluated. In the January 2015 Safe Cities Index released by the Economist Intelligence Unit (EIU), Tokyo was again rated the safest city on the 4 survey/research factors: 1. Digital, 2. Health, 3. Infrastructure, and 4. Personal Security. Singapore (same hot-as-hell temperature all year because it is pretty much on the equator), and Osaka were next. Next Asian city was Hong Kong at #11, Taipei #13, Seoul #24, the big 5 mainland China cities between 30 and 38; Bangkok #39, Delhi #42, Mumbai #44, Ho Chi Minh City #48, and finally Jakarta #50. By all means, please get over to, or set up in our safe and sweet, juicy Big Mikan/Tangerine.

Omakemono/Something extra — 5.6 acres (6,860 tsubo/22,638 square meters) on the New York side of the Saint Lawrence River—if you want a beachhead, without eroding sands, hurricane-free, flood protection from locks, and one of the most scenic boating areas in the world, check out The Thousand Islands, on the Saint Lawrence River. But for Frosty the Snowman in winter! You can build your compound and dream house or two right on the river. This must be the river with the clearest looking water among major rivers in North American. You can see pebbles on the river bottom even in a few meters of depth. Why? I have no idea. Except to say no mud, no delta inflow, pure melting snow fed? Beats me. It is Canada's Florida—freezing in winter, perfect in summer. I happen to own the largest untouched forested piece of land along the river, except for those parks, including Nevins Point, further north. Nothing to do with me. My land is 5.6 acres, with a driveway just off State Route 137. The shoreline gradually gets deep, so safe for even kids to swim. If you Google Satellite the New York State side of the river from Clayton and the 1,864 picturesque Thousand Islands, many with their beautiful island homes, you will see that what I say, about the last undeveloped virgin land is true. And there are very nice houses on either side of me. I have family and friends in the area to help strangers get started. So 'making a move' to this beautiful area, very safe from climate change also worth a thought. A perfect setting to enjoy global warming! I will 'stay put' in Tokyo. From your dock, without lifting a small yacht out of the water, you could boat to Montreal, Quebec, Ottawa, and even Toronto if you hug the northern shore of Lake Ontario. Watch out for going around by way of Lake Ontario's south shore. As you might go down Niagara Falls—barrels, yes. Your little boat with a cabin, probably not! If you are a crazy person, with a bigger yacht, and a sail or two, and you love fishing and eating delicious cold ocean sashimi, you would not even need a stove on board. But you have to be good with a sashimi hocho/carving knife. You can keep boating north to Hudson Bay, Baffin Bay, Greenland, Iceland, Norwegian Sea, Greenland Sea, North Sea, and Baltic Sea. You can boat all the way to Saint Petersburg, Russia, and make it to Mr. Vladimir Putin's Birthday Party on October 7. Enjoy the Russian bear meat at the big log cabin (above). Winter in Saint Petersburg, and sail back in the spring. Maybe going through Gibraltar, and wintering in English speaking Malta, or in Croatia, Montenegro, Greece, or Cyprus is a better idea. Sounds like fun. For you yachtsmen, and yachts-ladies it is a much shorter trip than leaving from Florida. Better to avoid the Bermuda Triangle. A lot cooler too.

Passing on What We Know about Human Resource and Labor Consulting to Stronger, More Powerful Parties that Can Leverage it to make a Bigger Difference.

And Finally Down to What I really Know and Do— Helping Out, and Making a Bigger Contribution with our New Stronger Partners in the Human Resource, Manpower Development Area, and Labor Consulting Business.

377. For over 30 years, Nevins/TMT's clients saw and appreciated the difference we made for them. <u>On our website (www.tmt-aba.com) 87 of these case study/ testimonial letters can be read. They appear with signatures in the hard copies of those books</u>. I think it is unusual for clients to do that for a consulting company.

And indeed, about half of the clients I asked told me that corporate policy did not allow those firms to issue such letters. The 87 letters represent perhaps 5 to 10% of the client relationships we have had. Unfortunately those letters appear only in English. I suppose free or reasonable translation software can provide a rough enough idea of the content.

378. Their existence is important for it is ludicrous and silly for a consultant or anyone to say that they are good at something. It is only ones good works, and the evaluation of others that prove that.

379. I was lucky that at the beginning of my long career, I had chances to be paid by renowned mainly US-based university professors (such as Professor Walter Galenson (1914-1990) of Cornell, and especially Professor William B. Gould IV of Stanford) to translate from Japanese into English *hanrei*/court case precedents, *hanketsu*/ legal decisions, and scholarly interpretations. They all involved Japanese labor law and trade union law. I had first been sent to Japan as a student by one of my professors, Alice H. Cook, from the School of Industrial and Labor Relations at Cornell University. For someone who is not an attorney, and never went to law school, just as important as learning labor and trade union law, was learning about practices, differences in corporate cultures, compensation, benefits, management structures etc. Indeed I studied those things and the Japanese language very intensively for many years. I also had a chance to work part-time in a number of Kokusai Roren (s)/ International Trade Union Federations, and in large Japanese companies and organizations. Next I started a Labor Consulting company in 1978. I called it TMT, and founded it on Halloween Day. Indeed, there have

been some 'tricks or treats'. We did not get into Executive Search until 1982.

380. My first book written just by me was published by JETRO (Japan External Trade Relations Organization) under the administration of 'the notorious' MITI (Ministry of International Trade and Industry). This was in 1980 when it was thought in some circles that Japan would become #1. It was about US style labor law, practices, and Employee Handbooks, which perform the function of Japanese Rules of Employment (ROE). My two *Japan Times* books were published in English. <u>Actually, they were compilations of articles that had appeared and been printed in many credible Japanese and international newspapers, magazines or university published books about Japan.</u> The material was out there to have any inaccuracies exposed to the criticism of letters to the editor etc. Yet there was no such criticism. I suppose this helped to make those books all the more credible.

381. At least to me, each of my books is very different, and I rarely present the same material in the same way. As per usual in the case of my books, this book need not be read like a novel from cover to cover. I deliberately put in a wide variety of material into this book. I realize that all readers may not be particularly interested in all the content, and the subject areas presented.

Time to Pass it on, and Pay it forward. There is so Much more that needs to be done in Japan. Our Consulting Methods and Process will also Work Better than Standard, Traditional Approaches Used in Many other Countries.

382. With this book, and at this point in my life, it is time to try and help Japanese people, companies, and hopefully even to some extent the economy. And at least where possible, to do the same for Japanese and non-Japanese companies in some other countries. I hope we can do this on a much larger scale than I and TMT have done in the past. I was a single *gaijin* labor consultant with a few support staff, (and in easier, less competitive days 15 to 20 executive search consultants). Clients come to us through mass marketing, articles, my books, advertising, and a CNN television commercial, which we ran pretty much at least once a day for many years. Also ran it on BBC at times. I came to realize that I needed to pass on what I have learned in the human resource and labor consulting area. There was never anything that unique and special about the recruiting side of the business. I got into executive search a few years after doing my specialized labor consulting. I personally was kept busy with my Labor Consulting not our recruiting. ***Now I would like to better leverage our unique consulting perspective, approaches, strategies, policies and tactics to firms much larger and stronger than mine. Yes. It is time to work toward something much bigger than myself, my little firm, and what we were able to accomplish all these years.***

383. One of the big challenges to the Japanese economy is the fear shared by so many firms concerning the risks and expenses of hiring seishain/regular employees. Because of this, too many people face a lack of job security, and low wages. This is much more than an issue of costs to the companies that use so many dispatch and term contract workers. The real, perhaps higher cost of this growing trend is not always so visible. There is the premium that is paid to temporary help dispatch companies. There is the

impractical, and less than ideal situation of hesitating to waste money on training and growing staff and managers. This is because they cannot and will not be retained because of these contract term regulations. <u>Therefore the actual savings to these firms using temporary dispatched staff cannot be that great.</u> Clearly in this less than optimum employment environment there are great wastes, great costs, and many great opportunities lost. There are the laws that require that dispatch staff can only be in their jobs for a limited number of years. They then must be replaced by another temp, go into a different job, or be replaced by a regular staff. Or they are finally given regular employment but only after such a long period of time working in that company. <u>Therefore much flexibility and efficiency is lost.</u>

384. It would be good to have great growth in the numbers and percentage of regular, non-term contract staff. However, a problem is that it can be too difficult to terminate a poor performing, troublesome employee who threatens to, or who actually goes to court. And this is one of the main reasons that so many firms are gun-shy about offering regular, full-time employment, more job security and better jobs to their employees. ***More good people should be able to get good, and higher paying jobs!*** People, who are not performing should be given other options within that firm, and probably at a lower pay level. But if they are still a problem for their employer or fellow workers, they need to take responsibility and work on themselves. They must be freed up to look for something more in line with their skills. Or they must get better at what they do. It has to be easier for their employers to help them take responsibility for their behavior, and lack of performance and contribution. They have to make sure

they get skills and can do better in their next job with a different employer, <u>or perhaps in a different more vibrant and growing industry</u>. Or such underemployed and less needed staff and managers must go off and do something entrepreneurial and enterprising for themselves, their society and economy.

385. Voluntary retirement programs, as carried out mostly at some large famous companies, are not legally required. <u>Severance packages read about in the newspapers can sometimes be very large. That is why they made it into the newspaper or media!</u> Most companies cannot afford such severance packages. Most employees cannot receive and enjoy those generous severance packages. And *kibotaishoku* voluntary retirement benefits offered to everyone definitely do result in many of the firms' best and brightest people leaving those firms. <u>If they are joining a Japanese competitor, it's not a very smart or rational way for their employer to do a staff reduction.</u> In these cases it is usually salaried inner-circle executives who design and execute rich voluntary retirement program severance packages. And all too often those good managers and skilled staffs are planning to leave with those rich severance packages! Yet less confident, less skilled staff still cling on to their jobs. Many large employers seem to be unwilling or unable to do very much to improve and ameliorate this situation. The result of strong people leaving helps competitors and also triggers a brain drain of technology, skills and products to competing companies, and to competing nations. Japanese companies like Sharp, Sony and Matsushita, and foreign companies' operations outside and inside Japan such as IBM, Kodak, and DuPont, have been greatly weakened by these practices.

386. In this small number of very large firms maybe these practices will continue. ***But it is clear that at an owner-controlled company, if the owner knew that there were much more effective and fairer approaches to restructuring that work better, the owner and shareholders would be interested***. I hope that with a strong team of collaborating companies, we can provide an important service especially at companies of 100 to a few thousand staff. Or at any other even larger owner-controlled companies. And also when other companies, private equity firms, venture capitalists, or investment banks have control of the situation, and are determined to get the best and fastest results possible.

387. In these situations, the important and key thing is that the restructuring program planners and all strong managers and staff have no chance to get a large voluntary retirement benefit. When this is the case, these same decision makers will make sure the severance packages are less rich. Valuable and limited funds should instead be made available only to the poor people that are subject to *kata-tataki*/shoulder-tapping pressure to leave the employ of the company. If the strongest staff and managers are able to leave the firm, gradually the company becomes unable to support the majority of less-confident staff and managers who cling to their jobs and their companies. We have seen this over the years in many Japanese industries, and in once great non-Japanese corporations outside Japan as well.

388. Usually, the very smallest owner-controlled companies of a very small number of staff are better at being able to dismiss or carry-out staff reductions at a more reasonable cost level. But even the smallest owner controlled firms of 10 or fewer staff have had to come to me/TMT for help.

My Dream has become a Plan and a Program. Governments are proving They Cannot Do this for us. Governments Can Also Come Up with Unrealistic and Harmful Fixes!

389. I have a dream! It has become a plan and program. It is to try and bring what I have developed to collaborative firms who will learn my and TMT's unique know-how and skills. Then with these large operations we can have a much greater and more positive impact on a much larger number of Japanese and other companies that need a new approach and more effective help. I alone with my small staff support was, of course, not able to do this. The *gaishikei*/foreign capital company market I worked was never more than 1 or 2 % of the Japanese economy. I want to work with partners that have the client relationships, established trust, and respect of hundreds if not thousands of firms where together we can make much more of a difference. <u>I want to do my best to provide training, OJT working on projects together, and passing on our methods, skills and human resource policy software products</u>. We have also been developing new training materials to better help achieve this, and pass it on to new parties.

390. It has proven difficult for enough to be done by the government and through government policies. From the time of Prime Minister Koizumi on to Mr. Abe today, efforts to have a more flexible labor market and to make it easier to dismiss employees have not been able to pass the diet. But when we think about it, these are not issues and practices involving laws and statutes, unless a maximum severance payment amount law gets passed. I wonder if such a new law would be supported in Japanese courts of

law by the Judges. <u>The termination law in Japan, Article 20 of the Labor Standards Law, makes it extremely easy to terminate staff. It can be done with just 30 days' pay or 30 days' notice, or a combination of the two, WITHOUT just cause.</u>

391. However, look at the situation we have. Most reasonable staff accept their share of responsibility, and quickly, smoothly, and at minimum cost agree to cooperate and leave their employer if that is what that company is requesting. But far too many staff and managers have been terminated many times, and used the same lawyer to become reinstated. Too many people try to enrich themselves through termination litigation using the courts, or through threat of court action. They become too much of a burden on their company and their fellow employees. This is a major reason so many companies do not want to risk hiring regular *seishain*. Instead firms want dispatched, or term contract staff. Years ago I read a study out of the USA that determined that just 3% of such troublesome staff account for 28% of personnel expenses. Japan is probably not much different.

392. There is another huge mistake the government is now making. Years ago, there was legislation proposed that if employees made over 4,000,000 yen per year, they would be exempt from overtime. Meaning not able to submit hours for overtime. This was opposed by unions, and the opposition parties and did not fly. More recently this threshold salary figure became 8,000,000 yen. Now there is a proposal that this amount be over 10,000,000 yen! I have even read about a 12,000,000 yen annual figure. <u>Prime Minister Abe, and his party would gain nothing by having such legislation passed! By reverse logic it would simply lead to demands for overtime payment</u>

from more employees paid less than those high-salary figures! *This absolutely flies in the face of any progress the ruling Liberal Democratic Party/LDP hopes to make in the area of labor flexibility, or making Japan a more competitive business environment for foreign or local Japanese investment.* I am absolutely flabbergasted at the utter stupidity of these policy makers. My apologies for the strong statement. But this is serious stuff. They are playing with fire.

393. They must live in a sheltered bubble, with no real-life experience, no clue about what happened all these years inside companies. Also no clue about the trusting relationship, and sense of fair play that the majority of senior staff, and junior staff shared amongst each other. The traditional practices of *kacho*/managers and above staff getting special allowances, and no longer getting overtime; or *gaiji*/outside activity, non-supervised sales etc. staff; or staff over a certain grade in a salary system; or announcements of "no overtime payable on Wednesdays and Friday nights"; or registerable overtime-hour limits decided by unions; or no overtime after 6pm without written signed permission in advance from bosses etc., was actually quite effective. What Prime Minister Abe's people are now proposing will turn right around and bite them in the *oshiri*. I don't want to write the "ass" word. It will greatly hurt business in general. And it will not be fair to the majority of employees who have common sense and are reasonable. Such a 10,000,000 yen rule will only make it easier for the scoundrels to continue to trouble their employers, and drag-down and demoralize their more reasonable, conscientious fellow workers. And the number of such self-indulgent loafers, trying to squeeze extra overtime money out of their companies without bringing enough value, will increase.

One Client in Particular Encouraged Me, and was a Trigger for Me to Develop Our ABCD Approach. It will Work in other Countries as Well. I'm Clonable. We Will Work at it, and Clone Even Stronger and More Effective Japanese Consultants, and Consultants Indigenous to other Countries.

394. At the beginning of my career in this field I was not much better than law firms or other consultancies that provide advice or consulting services in these areas. I, too, often merely consulted on the outside and could not and did not actually help implement the solution to employment and labor problems. Actually, one reason for triggering my change in methods was one client, a Japanese personnel manager, who asked me to rent two more floors in our building—one for a seminar room accommodating 81 people, and another floor for an outplacement/ career center with 18 cubicles, phones and PCs. This client did not want any of the staff-reduction and cost-saving work done in his own company. This Japanese personnel manager wanted my help based on my track record with him and his company over several years. Up until then I had often explained directly to groups of staff about the changes in Rules of Employment (ROE), salary, retirement benefits etc., or the need for, and details of separation packages. I already had been going out and was taking charge of a lot of union negotiations.

395. But at our own in-house TMT facilities, we further developed and perfected new methods, approaches, and communication processes. Of course, if many hundreds or thousands of staff were involved, getting everyone into a large hotel banquet facility, and

making sure everyone got the same message and Q & A process at the same time was important. To do this the same day was much more efficient and the right way to do it, rather than have the process prolonged over several days in our seminar room of limited space. *Gradually, I came to call and label these methods the ABCD approach—All-employee Behavioral Communication Dynamic. Without needing to know all but a very few details of a given country's labor, compensation and termination laws, this method, this ABCD process, can be used in any country. It results in greater fairness, and in fast, smooth and painless implementation. ABCD certainly speeds up any restructuring or changes to employees' wages, benefits and treatment.*

396. Of course that is just one part of our consulting offerings and method of intervention. Our collaborators are getting very good at ways to handle even single poor performer separations, major or minor adjustments to human resource/HR systems, union negotiations, staff reductions, and various forms of communication and participation from managers and staff. We believe that with the right team of strong collaborators, and with diligent application of new ideas, programs and methods, we can have a great impact on establishing more effective startups' Rules of Employment (ROE) or other countries similar work rules and salary system etc. We can also carry out fair and rational corporate closures. And more importantly by fixing the HR foundation, we can make sure such closures, or staff reductions do not need to take place in the future. Instead of a closure, less drastic cost reduction and restructuring is preferable.

397. With these strong collaborating Partners, we can also train-up and have large numbers of highly qualified professional consultants to meet our clients' needs. Together we can identify candidate firms that can benefit from mergers or acquisitions. We can encourage joint ventures that will work well for both firms. We can assist firms or broker joint ventures coming to Japan or going out of Japan to any other country. We can more effectively restructure businesses already inside and outside Japan. We can also help assist Japanese companies that wish they were more global, but can now gain confidence and be determined to go more global and succeed at this.

Birthrates and Populations are shrinking in Many Countries. Older or Retired People can Work longer and at Better Jobs if We Make those Jobs Available. With Good Elderly Nursing Homes, and Especially Company In-house Childcare Centers, We Can Relieve People of these Burdens and Increase the Workforce Participation Rate. Better Training and better Matching of Skills and Labor Demand is Achievable.

398. A challenge and problem for many advanced economies are shrinking and aging populations. Let us work toward ways to make better use of older, experienced workers who want to work. But they feel they have little choice but to retire do to slim chances of getting work in good fulfilling jobs. Let us free up more parents with young children, and increase the labor participation rate of mothers and fathers at home. Let us do more for parents now only able to do lower level and poorly

paid part time work. Single parents should also be able to find it easier, and less compromising to work at fulfilling careers. In Japan, child day care centers have been rejected by many neighborhoods because of the noise from children at play. With the shrinking populations, and small percentage of children in many countries, many school facilities have been closed and abandoned. Let us use these school buildings for child day care centers. Because of the internet, e-books, and ease of online purchase and delivery, many libraries in many countries have been closed. We can use these schools and these shuttered libraries for training facilities to give people the training they need for today's economy. We can reduce the wasteful miss-match of workers' abilities and the skills needed now by the corporate sector. This challenge exists in many countries, not just Japan.

399. In Japan, and probably many countries there are empty factories and buildings. Land prices are way down, especially in outlying areas. With the internet, and internet and drug addiction and abuse, and with uncertainty about the future, there are growing numbers of people suffering from depression and other mental illnesses. We need a better cross fertilization of hospitals, and protected health care environments, combined with group living, and exposure to training and work. This will get these people rehabilitated back into regular society as quickly as possible. These people can productively work and contribute. There is room for the private sector to get more involved and launch into such new growing business areas.

400. The ideal child day care center is one that is directly within company facilities. This eliminates the problem

of noise in the neighborhood. It also allows very young mothers to more quickly get back to their careers as baby nursing can take place at a workplace onsite facility. In Japan and many countries, if there was a humane restructuring of underemployed, less needed staff, if there were some fair adjustments in pay levels, and if some wasteful unneeded benefits were cut back, there would be more than enough space and budget to create and support such in-house child day care centers. As populations age, having care facilities for employees' elderly and sick parents on the premises or nearby would also be good for employers, the employees, and for overall economic growth.

401. Mothers or fathers commuting with small children to their work place childcare facility on crowded commuter trains is of course an issue. Also not being able to use baby/small child strollers on trains during peak rush hours is another issue. Perhaps if employees in this situation were able to work in an early and late shift, the working parent and child would be able to comfortably use the public transportation without inconveniencing other passengers. If their workday started at 7 am, they would be able to more easily reach by telephone their operations, counterparts, or customers in other countries that are otherwise difficult to reach during regular Japanese working hours. For example, 7 am in Japan is 5 pm in NYC, 4 pm in Chicago, 4 pm in Mexico City. This early shift could end between 3 or 4 pm in Japan. So the commute home would not be crowded. The late shift for these staff commuting with children could start at 11 am and go until 7 or 8 pm. At 8 pm it is easier to reach some locations otherwise difficult to telephone. At 8 pm in

Japan it is, 11 am in London, 9 am in Sao Paulo, and 4:30 in New Delhi. Such new and flexible approaches will be well worth the effort not only in Japan, but in other national economies as well.

The Old Testament

Aimed a Bit More at a Japanese Reading Audience, but Hopefully Interesting Enough for All. Also More Content in the Human Resource and Labor Consulting Area, and Tips Helpful for Young or Old People, or Japanese or Foreign Capital Firms 'Staying Put' in Japan, or 'Making a Move' Offshore. Something on Avoiding Real Estate Problems, Global Natural Calamities, and Ideas for Japanese and Non-Japanese to be Able to Communicate and Understand Each other Better, and Share Even More Friendly Ties.

Who is The Old Testament for?

I deliberately wrote this book for a number of different categories of readers. There are different focuses and subject areas. But aren't there different sides to all of us? We face different problems and challenges at different times. I could not cover all areas of our personal and business lives when living abroad or in Japan, so I selected some areas and focuses with new ideas and approaches. I believe much of this book's contents has never been written or talked about before.

I put in a numerically recognizable table of contents, with numbered subtitles so you can be able to easily remember your place when you read in quick spurts. No one has to read this entire book in order. Reading it in the bits and pieces that interest you under changing circumstances is probably best.

There is something for those working on your manufacturing or office site acquisition. Chapters 4 and 5 detail the horrible experience I had. I hope to save as many people as possible from such unpleasantness. It can help individuals in Japan, or those entering a new country and wanting to buy or rent real estate. I painted a picture of what a nightmare I created for myself—with some good help from uncooperative and ungrateful landlords, and a puzzling and mysterious District Court Judge. Whether you are in Japan, or whatever country you go to, or stay on to live in, do try and not fight battles where you could end up facing the whims of "justice". Empathy with the specific circumstances, understanding of the situation faced, and the appropriate justice may not be there.

In this book, I felt I could not ignore the 3/11/11 earthquake/tsunami/radiation that has impacted all of our lives, and ended the lives of people we may know. It has also robbed money from many of our pockets—a terrible encore to the Lehman shock. It has affected our and the world's outlook on nuclear energy and risks. In Chapter 8, I wanted to remind ourselves and the world that even greater, although sometimes different, natural and man-made risks exist everywhere. At least for a few more years, wherever you go, the subject of our 3/11/11 tragedy in Japan will come up. But this tragedy also needs to be put into perspective. We cannot allow that people and industry are afraid to visit, or to stay in Japan.

Chapter 3 backs up my beliefs and my hope that quickly moving too much industry out of Japan may not be necessary. Hollowing out the industrial structure of this Japan that we love is something that requires deep and careful reflection. Again patience and smaller corporate profits temporarily may be called for. There are things that we can do in Japan, to keep jobs in Japan. I did not want to write about the things that everyone writes about—lowering corporate tax rates, attracting investment and jobs with favorable industrial zones, some areas that could use deregulation, or less bureaucracy etc.

No matter what we try and accomplish in terms of personnel policies, corporate strategy, and management techniques, it all works better when we get the basics right when it comes to communicating with people. Everything has to be done through animals that walk on two legs, sometimes don't listen, and talk or scream back at us. This is what Chapters 7 and 9 are all about. We all need to improve and get better, whether it is two Japanese people trying to understand each other in Japan, or a mix of different languages and cultures anywhere.

Being able to make friends in a foreign country, especially among fellow guys, when one's local language skills are not too strong is not easy. I hope Chapter 10 gives a few helpful and rather fresh insights in this area.

Without writing a long autobiography of myself, or my life in Japan, and my interactions with Japanese people—most of them very helpful and pleasant—I also wanted to give some insight into what it can be like for a *gaijin* like me living in Japan. Yes. I am a *'gaijin'* in Japan. Perhaps more than I am seen as a USA-American. If you are Japanese, when you live in a foreign country, you may be seen more as a Japanese person than as a foreigner/*gaijin*. Does it really matter? There are growing chances people will think you are Chinese or maybe even Korean. That should not matter much either.

However, I would not hesitate to quickly but quietly and calmly point out that you are Japanese. I think in the world today, Japanese are very well thought of. Without arrogance, and as appropriate: be proud of your birthplace, your culture, your country. I am proud of my chosen home. Japan really is a wonderful place. You are lucky that especially in these recent years the world has a lot of respect, admiration, friendship and warm feelings for the Japanese people.

Only about two years ago in Istanbul, Turkey, I bought some caviar with my Asian-looking Japanese wife. The Turkish *ojisan*/man in the store on the *shotengai* narrow shopping street offered, "She must be Japanese. The Chinese stop by and just argue, haggle, and don't buy like the Japanese. I miss more Japanese!" I think he was being more than just a *gomasuri*/ flattering sales guy because we had already handed over the money for the caviar. But it is also a wonderful thing that the Chinese are doing so well these days. Mainland China had not done very well for a very long time. Let's hope we all can be as happy as possible in a peaceful and prospering world.

Stay Put? Make a Move? From Lake Waccabuc to Omotesando

The Old Testament

Contents

you by the landlord. Make sure you negotiate. Whether it is your company lease, or for your private residence

4c. You should not trust people too much, even in Japan! The worst experience of my life

4d. Sometimes we can gaman/persevere too much. We should have complained and triggered a problem with the landlord much sooner

4e. Things with our landlord started on a downward spiral

4f. We tried everything to be able to buy the building if we could not get the rent lowered

4g. With no chance to buy the building we were in for 24 years, we had no choice but to buy and get ourselves into another building as soon as possible

4h. We were ripped off by 63,000,000 yen just in electricity overcharges!—by the landlord, not TEPCO. This is illegal in most countries you might come to live

CHAPTER 5   325

The District Court Judge Ended Up Giving TMT/Me an Even More Hellish Nightmare, and Just Before Christmas on the Shortest, Darkest Day of the Year—12/21/11

5a. In real terms our damages just from the electricity overcharge during the last 7 years was greater than actual monetary damages to the landlord

5b. I learned that sometimes no matter how right you think you are, and how hard you try, you cannot succeed

5c. After many, many months in court, and about 5 months before the *hanketsu*/decision, I finally touched an issue of possible racial discrimination by the landlord

5d. The landlord started to look better to me than the judge. Could that have been the judge's plan?

5e. I tried to do my best to communicate to the judge that I was hoping for his guidance, and that I would follow that guidance

5f. It seemed the judge squeezed the pinchers on TMT/ me toward the end when I was giving up and greatly compromising

10a. Among "American" and fellow native speakers of English, there are things even we should watch out for

10b. From noodle slurping to handshakes

10c. Convenience store training manuals can affect cultural habits—at least until the manual gets changed

10d. Two very different uses for handkerchiefs—more on customs you don't need to copy

10e. Cultural reactions and treatment between men and women will naturally vary

10f. There are different advantages, but good possibilities in just about any country you go to live

10g. 'Ladies first' is still there, but is getting more complex

10h. Is giving everyone's age in brackets on Japanese television unique to Japan?

10i. Other ways for you to make friends when living abroad—guys with guys is especially difficult

10j. Being a little foolish and fun to be with helps

10k. Insight from a reunion meeting with Professor Haruo Shimada

CHAPTER 1

What Kind of a Gaijin in a Foreign Land Do You Want to Be?

I have lived, and now live, in two of the nicest places on this earth—on the shores of Lake Waccabuc, Westchester County, New York State, and Omotesando straddling Minato-ku (ward) and Shibuya-ku in Tokyo. But there are thousands of nice places in our world, and you too probably have lived or live in one of those places.

Maybe you are already working outside Japan in a foreign country. Maybe you are looking forward to living and working abroad. Maybe it is about the last thing you feel you want to do. There is that Japanese expression, "Sumeba Miyako" ("home is where you make it")—maybe, maybe not. But this is largely a state of mind, and the way you look at the opportunity. Yes, the country you are going to, and how well you will be supported there by your company, if you are going with a company, and so many other factors will affect your experience.

Japan in my life was an accident, at least in the beginning. I did not do well in H.S. French, and one reason I went to the School of Industrial and Labor Relations at Cornell U. in Ithaca, N.Y., was that I would not have to study a foreign language. I never would have guessed that I would decide to study Japanese at Cornell my senior year there. The reason was a professor at Cornell, Professor Alice H. Cook suggested I go to Japan and help her with her research. She knew that I drove from Ithaca, N.Y. to Alaska the summer after my freshman year. After her class, she asked me in the hallway if I was "Going to someplace exotic again for your summer vacation?" I answered that I had to go to Katmandu, Nepal, on a challenge from my Fraternity Club Senpai/Senior. She laughed and said, "It is a long way to go. I have an idea. Come to my office." Short story is we planned on me taking a semester off. Out of the 7 months of travel around the world, I would spend about two months in Japan doing research to write a paper for and with Professor Cook.

So I was very lucky. Her connections, mostly among labor union leaders and scholars, led to face-to-face meetings with famous labor union leaders such as Ohta Kaoru, who established Sohyo (General Council of Trade Unions of Japan—the largest trade union federation comprised mainly of government sector or more left wing unions), conceptualized the annual Shunto/spring wage struggle, and ran for mayor of Tokyo against Shunichi Suzuki. I also met Takita Minoru, who from Zensen Domei (National Federation of Textile Industry Workers Unions) founded the Domei National Center—the second largest trade union federation mostly comprised of private industry firms and more right wing. I had a long meeting with Shioji, Ichiro, head of Jidoshasoren (Confederation of Japan Automobile Workers' Union), and up from the Nissan labor union.

Later on through these and other connections, when I came back to Japan after graduation from Cornell in 1972, I worked part-time in many of these labor unions. I also got a part-time job at the NTT (Japan's telephone monopoly company at the time) union Zendentsu. Mr. Akira Yamagishi who later on would unite Rengo, was the *shokicho*/general secretary or number two at Zendentsu. Sometimes before he would take a trip abroad we would warm up his English a little bit. Mostly my jobs were translating documents, and writing or correcting English letters or papers written by others.

1a. My early lucky breaks continued, but I was working/ studying hard at the Japanese language and Japanese labor/ personnel issues, to be prepared to be able to meet these opportunities

Many of these people, and the officers and staff below them, did not speak much English. Yet they were very broad-minded and very international in their outlook. Some, of course, had excellent English. They certainly were nice to me, and helped me greatly. One of the jobs I got as an advisor—all this before starting my company TMT in 1978—was at Kokusai Kotsu Anzen Gakkai/ International Association of Traffic & Safety Science. This was a foundation set up by Mr. Honda and Mr. Fujisawa of Honda Motors. It was located in Honda's old head office in Yaesu, after the main head office had moved to Aoyama 1-chome, on the corner of Aoyama Dori. The *jimukyokucho*/general director there, Mr. Suzuki, Tatsuo, was one of the most international Japanese I have ever met. His English was not so strong, but he had interpreters all around him. We had many famous scholars from around the world come to our symposium. I translated many of the Japanese language papers into English. I also made the first English translation of *Doro Kotsu Ho* and called it *Rules of the Road.* This was one of the many *itaku*/contracted out projects we received from *Keishicho*/National Police Agency, and *Sorifu*/the Prime Minister's Office. I was indeed lucky. The *jimukyokucho*, Suzuki-san, suggested I start my labor consulting company. He said, "All this transportation, and human/car traffic movement, behavior and psychology is not really your specialty. You are young, but you should focus on what you really know and love." So at least for a year or so, I was able to have a *renraku jimusho*/liaison office of my labor consulting TMT at this Honda Kokusai Kotsu Anzen Gakkai office. I was able to stay on a bit longer as an Advisor there.

I wonder how important the quality of life is when you start out in a foreign country. My next-door neighbor now lives in a beautiful house in Omotesando. He started out in the restaurant business in Stockholm washing dishes. Now he owns about 70 restaurants, many of them very famous. If you live in Japan, you would know, and have probably often dined in many of them. A few of them are in foreign countries. It is helpful that his English is so good. My first 3 years in Japan, my apartment was a 6-tatami mat room with a 2-mat size single burner kitchen. There was a squat toilet and no bath. I went to the *sento*/public bath in Minami Asagaya on Omekaido just across from the entranceway to Pearl Center. I was happy, and it was a good way to learn Japanese, and learn about the 'real Japan'. I think many of my friends who spoke no English were especially international, because they were willing to spend time with me, even though they were not practicing their English on me. A couple of the policemen at the *koban*/ police box on Omekaido across from Pearl Center got a kick out of speaking with me. They had me sit in the koban and talk to them quite a lot. People in the neighborhood must have thought, *my that young Gaijin gets in trouble a lot!* These friends just treated me pretty much like a regular Japanese guy. (Although sitting and chatting in a *koban* was a bit unique.) They never asked me if I could use chopsticks. They did not tell me my Japanese was 'jozu desu ne' (good). If anything they told me I was still terrible. They had fun teaching me all the bad and dirty words. (Not the police officers.)

1b. I first arrived in Japan the month before Yukio Mishima committed suicide

Before I found that first apartment in Narita Higashi off Omekaido, I lived in Seijo Gakuenmae with a family where everyone had lived abroad, worked at foreign embassies, or taught at universities. They were also incredibly international, speaking with me as much as possible in Japanese, and teaching me so much. I remember my first autumn in Japan was also the autumn of Mishima, Yukio's life—the time when he committed suicide at the Jieitai (Self Defense Force) headquarters in Ichigaya. That deeply affected my Seijo friend, and I remember he shed a tear when he tried to describe what Mishima's life work had meant to him.

I think as you go out and live in a foreign country, you will also most appreciate the people who speak no Japanese. Perhaps know or care little about Japan. But they still care about you. They want to be your friend. Especially in Tokyo, there are many Japanese who speak good English. Sometimes when they see a foreigner, they react by speaking English, or asking him/her if she can use chopsticks. More in the 'old days', when I first arrived, they might mention 'Osaka', and ask me if I know where it is. If anything in some foreign countries, I know in the USA, they expect everyone around the world to know a lot about the USA. I don't know which approach is better! It is just the way it is.

I think it was 1979, when I was chosen from the American Chamber of Commerce (ACCJ) in Japan to represent the ACCJ in joining a JETRO, US Embassy, and USA Dept. of Commerce sponsored investment mission to the USA. I believe there were 52 Japanese presidents branching off and visiting 19 states or USA cities in 16 days. Anyway, some crazy schedules like that. I remember sitting at or near the head table with the various city mayors, Ed Koch of NYC, Jane Byrne of Chicago, Tom Bradley of Los Angeles. There were also several state governors. I noticed there were quite a few Japanese Japan-born consultants living in the USA, and there to help the Japanese with their investments. I suppose that is what I have been doing for the foreign capitalized companies here in Japan. I wish the reception I got here in Japan from some of the Japanese executives at these foreign companies was a little bit more open to the help I bring. But their resistance to a knowledgeable outsider who has some new and different ideas is also very understandable. One Japanese president was honest enough to tell his USA boss who was based in Singapore that, "I don't want this Nevins involved, because you will believe him more than me." Some of the Japanese executives, once they get used to the idea of working with me, and once they see the great results we can win together, become strong allies and good friends. Certainly in the recruiting/executive search area, there is less resistance and they welcome our effective approach toward introducing good people who really make a difference and greatly help them achieve the results they need to achieve.

1c. Hopefully you will meet some local people in a foreign country who will be a big help to you

So probably like me, when you are stationed in a foreign country, you will also continue to deal with both fellow Japanese in that country and with the local "foreigners". I remember that Mr. Shinsaku Sogo, who was the son of the father of the *shinkansen*, Mr. Shinji Sogo, was very international.

His English was excellent. He was the head of JETRO (except for the MITI *Kacho*/Section Chief always above the head of JETRO!). Sogo-san always spoke to me in Japanese. I guess he remembered that from when he lived in New York. He was determined to have the Japanese community mingle more with the local New York businessmen/women. Mr. Sogo enjoyed being immersed in that English speaking, USA world. He thought foreigners like me should be treated the same way, speaking Japanese since they were in Japan. He was an incredible man, who was instrumental in getting my 1980 book published by JETRO.

You will have many amazing experiences living in a foreign country. Especially if you have a forward-looking attitude, wear a big smile, and are friendly. It does not matter if you make mistakes with your English (or Japanese if you are a *gaijin*), or the other foreign language being used around you. I still make mistakes with my Japanese. I think people in some foreign countries will correct your use of their local language more than the Japanese tend to correct foreigners' Japanese. But I am not so sure about that... If you ask for people to correct your mistakes, it is more likely they will.

1d. I did Tora-san aisatsu, and then sang, "Otoko wa Tsurai Yo," to Atsumi Kiyoshi at Haneda Airport—chotto hen na gaijin deshoo?! (pretty weird gaijin. Right?)

Japan was especially interesting for foreigners like me, and especially in the 'old days' before many foreigners spoke good Japanese. When I was at Haneda airport sending home my visiting parents before there was a Narita airport, I saw Atsumi Kiyoshi with a large group of his tsukibito supporters. I went up to him and gave him the, *"Watakushi umare mo sodachi mo Katsushika…"* ("I was born and raised in Katsushika-ku") The whole thing—I had just memorized it. Then I sang, *"Ore ga itanja, oyome nya ikenu…"* (Check-out the song on the web or rent or download a movie!) The whole thing memorized from the movies and the radio. They all stood up and applauded. That was fun. My parents stood by and watched in confused amazement. But my dad also shook hands with Tora-san. I don't suggest that you go up to Tony Bennett if you see him at an airport, and sing, "I left my heart in San Francisco" even if it is San Francisco airport. So there are some differences between you being a foreigner in a foreign country, and us being foreigners in Japan. This is especially true in the "old days", before all the Australians, Asians and others studied and learned Japanese so well even from the junior high and high school grade level.

As for discrimination, sure we both will sense it in different ways. Did you imagine this? I can speak in Japanese on the phone and people often assume I am Japanese. But if they see me when I ask a question with a Japanese-looking person standing next to me, 85%, maybe 95% of the time the Japanese will only look at, and give the answer to the Japanese looking person standing next to me? But we just have to get used to that.

I remember a Japanese president that we placed into a foreign company here in Japan was complaining that when he flies with United Airlines, or anyway many such foreign airlines, he does not get treated the same as the non-Japanese executives. I told him a true story. I recall a time when a client flew me first class on JAL to Los Angeles for a consulting project there. There was only myself, and a non-famous Japanese face in the first class cabin with me. (I also confirmed later on with one of the flight attendants, that that Japanese gentleman was not famous. She did not know his name from the media.) During the flight, and within about an hour, one of the flight attendants spilled orange juice on me. She was the only flight attendant who helped clean it up. No other cabin crew came over and apologized. But later on when the same orange juice was spilled on the Japanese passenger, about seven cabin crew including the male chief purser came over to that passenger and profusely apologized.

1e. So let's not take the discrimination we feel we receive too seriously. It is atarimae/*comes with the turf of living in a foreign country*

If we are going to be *chuzaiin* with a company behind us and supporting us, or regardless of what capacity, and in what level we live in a foreign country, we cannot be worried about things such as the above. My Japanese wife also tells me that when she lived in foreign countries, even in the USA, which is supposed to be a melting pot, her treatment at cash registers in retail establishments, or wherever, was a bit different than that she perceived other mainstream, non-foreign Americans were getting. We also decided we are stared at a bit more, and stand out a bit more in certain other foreign countries in Europe, and central Asia. She probably notices such different treatment more than I do when we are outside Japan. I am probably more sensitive to different treatment within Japan.

But none of this is very important. The advantages, challenges, stimulus, and things we learn, and fun we can experience in foreign countries should and will far outweigh such issues.

CHAPTER 2

More about Me and Why this Book

The first book I wrote with a collaborator was called *Passport to Japan* (BII 1978). It was aimed at helping foreign businessmen understand Japan. I came up with the cover idea. I got the idea to put them in boxes standing near the cash registers of Japan hotel lobbies and the hotel bookstores. In those days it sold especially well off the Hotel Okura Honkan tobacco/newspaper/candy counter near the exit. It had a gold chrysanthemum on a black background cover, the size of, and looking quite a bit like a Japanese passport. The second book I wrote was published by JETRO in 1980. It was titled *The Complete Handbook of U.S. Personnel and Labor Relations Practices for Japanese Corporations*. Some of the older of you may remember that iconic Japanese red sun in the middle of the red white and blue American flag. The famous and greatly influential Professor Shimada, Haruo of Keio University...and now president of Chiba University of Commerce agreed to be the kanshu (advisor and supervisor of the translation) for the book. It was toward the start of the great "Japan as No. 1" industrial juggernaut during Japan's first big expansion abroad. I tried to do my part, and help the Japanese successfully invest abroad. But I had decided to base myself in Japan. I would instead help the foreign management better manage their Japanese staff. Many gaijin bosses in Japan bought my *Japan Times* books, *Labor Pains and the Gaijin Boss* (1984), and *Taking Charge in Japan* (1990).

In 2012 and 2013, even after the great earthquake and tsunami, for reasons that surprised us, the yen was strong. So strong, that it was driving manufacturing operations away from Japan. So if you are reading this book, or if your company bought copies and gave it to you, chances are you headed out to do your part to be a *Nihonjin Gaijin Chuzaiin* or staff or maybe a boss somewhere. Maybe you are a young or older person, who had some strong yen to cash out. You want to buy into and make a move to a new adventure and a new life in a new country. Then in 2014 and 2015 the yen got weaker than it had been in years. Good reasons for manufacturing and you to come back to Japan!

2a. People are basically the same. You can make them angry. You can make them laugh

It really does not matter so much where you go, because wherever you go you have to deal with people. People and human nature are pretty much the same everywhere. You can make people angry, or you can make them laugh. You can teach them. You can be taught. Listening is always more important than talking. Yes. Communication is the key. Probably 70% of communications is non-verbal. Even if that number is 50%, you can still do a lot whether your foreign language skills are excellent, or laughable. Having a sense of humor, and getting people to laugh is important. If you can do that just by speaking their local language, you don't even have to learn any jokes ☺.

As can be seen from my books, and on our website (www.tmt-aba.com), since 1978 TMT in Tokyo has done big important work for hundreds of foreign capitalized companies in Japan.

Sometimes this has been for their joint ventures with Japanese companies here in Japan. There is a bit of "Japan-passing" now by foreign capital companies. There is the earthquake scare, Fukushima radiation, and an overall feeling that there is not much growth in the Japanese economy. This has resulted in some Asia Pacific regional offices moving to Hong Kong, Singapore, and other places. There appear to be not as many *gaijin*/expats in Japan as their used to be. Together with TMT's vice president of Business Development we got the idea of turning the clock back to the 1980 JETRO book. We decided to write something to help the Japanese executives and staff forced to ride the endaka/strong yen tsunami to distant shores outside Japan. Then before you know it is enyasu/weak yen times again!

I have written some very long books. In 2004 we published a 620-page book titled *Japan True or False—People Problems, Costs, Restructuring.* Parts of this book were translated into Japanese. One section of 63 True or False questions became a booklet titled *Gaijin Boss's Power Pill*, revised and updated in 2010, and then further revised and reprinted in 2011. The point of these questions is to go up against and refute some of the stereotypes and mistaken interpretations of what can and cannot be done in Japan. Many of the great, effective consulting projects we carried out at foreign capitalized firms in Japan might have been interpreted by some *gaijin* and Japanese executives, the personnel managers, and outside attorneys, to be impossible to achieve such great results so quickly—quickly and with so little pain on the part of the employees. Yet through good strategy, fair severances packages, tactics, and most of all communications, difficult staff reductions, or cost saving programs became possible. They were executed very smoothly. The staffs remaining in the company were happy and motivated.

2b. Approaches and methods that worked for us here in Japan, can work for Japanese staff or anyone working with and managing local people in foreign countries

When it comes down to execution, the ABCD—All Employee Behavioral Communication Dynamic — I have developed with clients has been helpful in gaining fast and smooth results. The concepts, dynamic, and methods will work in any country and in any language. I am hoping that Japanese or any executives having to get good results in managing people and labor problems in foreign countries will be able to make use of these approaches. And/or have their local non-Japanese managers read the English version and together use these methods.

In Japan there are parties that believe that staff reductions must be done, or should be done on a voluntary *kibotaishoku* basis, where even a firm's best and most needed people can resign and get an extra severance package. Yet, obviously the owner of a sushi shop, or even the owner of a medium-size company of a couple hundred staff, would not be so unwise to let his best managers and staffs resign and get some extra severance on the way out. Instead the effort would be to gracefully have the least productive, or least cooperative staff leave the firm. At the same time a smart owner of a medium or smaller company, or dedicated and determined top executives of a large corporation would want to keep all of their strongest and most needed human resources. But they have to believe that that can be done. They have to learn how they can do it.

WARNING: There may be local executives, staff, and perhaps attorneys in the foreign country where you are working who will tell you that some of the things you want to do are impossible or will not work. Frankly, in Japan, I have often run into this kind of resistance, from Japanese executives here in Japan, and from the company's legal advisors. Among the bilingual Japanese working at *gaishikei*/foreign capitalized firms in Japan, there are quite a few who are confident they can find another job. They may want to have a voluntary staff reduction, where they can get an extra severance package, and go out and find another position. Fair enough. If you are, or when you were an executive working at a large Japanese employer, maybe you would also want to raise your hand for a voluntary retirement benefit if you could get it. Fair enough. You had the courage to leave while others needed to cling on to the company, due to their lack of confidence, or refusal to cooperate and retire from the company.

2c. What do you do when you are part of a team entrusted to get the best results for your company and your colleagues?

But now that you are the boss or a key player at your Japanese or company of any country in a foreign land, or in your own country, the shoe is on the other foot. Like the expat *gaijin* bosses who have been my clients in Japan, if you possibly could, you would rather not incentivize your stronger needed locally employed executives and staff to leave your firm as part of a kibotaishoku/voluntary staff reduction. As an expat, *nihonjin gaijin* staff or boss outside Japan in a foreign country, you know that you are on a different career path. You belong to the head office, and will/would go back to Japan, or to another country. Even if you wanted it, you are not part of a local employee staff reduction. You cannot get the extra severance package.

So this book, and TMT developed human resource consulting methods are your ally. This book, these concepts and tactics can help you get started in the right direction toward needed changes. In Japan, at Japanese companies, when reaching certain age levels, or if the company has financial difficulties, salary levels are reduced quite often. It is said by many Japanese personnel managers and attorneys that 'you can't reduce people's pay unless they agree'. With the proper tactics, and communications, such stereotype sound bites become almost meaningless. You will hear much about what you can do, or can't do. "We don't do that in Thailand." "That is not the way we do things here in China." Fair enough. Natural enough. How many times have Japanese executives and staff said that to their *gaijin* bosses in Japan? Yet like the challenge you face, or may face, things need to get done—sometimes difficult, unpleasant things that have a negative impact on people and their livelihoods. This book, our consulting approaches, are based on over 30 years of experience in Japan of me being on the front lines, getting difficult things done with clients. It can help you. We focus on getting them done most effectively, while keeping your operation strong. The result is your surviving local employees are happier and more motivated than they could ever be after a voluntary *kibotaishoku* staff reduction.

Unlike my 1980 JETRO book that was focused only on the USA, the discoveries and experience you will gain from this book, with our follow up consulting advice, will work in any country. People are people the world over. There are poor ways, good ways, and great ways to communicate and accomplish goals. There will always be differences in some specifics of local labor standards, practices, statutes, and case law. An expert on your staff will know those things. You can quickly get a grasp of that. In any country, and generally more so than in Japan, you will have to be careful about sexual harassment, and age, gender, race, or religious discrimination. Japan's approach to age discrimination, with age discrimination not being such a problem, is one outstanding difference. For example, in Japan, it is common to target a staff reduction or a pay reduction at staff over a certain age, and/or over a certain number of years of seniority. Most countries are more sensitive about that. It is often clearly illegal. Even in Japan, age discrimination at time of hiring has become a bit more problematic. But most countries are probably tougher on an employer for any kind of age discrimination than is the case in Japan. Another area that would be illegal in most countries is the rather common traditional practice in Japan that often includes pay scales that actually go up, then stay level, and then often taper down depending on one's age.

2d. Age and sex discrimination are two traps
that deserve special caution

In many foreign countries outside Japan, age discrimination especially kicks in if a younger person replaces an older person. Race or gender discrimination cases basically get started if one race, gender or perhaps religion is replaced by another. You must also be more careful with promotions and pay levels. Often you will get in trouble if women are not paid the same or promoted the same as men. *Ippan shoku* (lower level, non-transferable staff level) and *Sogo shoku* (higher level staff expected to change jobs and locations) distinction will not get you as far in most foreign countries. Clearly Japanese practice of different pay based on educational level and schooling degree is also an area where Japanese managers must exercise more caution. Some extra care in these areas in required. Other than this there are many universal factors in running a business, and also in interfacing and managing people. Never leave your instincts, or your common sense at home. Common sense about how something needs to be done is usually more important than concern for the possibility that some remote law might cause you problems later on.

Even if you disagree, and if you think Japan can't possibly be like that, or that something we are accomplishing with our consulting methods could never be done in Japan, the lesson is that it did work well for us in Japan. These were the ways I brought the most effective success, and in the fastest manner for a client who believes in me, himself and these methods.

So what does that tell you about the local staff, experts, and attorneys in the country outside Japan where you work or where you are headed? The point is they may tell you many things. You may be told by locals in the foreign country you were transferred to that certain things cannot be done, for X reason, or because this is Vietnam, Thailand, China, or New Zealand, or Brazil, or the USA or France. You will probably be given confusing guidance. Often using your common sense, intuition, and setting about doing the thing that will bring you the results you are after is the best way to proceed.

2e. You will have the difficult choice of figuring out who and what to believe

So the key is to not blindly believe everything you hear, read, or are told. And that includes this book of mine. I can tell you that our beliefs and methods have worked for TMT and our clients. My personal involvement and efforts may have had some influence on the success. I suppose I could be of use in some countries where English or Japanese (less likely) is a dominant language among the workforce. But I am best at doing these things in

Japan. There are 87 detailed case studies, and testimonial letters actually appearing with the individual client company executive's signature in those various *Japan Times* and other books. (They appear on our website www.tmt-aba.com without the signatures, to keep those signatures out of cyberspace.)

Now you will be a junior staff on up to a senior executive at your Japanese or at any company's operation in a foreign land. If there is a need for a staff reduction, as an expat staff on a different career path, you will have no option to take a voluntary retirement package if one is offered. You have the same challenge as my *gaishikei* head office and *gaijin* expat boss has in Japan. Do I want to do the staff reduction the way some local staff and executives want me to do it—probably on a *kibotaishoku*/voluntary basis? **_Or do I want to use a method that will allow me to keep all my strongest human resources, and at the same time allow me to smoothly remove the least effective and most troublesome staff and managers that work here?_**

I have had local Japanese staff and executives fight hard against TMT's consulting methods. You may or may not face the same dynamic in the foreign country you are assigned to outside Japan. Who are you going to believe? What should you do? How should you handle the project and meet the challenge?

But first, let's confirm that it really is necessary to close a Japanese plant, and replace it with one in a foreign country. If at all possible, let us strive to avoid that. Let us continue to provide as many good, higher paying manufacturing jobs to our fellow Japanese citizens as possible, even if that temporarily reduces corporate profits. Let us hold on to and keep in Japan as much technology and sophisticated manufacturing processes as we possibly can.

CHAPTER 3

A few Reasons to Keep as Many Plants, Operations, and as much Employment in Japan as Possible

Most importantly we don't want a hollowing out of Japanese industry. We should have as many higher paying manufacturing jobs as possible in Japan. If anything, with the deflation we have been having for years, wages and salaries have been going down in Japan. Salaries, and industrial strife and strikes have rapidly gone up in many countries. Japan used to think it was advantageous to invest in these countries. In recent years, foreign companies, and especially the rather prevalent Japanese investments in China, were targeted more by radical union action than the indigenous public and even private Chinese firms. There was that crippling flood in Thailand in later 2011. There are also growing labor shortages and difficulties in hiring skilled labor in many countries from China to Vietnam. Yet there is surplus labor, and unemployment, underutilized labor and women in Japan. It is also easier for Japanese to train fellow Japanese. It is a smarter and wise policy for the Japanese people and for Japan to build up the skills of Japanese people, rather than the skills of foreigners living outside Japan. Foreigners outside Japan will merely end up competing against us. Let's keep Japan as strong and prosperous as we can!

In Europe, and in many highly industrialized Western first-world countries, there are many family-owned and other companies. They have found that with technical innovation and automation they can continue to successfully manufacture and profitably operate even in Europe, Canada, Australia, and the USA. Yes, their profits may be somewhat less than they could be if they moved more manufacturing operations to low-wage countries. These privately owned family companies may like to keep their operations nearby. They may not want to travel long distances to overseas foreign operations that will be more complex and may be located in unpredictable environments. Just like in Japan, many companies in Europe and around the industrialized world feel committed to the employees and people in their towns and regions. Call it regionalism, national pride or even patriotism if you will. But don't we all want to live in prosperous and pleasant cities and towns, with happy, prosperous, and healthy people around us? There are a lot of smart privately held business owners who realize being reasonably profitable and in control of one's life, destiny and business, is more important than being the biggest most profitable player in the industry with the largest market share.

3a. In foreign countries, things and the future can be even more unpredictable than they are in Japan

Moving operations abroad where there are unknowns in terms of local laws, social stability, corruption, kick-backs, higher crime, kidnapping and ransoming of executives, more risk from extreme weather, power failures, flooding, drought, less protection of patents and proprietary technologies are indeed factors to carefully consider. Governments can rapidly change, with the ruling, political, social fabric, and local economy rapidly deteriorating. Certainly this was seen with the Arab spring throughout the Middle East beginning in 2011.

Yes. The yen was strong but now weaker. But the history of the yen since 1971 always shows that it will soon get weak as it did in 2014 and 2015. It will get stronger again. Perhaps, just after all your hard work in learning about a new country, or region abroad. A lot of the money and time you invested in that country can be wasted. The yen will, and pretty much has, weakened to levels that make all your effort in moving your factory or operation out of Japan unnecessary. It is true. In surveys today, a vast majority of Japanese companies answer that they are considering, or are moving in the direction of investing more and moving more operations abroad. Does that mean that we should join that trend with a group-think knee-jerk reaction?

Instead of rushing to move an operation abroad, it might be better to get our employees in Japan to make a few more hopefully temporary concessions in terms of accepting lower bonuses, or taking no pay increases. Hopefully, only in the short term, it could be better to reduce a selected number, if not all employees pay and benefits level. Labor unions in Japan have traditionally been quite cooperative in helping their companies in these areas. However, Rengo, the United Labor Union Center, and some political factions, and the judicial process in Japan have continued to be making a tragic mistake. These parties should not be making it so difficult for companies to lay-off, or to de-hire certain employees. The Labor Standards Office is never the problem. As long as the company pays at least the minimum wage, gives at least the 30 days' notice, or 30 days' pay to terminate someone, and pays out any retirement benefit that may be in the Rules of Employment, the Labor Standards Office will not interfere. What can often happen in courts and with non-labor specialist judges becomes the problems.

In some countries there are moderate, and fair fixed severance laws. In Japan it seems like the aggressive, non-compromising party wins. That is often the employee rather than the company. When a terminated employee demands a huge severance from a company, few judges control those employees and restrain those demands with the required authority and decisiveness. Although the judge hesitates, and really cannot write a decision demanding a company to pay a huge severance package, the judge often places too much pressure on the employer. The judge threatens to rule that the termination is an abuse of the employer's right of dismissal. That would mean the employee can come back to his/her job. Is the judge really even qualified to make such a decision, and to so interfere with a company's management? Let the judge take on the troublesome, incompetent, or employee of poor attitude, as that judge's assistant or colleague! Then the judge will get a taste of the real world, where we all have to work and live.

Of course, employees should not be easily terminated for unfair reasons. But usually if an employer is taking action against a given employee, there are reasons for that. That company is not trying to push out the other employees who are doing a good job, are cooperative, and have a good helpful positive attitude etc. So there is a need for a more effective termination law and a more effective labor tribunal where the case cannot be appealable to the non-specialist regular district court case proceeding.

A big reason there are so many term contract and dispatch employees in Japan is that so many companies have suffered with the difficulties of taking required disciplinary, job adjustment, or termination action against regular employee/ seishain. So if this practice of making terminations so difficult continues, Rengo and other union and political factions wanting to keep it difficult to fire staff are really shooting themselves in the foot. They are hurting their own cause. They are depriving Japanese workers of getting good jobs as regular employees. The stories of labor nightmares and difficulties of managing and terminating Japanese staff will also discourage non-Japanese foreign capitalized firms from investing in Japan. Rengo and such political thinking, and judicial process are making it more likely that more employers will hire more term contract and dispatch workers.

3c. Approaches to firing, and term contract time limits in Japan make impossible the flexibility, and more rational approaches that are needed

For example, law/practice that a dispatch worker (and often a term contract direct hire) employee, must/should become a regular/*seishain* employee after working only 3 years is also not very rational or helpful for that worker who must be let go because the term limit is reached. It is also not helpful for the company. Of course if there was more flexibility with the hiring and termination of regular/*seishain* non-contract employees, this would be much less of a problem. It is more likely the worker would be taken on as a regular/*seishain* employee. Yes. There might be an additional burden from the employee's newly acquired benefits as a *seishain*. But can these benefits be too much?

Cutting back some less rational, not legally required, extra benefits would also make it more attractive and possible for factories and operations to stay in Japan instead of moving to what are anyway now perceived to be lower wage countries. For example, paying such high commutation allowances to only certain staff, sometimes up to as high as 100,000 yen/$1,000 or more per month, is expensive, and not fair to staff living closer to the company. Instead companies could implement a maximum cap on this commutation allowance. Offering paid menstrual leave when only a small minority of women take advantage of this, is also not fair to the vast majority of other women who are stuck with the extra workload caused by those less dedicated women taking paid menstrual leave.

Paying 100% of salary repeatedly to a handful of staff who too often claim to be sick, also should be looked at—*kokoro no byoki*! (sickness of the heart)! Hah! Stressed from "power harassment"—hah! Sometimes there are genuine and unfortunate cases. But maybe, too often, some staff are a bit lazy and too unwilling to accept responsibility for themselves, and their own weaknesses. Instead they may be too willing to take advantage of an over generous system of long term disability leave. The time cycle of getting this benefit could be looked at—the between-benefit cycles greatly lengthened. The company could also get the 66% subsidy from the Social Insurance Office, instead of paying the whole amount to the employee. (If the company writes in the Rules of Employment, that the company will pay something, that amount is deducted from the 66%, which comes from the Social Insurances.) Probation periods could be lengthened from the typical 3 months. Staff could initially be hired on 6-month and then one-year term contracts, following the temp to perm (permanent employee) pattern. These ways employers would have less risk, and more of a chance to really test the skills, and get to know a newly joining employee.

3d. There are other benefits that could be cut back for the sake of fairness among employees. This could make it more possible to continue to manufacture more profitably in Japan

With 16 public holidays, Japan has more national holidays than just about any country in the world. It is true that many Japanese only take about half of their individual paid vacation entitlement. However, the acceleration of paid vacation—10 days/two weeks after just 6 months, and then 11 days, 12 days, 14 days, and reaching 20 days or 4 weeks' vacation in just 6 years of service is actually a faster acceleration than most countries in the world. Combined with the extra New Year's holidays, sometimes Golden Week holidays, and Obon holidays, Japan actually has more holidays than most countries. Japanese people and even the Japanese government officials don't seem to be aware of this. The problem with personal vacation benefits that are too rich is that only a minority of employees take all of their vacation. The employees that hesitate to do that because of heavy workloads have often told me they feel it is unfair. They are dissatisfied with this situation. You will not find as many extra New Year's, Golden Week, and Obon holidays in most foreign companies. Still these extra holidays in foreign companies as well might vary between 9 to 16 days. So it is a total of 25 to 32 of mostly working days of holiday—before paid personal vacation is even used.

Some of these reasons may seem like reasons not to be operating in Japan. But rest assured, other countries have their own labor management difficulties, including too much regulation and bureaucratic reporting. There are other costly, unnecessary benefits, and difficulties with age, sex, racial, and ethnic discrimination. And it is a lot easier to make changes and adjustments in Japan. Japan is the country a Japanese person really knows. It is easier in Japan than in a foreign land to try and get things strategically sensible and right, with employees you don't really understand. And maybe the local non-Japanese employees do not want to make much of an effort to understand their Japanese (or other foreign) bosses or colleagues. Instead it is easier for them to blame things on the "inscrutable, mysterious, strange, and unique Japanese".

From an employer's point of view there are also many advantages to managing labor in Japan. There are practices that allow a company more flexibility to manage labor than is possible in many other countries. For example, in Japan, based on reaching certain ages, it is possible to easily change employee's jobs, and adjust their pay down. In Japan, unlike in most countries, it is possible to carry out staff reductions of employees that reach certain ages or years of seniority without the fear of an age discrimination law suit. On the seniority issue, however, when it comes to wage and salary payment in Japan, probably the practice of increasing wages based on age or seniority should become less prevalent. Or at least the incremental increases should become much smaller.

3e. Japan's system of overtime payment is quite unique and strange when looked at by many foreigners

There are a number of other areas where Japan should be more rational. This would make it easier for Japanese companies to stay in Japan, and keep Japanese employees gainfully employed.

In most foreign countries, if employees went to the university, and if they do white-collar office work, even from directly after school graduation, there is no overtime. These employees are not able to charge, or to be paid overtime allowances—even if they work very late. They are considered to be "exempt" from overtime. Overtime is more strictly used mostly when a production line is moving, and a worker obviously must move along with the assembly line. Or overtime would be payable with certain workers serving customers on a shift, in line with the opening and closing hours of the retail establishment.

But overtime is not payable to most other categories of workers, no matter how many hours they work in the office. They are considered to be discretionary labor, just like software engineers, researchers, salesmen, almost all higher educated office workers, where efficiencies and speed in doing ones work greatly varies. Also everyone knows that many people inefficiently engage in their work, the internet (including their internet shopping and vacation planning), conversations, or daydreaming during office working hours. The Japanese have an idea that there is something wrong with "*Service Zangyo*" (overtime). There are occasional surprise inspections by the Japanese Labor Standards Office (LSO). The LSO position, that the log-in and log-out times of an employee's PC, have anything to do with the calculation of his overtime hours, and his pay is just ludicrous.

I have been called in several times by clients facing the threat of having to pay even tens if not hundreds of millions of yen, or several *oku* yen (millions of dollars) in "unpaid overtime". I will visit the Labor Standards Office, pointing out the civil servants in the Labor Standards Office talking about non-work related matters. I will show that there are non-work-related PC screens. There is someone reading a newspaper, or someone sleeping on his/her arms at his/her desk. These civil servants are not particularly lazy, but virtually no employees work at full efficiency all day long. Pointing out the realities of any work environment, helps the bureaucrats get the message and is one tactic, among many more messages and policies, that helps get them to be more understanding and to be more flexible. I have saved my clients even hundreds of millions of yen in such unpaid back-calculated overtime. Japan is not a strange country because *"Service Zangyo"*/voluntarily overtime work exists. It is a strange country because this expression in its usual context exists.

It is also true that the Japanese have a tendency to want to stay in the office more than people in most countries. But one reason for this was that until they became *kacho* (section chief), and got a special *kacho*/management allowance, they were often paid for that time when they were hanging around the office. There have always been people who do not work efficiently all day, and instead look forward to inflating their pay check with overtime. And this is often welcomed by their wives, or husbands. There are, of course, many employees who go out of their way to work fast and efficiently, and try to save their company's overtime money. These conscientious staffs are deeply distressed and unhappy seeing some of their colleagues deliberately trying to earn extra overtime pay. This strange practice of overtime being payable to higher level white-collar employees will not exist in most countries you might be transferred to.

CHAPTER 4

Some Thoughts on Real Estate—whether to Lease Land and a Building, or to Buy Them. Toward You or Your Company Avoiding the Nightmarish Worst, Most Unfair, Discriminatory Experience I have had during these 43 Years in Japan

(I wrote Chapters 4 and 5 immediately after learning of the shocking court case decision of 12/21/2011. I wanted to turn this experience into a positive direction by making sure readers would not suffer a similar fate.)

This is one of the early decisions that you and your company have to make when you go invest in a foreign country. If you have decided to go off to a foreign country pretty much on your own, for your own reasons, the way I settled in Japan, I would also recommend that you buy a condo or a house, rather than rent. With the current low prices in many countries, you probably cannot go too wrong. In the case of my company in Japan, the cost of rent was our second largest cost after the payroll and incentives we paid our people for quite a few years. This may not be the case of a manufacturing factory with material costs, or a restaurant with food/beverage costs, but for many businesses it may be the case. You are better off buying the land for a factory, or for your campus-style office in the suburbs or country, or even a building in the middle of a city or town. You will have a lot more control over the property, how you design it, build it, maintain it, and how it looks. Do you remember the Nakatomi Plaza building, supposedly in Los Angeles in the first *Diehard* movie with Bruce Willis? Do you remember how there were waterfalls, ponds, and beautiful Japanese gardens, scenery, and design that matched the Samurai statues and other artwork etc.? This was on a top floor of the skyscraper building. If Nakatomi was renting, can you imagine what the *genjokaifuku*/restoration costs would be to restore those premises to its previous state!?

On a much smaller scale as well, or if you want to have something like a nice Japanese garden for you, your customers and employees to enjoy, things are much less complicated if you own the land or building. Land prices are going down even in China. If you are going to rent, take a more careful look at your rental agreement than I ever did in Japan. Especially in these times, when the market is favorable to the renting tenant, it should be possible to make sure the rental agreement gives you 'first right of refusal'. This will give you an opportunity to hear in advance of any sale of the property. First right of refusal means that you are always informed if a building or land is going to be sold. This way the building cannot be secretly sold, even though, for example you have been paying rent on a majority of the building for years, and remain very committed to the land, location, or building.

4a. Make sure you have a 'first right of refusal' clause

First right of refusal is very common in many countries. And it probably should become more common in Japan. The seller has to be able to prove that the property was sold for more than you, the major long-term tenant, would have been willing to offer. But before that you must be given a chance to make that offer. Sometimes, the offer you make can be a certain percentage below the other higher offer, or a designated percentage less than the estimated market price. These matters should be detailed in the rental agreement.

In some countries, it is also possible that a small percentage of the rent you pay can be used to reduce your purchase price of the property, should you decide to buy the property in the future. This "rent to own" or "rental purchase" practice began in the 1930s in the UK and Europe. It reached the USA. and many other countries by the 50 and 60s. This clause should also be in the property rental or lease agreement. I am certainly no expert on real estate. But I am sure that even in Japan, if you insisted in having first right of refusal in your rental agreement, and if the landlord/building owner accepted this, it would legally mean something. It would give you more of a fair chance to know about, and to bid on the property. Nowadays, especially for small buildings, perhaps for even some larger buildings, and for leasing land, it is very much a tenant-favorable market in Japan. So the owner of the property might be willing to have a first right of refusal in the rental agreement. If the property owner does not agree, you keep searching for another property until the owner of that property does agree.

Actually, first right of refusal is not even necessarily disadvantageous to a property owner. The owner might be surprised that the party already renting the building is more willing to pay a higher price than an outsider considering buying the building. There is really no good reason to secretly sell the building without a long-term majority tenant being told that the building or land is going up for sale. A building owner might believe that if he tells the long-term majority tenant that the building is up for sale, and if the tenant wants to buy at a slightly lower price, and if the owner does not agree to that price, than the tenant would threaten to leave, or would actually leave the building. In any case, this might happen anyway after the secret sale. However, that tenant has been renting a majority of the space of the building for many years. Perhaps already paying in rent much more than the worth of the building! Isn't it reasonable that the tenant finally has a chance to get some benefit after supporting the building, or land owner for so many years?

4b. You don't need to accept the rental agreement as given to you by the landlord. Make sure you negotiate. Whether it is your company's lease, or for your private residence

In foreign countries and in Japan, watch out for unnecessarily one-sided clauses in rental agreements. <u>For example, do not accept having to pay a large extra penalty amount—sometimes double the rent amount—or large interest payments if your rental payment is delayed. What if you reach a situation where you run out of cash, or cannot get access to cash? You cannot pay the rent, but you are trying to get out of the building as soon as possible. If the tenant is so making their best efforts, why should the tenant be penalized and have to pay double the rent amount? If the landlord eventually gets the normal rent level, the landlord does not suffer financially, and faced no damages.</u> Also avoid or negotiate down the number of months, or amount of building deposit you must put down. Avoid long periods of notice, and negotiate to shorten the terms of notice.

I am writing about real estate, because a problem TMT had with our building is probably the largest shock, and most unpleasant and unfair thing that has happened to me in Japan. TMT has never had more than 28 staff, but from February

1, 1986 until April, 2011, for 24 years we rented on average 5 floors, and as many as 6 floors, out of the possible 7 floors of the building. It was a small building. Except for the 1st and 7th floors that were slightly smaller, the floors were 38.03 tsubo, or 125.49 square meters (1,358.8 square feet) each. At one point we paid in rent as much as 29,500 yen/$295 per tsubo/3.3 square meters (36 square feet). This roughly came out to 6,700,000 yen/$67,000 of rent per month. At one point we had as much as 72,000,000 yen/$720,000 in the form of building deposits. During the 24 years we estimate that we paid well over 10 *oku*/1,000,000,000 yen/$10,000,000 in rent. The man who had a wooden house on this 67 tsubo (221 square meters/2,379 square feet) land lot was able to do a *toka kokan* (basically get a building built for him for free), get an 8-storey building built, get rent from just over half of the floors, and get to live up on the 8th floor. Ah!—the beautiful bubble days when construction companies/developers would do that for land owners!

4c. You should not trust people too much, even in Japan!
The worst experience of my life

The building owner upstairs on the 8th floor became a friend of mine, and he would often thank me for supporting his life so well. He would say that I did much more for him than anyone else. He said he was lucky, and I have done more to support the building than anyone. For years we were the only tenants, and only the 3rd floor of the building was usually open. Indications were, and there was periodic talk of me being able to buy the building. But alas, when two sales actually took place, both times they were secret sales without me being informed. The second sale in 2003 was shortly after the sudden death of my friend the owner. I and my staffs were not told of his death. Later on staff heard from the real estate agent something about the new owner. In 2003 that owner's father bought him the building for 5 *oku*/500,000,000 yen/$5,000,000. During a conversation in about 2008 or 2009, the real estate agent told one of my staff that now the building is probably worth only 4 oku, or 400,000,000 yen/$4,000,000. By 2011, the 25-year-old building would probably be worth less than that.

In 2003 our *kanrinin* (fulltime building security and maintenance and cleaning person) who had cleaned, done maintenance, and emptied the garbage cans everyday—even on Jan. 1st — for over 15 years, told me that he heard that very same day that the building was sold. He said he was fired with one day's notice and "Can't come tomorrow to empty the garbage, and be in my *kanrishitsu* (his room) during the day to help you." Our *kanrinin* had attended our *bonenkai* and *shinnenkai*/year-end and year-beginning parties every year playing the *shamisen*, *koto*, harmonica, and singing. This *kanrinin* had been in the *kanrishitsu* (his room) every day and for most of 15 years all day to help us with anything and everything he could. For a few days after the secret building sale, and after our *kanrinin* was fired we had no one coming to clean, or take out the garbage. There was no word, *aisatsu*/greetings or apology from the real estate agents or the new owner until there was a meeting at the real estate agent's office. I am sure that the new owner who secretly bought the building, and the real estate people involved knew that I wanted to buy the building. They knew that subject had come up informally several times with me.

4d. Sometimes we can gaman/persevere too much. We should have complained and triggered a problem with the landlord much sooner

Obviously my staff and I were not happy with the situation. We asked for a rent reduction because there was no longer a *kanrinin*, and sometimes no one would show up in the morning to clean. Unlike before, the cleaning people kept changing etc. This was also not very good for security. The rent decrease we asked for was refused. I was unhappy, but I decided not to fight. I tried not to think about the situation. I can be as good as the best Japanese at such *gaman* (perseverance). But sometimes that is a mistake. I knew from past experience that when you start to complain about maintenance etc., relationships with landlords often get irreparably damaged. Problems between landlord and tenants are not pleasant. So the outside of the windows were not washed for 7 years. A door to the outside of the elevator lobby would not close unless pulled each time. The all-too-often open door wastes electricity and money especially in the middle of winter and summer. This door on my floor where many clients come also had large patches of missing paint. The landlord wanted to wait to fix it until all the doors would be painted. So we waited and waited.

Black soot came out of the ceiling air conditioners. Some of our staff had swollen eyes and coughing from air impurities. You get the picture. It was a really messy building, with poor cleaning and maintenance. It had many things needing repair. If this were your own building, as I wrote in the beginning of this real estate section, you would be able to control all these frustrations. I, for one, would never want to deal with a landlord again. I managed to cheerfully enough greet the new landlord living on the 8th floor beginning from 2003. With the exception of his wife who knew how to greet people and talk to people, her husband would enter and leave very fast and avoid eye contact with me and all but one of my female staff. I always thought his avoidance of eye contact with us, and lack of greetings was because he knew he did a very inconsiderate and financially damaging thing to me and to our staff at TMT. If we had been able to buy the building, how much easier life would have been if for many of those years we had earned a little rent from others rather than have to pay it?

4e. Things with our landlord started on a downward spiral

One day, one of our staff told me that the landlord wanted to give us a new plant as a gift for one of our first-floor display windows. On December 2 2009 we met. It ends up our landlord living on the 8th floor was apparently irritated by our very expensive but not often changed *Ginza Mitsukoshi* or *Matsuya* department-store-bought artificial flower vase and arrangement. The landlord fumbled along saying that if such plants were not periodically changed, the whole atmosphere of the building is negatively affected. (Later on in court he denied in writing that he said this, even though his wife, his vendor who was going to give us the new plant, and another TMT staff were attending the meeting. We all heard/witnessed his comment on our needing to change our plant.) He also wondered why we blocked off our first-floor entrance door. We had always had another conference room at the front of our first-floor office. He did not even realize that if the door were open, TMT would have to meet and greet and *annai/* guide everyone entering the building. That entrance door out-front belonged only to the first floor! By plan, design, and necessity, everyone else had to come along the side of the building toward the main building elevator entranceway. This is not an uncommon design/layout.

After the Lehman shock business was bad. In January 2010 one of my staff wrote a long letter asking for a temporary rent decrease of 3,000 yen/$30 per tsubo (3.3 square meter/11 square feet). This was turned down the next month in February with just one and a half lines of text. It seemed like both sides now were trying to make the other party angry. At the same time we wrote that we finally wanted to have a chance to buy the building TMT had rented all those years. I would renovate the top floors for our residence. TMT had 44 printed items; some of them were thousands of copies of expensive full-color booklets and brochures. They all had that building and its address and telephone numbers on them. Leaving that building was something that I always felt would be impossible. The owner living above us upstairs refused to give us a chance to buy the building, unless we would pay 6 or 6.5 *oku* yen (600-650,000,000 yen/$6,000,000-6,500,000). This was more than the landlord paid and about 50% more than the value of the building. We had already spent about 2.5 times the building's worth in rent. Our position was if we cannot buy the building, at least please grant us the temporary rent decrease. With the lease expiring March 31st 2010, we requested a chance to meet to negotiate down the rent. This was rejected along with a threat to cancel our lease agreement. Before we reduced the rent by 3,000 yen, the lease agreement was essentially cancelled.

4f. We tried everything to be able to buy the building if we could not get the rent lowered

Another reason we decided to decrease the rent was that we needed a dispute to be able to get a chance to buy the building. This dispute over rent, and the actual rent paid when compared to the invoice from the landlord, would prevent the landlord from secretly selling the building to someone other than me/TMT. I was sure no other party would buy a building under dispute, which might give us a chance to finally buy the building.

With many companies in small buildings, and especially with small-scale landlords, one can never be sure if the building deposits will be returned from the landlord to the tenant. That is why often tenants draw down deposits. We did not stop paying rent until our lease was cancelled by the landlord, and about this time the landlord/owner did not invoice TMT for the rent. The landlord continued to refuse to sell the building. To me and my staff, it seemed pretty much the same as a forced eviction. After all those years, paying all that rent, and cooperating with the landlord even after he secretly bought the building, the situation seemed very unfair. The refusal to give us a chance to buy the building, and the landlord's fast steps toward cancelling our leases, instead of granting a temporary rent decrease, all seemed like an abuse of the landlord's contractual rights.

4g. With no chance to buy the building we were in for 24 years, we had no choice but to buy and get ourselves into another building as soon as possible

Now the problem we had was to find another building to buy. We moved as quickly as we could and looked at about 15 properties. The other problem was that it would take several months to renovate any building we bought. If we had been able to buy the building we had been renting and committed to for 24 years, we would have had none of these time delay problems. The reason for this is we could have sold our condo residence and moved into the eight floor residence immediately. Enough floors were open in the building TMT had been in, such that we could have moved extra furniture there and immediately begun renovation of the seventh floor to go along with the eight floor that was already the landlord's residence. TMT had recently left the seventh floor and it was open. We could have moved our residence to the eighth floor immediately and immediately begun renovation of the seventh floor into additional residence.

The problem went to the courts. At the first court session in October 2010, I was able to announce that I had just bought an alternate building. Soon after that my TMT staff discovered that since 1986 we had been paying 35 yen (about 30 cents) per kwh of electricity. TEPCO told us TEPCO was only charging the building at our address 12.65 yen most seasons, and 13.75/kwh between July and September. We also confirmed that during the previous ten years, and just before late 2010 and 2011, electricity rates were closer to 10 yen/kwh. Each floor had its own electricity meters, so it was very easy to see how much electricity each floor used. Each month an exact different number of kWh was consumed and invoiced by the landlord, not by TEPCO. The thing that was so wrong was that since 1986 we had been invoiced 35 yen per kwh, instead of about 10 yen. We never imagined that tenants could be so blatantly overcharged electricity. We were overcharged more than 3 times the normal business rate.

4h. We were ripped off by 63,000,000 yen/$630,000 just in electricity overcharges—by the landlord, not TEPCO. This is illegal in most countries you might come to live in

This meant that TMT had paid an extra approximately 63,000,000 yen in electricity since 1986 and about 17,000,000 yen/$170,000 under the current landlord since 2003. In many countries such as in the UK it is absolutely illegal for a landlord or building owner to pass on any extra charge to the tenant over what the property owner is charged by the utility. This is another reason why I started this section out encouraging you to buy your real estate to avoid all these troubles. Better to be billed directly from the utility company. I know that everyone I talk to is shocked when they hear about this electricity overcharge. Like us at TMT, they all believed they could trust building owners not to do such a thing, especially in Japan. In Japan, in so many ways people are so honest, and there is little such corruption and commercial fraud.

CHAPTER 5

The District Court Judge Ended Up Giving TMT/Me an Even More Hellish Nightmare, and Just Before Christmas on the Shortest, Darkest Day of the Year—12/21/11

I hate having to write about all this. I wish it had never happened. I wish someone had told me to put a first right of refusal clause in the rental agreement. I wish I had not let myself get misled and played by my old friend who lived upstairs on the eighth floor of the building. I wish we had complained more about the terrible maintenance and need to fix fixtures, such as the heating equipment and outside floor sign markers. Because if you don't complain it can hurt you later on in court! I wish I had gotten angrier sooner at my-building-secret-purchase landlord. I wish we had not been trusting about the amount of money we were charged for electricity. I wish we had checked with TEPCO sooner. The judge ruled that because we had always been overcharged electricity, that the overcharge was alright! Didn't it matter to the judge that we were so abused and mistreated? We believed that in reality we were being forcibly evicted from the building with no fair compromise from the landlord. In retrospect I wish I had paid the full rent level, and then tried suing for the 17,000,000 yen/$170,000 electricity overcharge later. But then again, at least one district court judge ruled that it was okay to be overcharged electricity by a factor of about 3 — because we at TMT always had been so overcharged! And because we did not know we were being overcharged!

To make a long story as short as possible, 8 days ago on 12/21/11 a *hanketsu* was dropped on us that was about 3 times more expensive than the 9,000,000 yen/$90,000 *wakai*/settlement offered by the landlord before the *hanketsu*/decision. I had agreed to pay the landlord this. Believe me, it was not easy for me to come around and agree to pay 9,000,000 yen to the landlord under these unusual circumstances. I had always believed that my real damages from being committed to a building I got no chance to buy were much greater than the landlord's damages. Especially when we learned that since 2003, this landlord had overcharged us 17,000,000 yen in electricity charges. We felt that if we had not been stubbornly refused a chance to bid on and buy that building at or slightly above a market price, we would not have had the delay of staying on in that building because of the renovation period on a different building I ended up buying. Before the judge's *hanketsu*/decision, I told the Judge that I need no damages. I also told the judge that I don't feel it fair to pay damages to the landlord. I told the judge this to help the judge push both opposing parties to *wakai*/settle the case, thereby saving the judge the need to write a *hanketsu*/decision. I became willing to pay the 9,000,000 yen when the judge, who had listened sympathetically to our side suddenly, got tough on us and declared that the landlord would not have to come to court to testify, and to be cross-examined by our side.

5a. In real terms our damages just from the electricity overcharge during the last 7 years was greater than actual monetary damages to the landlord

According to our calculations, the actual loss of revenue, or financial cost to the landlord, including about 4,500,000 yen/$45,000 *genjokaifuku*/premises restoration costs (that was very much cut back by the judge in the *hanketsu*/court decision), was about 1,800,000 yen/$18,000 less than our 17,000,000 yen overcharge of electricity. These details and the basis of this calculation were presented to the judge. This means just our overcharge on the electricity during that landlord's 7 years was more than the real and actual financial damages or disadvantage to the landlord caused by us not paying the rent as we left the building. ***Even the landlord had deducted 8,600,000 yen/$86,000 of overcharge in electricity when drafting his settlement demands. Yet this judge ruled the electricity overcharge was alright because TMT had been overcharged for 24 years***! The reason the landlord only deducted 8,600,000 yen was that the landlord wrote that we were able to get the 35/kwh rate from some companies that we had subleased to. The landlord wrote that this meant TMT itself was not financially damaged for the sublease portion, because our sub-lease companies paid TMT for the electricity they used each month. Does this ruling by the judge that it is okay to charge about times the actual electricity rate make it easier for landlords in the future to do that to trusting Japanese and foreigners? Even here in Japan, there are court case precedents where it was ruled that the amount of overcharged electricity with penalties must be paid back to the tenant.

We — me, my lawyer, and my staff — really worked hard at communicating the situation and the facts to the judge. For example, the reason the landlord would not cooperate by temporarily lowering the rent was that we were giving up one more floor of the building. A company on the 5th floor of our building wanted more space, and wanted TMT's first floor for a warehouse, and probably the 2nd floor for the seminars that they give. Therefore we were no longer an important tenant to this landlord. It ends up that this other company was able to get more space in the building next to ours. All this information had been conveyed to the judge in writing and verbally mostly by me.

5b. I learned that sometimes no matter how right you think you are, and how hard you try, you cannot succeed

<u>But it seems like the more we explained and the harder we tried, the more the judge just wanted to focus on the rental agreement itself. Not the situation.</u> Not what was really going on between fellow human beings on this planet we call earth. Real estate agents that I talked to all agreed that it would be unfair, unusual and risky for someone to come in from the outside like that in 2003 when TMT was renting 6 out of the 7 floors of the building. The real estate agents and most people I talk to agree that it would not be a polite or considerate thing to do. That it is against good business manners and protocol. After all, the chances that a company owner who paid so much rent would want to buy an inexpensive small building are very great.

The landlord knew from the Japanese language articles in our first-floor display window that TMT was a privately held company. We believe that before he bought the building, the landlord had heard that I wanted to buy the building. All the landlord had to do was ask me. But the landlord already knew I wanted to buy it, and bought the building anyway. The reason it was an advantageous buy is that you cannot find another small building like that in Tokyo where almost all of it is rented by one company for so many years—24 years. Companies will either go bankrupt, or leave to an even smaller building. Or they will leave the building and go to a larger building and be on 1, 2, or 3-floor plates instead of 6 separate floors. So it was a good building buy for an inconsiderate, brazen, uncaring person — at least for the 7 years since the landlord's father bought his son the building. But now we are finally gone.

5c. After many, many months in court, and about 5 months before the decision I finally touched an issue of possible racial discrimination by the landlord

I was never one to complain about racial discrimination, or unfair treatment in Japan. However, I finally put in detailed writing something that I am convinced was happening and is true. The new landlord was planning on living above us on the 8th floor of the building. We were renting 6 out of 7 rentable floors. The new landlord buying the building would definitely have read the Japanese language articles readable through the 1st-floor display windows. The landlord knew all about me, and that TMT was a single-owner private company. TMT had rented almost the whole building for those last 17 years. The landlord knew there was at least talk of having me buy the building.

If I were a fellow Japanese small company owner, I am convinced that the landlord who was also a small company owner, would hesitate to buy the building. The landlord and his wife would not want to so impose themselves on a Japanese company owner. They would have to be constantly meeting. It would not be pleasant. If I/TMT were a fellow Japanese renting, who wanted to buy the building, there is no way the Japanese landlord buyer would come in from the outside and impose himself on a fellow Japanese, without first checking if it was alright to buy the building. The landlord and his wife would feel guilty and uncomfortable coming in and out of the building, constantly having to meet, greet and interact with a fellow Japanese person and his wife. But a foreigner is still a different animal, and can be largely ignored. Shared feelings and relationships are not as important and intense as those among fellow Japanese. It was worth the risk with a foreigner—a small building consistently providing rent over many years. And there was also the extra bonus of a foreigner not checking up on his electricity bill.

5d. The landlord started to look better to me than the Judge. Could that have been the Judge's plan?

It is mysterious to figure out why the judge ruled so harshly against me/TMT. I had come to agree to pay the *wakai* settlement of 9,000,000 yen/$90,000 demanded by the landlord. We had only slightly disagreed on the timing of the payments. Three days before the *hanketsu*/decision, I had even agreed to the landlord's schedule of the timing of the payments. But the landlord's lawyer said, "Let's wait for the *hanketsu*/judgment." I have learned that very often a judge will call the parties before the decision is announced, and encourage settlement. Judges will readily hold back on delivering the hanketsu, or delay the hanketsu. But this judge had made up his mind, and his behavior and thinking was different from many judges.

As I mentioned above, my lawyer's and my first surprise was when the judge suddenly declared that the landlord would not have to come in and testify or be cross-examined. That seemed wrong especially since there were some lies that deserved to be examined. I pointed this out. My lawyer complained about that unusually fast handling, and skipped procedure. The judge did apologize, and said that he thought he had warned us that that was what he was going to do (not call the landlord in to court). <u>I suggested verbally to the judge that if the landlord had to come in and testify, to avoid that, the landlord would probably lower his settlement demands, and be more flexible on the timing of the payments</u>. In order to help the judge avoid the risk of appeal to the Superior Court, earlier on, I had also told the judge that if he wrote a decision to the effect that I had to pay up to the 9,000,000 yen, that I would pay it and would not appeal. <u>Maybe the judge found these frank communications, and my efforts to solve our problems, irritating and offensive</u>. There may have been some clashes of cross-cultural communication going on? Perhaps this judge got his nose out of joint because my lawyer and mostly I were giving the judge such "brainstorming" help and feedback. Although we were very polite and careful in the way we conveyed such feelings to this judge.

5e. I tried to do my best to communicate to the judge that I was hoping for his guidance, and that I would follow that guidance

From the time we suddenly learned that the landlord would not have to testify, I asked the judge if he would please give me more feedback about how things were going. <u>I indicated that I would settle even if I had to accept the entire landlord's terms if that is what the judge would recommend to me. All the judge had to do was recommend that I accept the 9,000,000 yen settlement, with the payment installment timing that the landlord had put forth</u>. But there was no such helpful feedback from the judge. He was the second judge, taking over from the first judge. <u>My lawyer told me from the beginning that it would be a difficult case if I did not pay the full rent level, but neither of the judges ever told me that</u>. They seemed to listen rather sympathetically, and gave no guidance as to what I should do. My brother who is a N.Y. and N.J. Attorney told me that I should be on fairly safe ground because the Judges were with the situation and interfacing with me pretty much from the beginning. They never told me, "Anyway you had better pay the full rent for now." They never indicated I have a weak position. This time it was not a very helpful judicial process.

Our common sense in Japan is that judges are supposed to get things settled through *wakai*/settlement without having to write a *hanketsu*/decision. Indeed the decision was 23 pages and must have been quite troublesome for the judge to write. We are trying to figure out why it was such a harsh decision under these unusual and complex circumstances. ***Even though the landlord deducted the electricity overcharge why would the Judge not deduct it? Why did that judge not give me more guidance and direction when I really needed it from him?*** Under those circumstances when we had to, and were leaving the building as quickly as possible, why should we be penalized with a double the rent penalty? I also asked the judge for guidance, face to face, clearly seeking and needing the judge's help. Did I make him mad? I tried to be very polite. I did ask the judge and my lawyer to speak louder and slower so I could understand better. I also said things like, "If you were going to buy a building, I don't think you would buy a small building where someone was renting almost all of the building for so many years. I would never do a thing like that, would you?" (There was no clear answer from the judge.) I went to every court case hearing. Maybe the judge just got tired of seeing me and listening to my Japanese.

5f. It seemed the judge squeezed the pinchers on TMT/me toward the end when I was giving up and was greatly compromising

From a few months earlier our side dropped talk of financial damages, and I gave up on getting electricity overcharge returned. I said that, "I just want to finish this case, and don't need any money, but don't want to pay any money to the landlord either." It seems from that point the judge got tougher on us, and moved over to the less compromising landlord side. After I said I need no damages or money from the landlord, the judge said the landlord would not have to come to court and would not have to testify. I pointed this out to the judge, I thought in a very respectful way, and maybe the judge did not like me saying that. One of my Japanese friends said, "Maybe the judge is jealous and does not like the idea that a locally home-grown *gaijin* consultant can buy a little building in Japan…"

It is important to realize that the venue for almost all the 'court' appearances was a small, private conference room. It is not a court room. At some points both the plaintiff and defendant sit together with the judge around this small table. Then there is a chance for each side to be alone with the judge. This format should be able to lend itself to much more frank and direct communication, working toward solving such disputes. Instead of hitting and surprising one side with a 'gotcha' blow, I would hope the process could be more helpful.

We cannot help but wonder if the judge might be prejudiced against *gaijin*. Maybe he was a foreign exchange student in a foreign country and felt he was not treated fairly. Maybe his family owns and rents out buildings and charges too much for electricity?! Maybe he only could focus on the rental agreement, and not the timing of events such as when the rental agreements were cancelled? Who knows? It was all a big shock and mystery to us. New Year's holidays started from the next day. We had only two weeks to appeal the decision, so we appealed to the next level, higher Superior Court. I have to try not to think too much about this over this New Year's holiday. The best I can do is picture my landlord choking on some *mochi* /soft chewy rice chunks (just a 5-minute choking struggle) and the judge slipping on the ice. Actually, now my landlord looks better to me than the judge. Could that be what the judge had in mind? But such a decision of close to 30,000,000 yen/$300,000 penalty is much too much, and had us a bit bewildered. My staffs also wondered what it means. <u>TMT staff unnecessarily worried for their futures, and the future of TMT. So a judge's inconsiderate, very cold, harsh, extreme decision, and unusual behavior has many damaging effects. It seems this judge did not concern himself or worry about the ramifications of his decision.</u> Yes. It was our frustrating predicament and challenge, not this judge's problem.

<u>The judge's decision made me more reconciled to pay the 9,000,000 yen the landlord wanted. Even though our 17,000,000 yen electricity overcharge was more than any unpaid rent and costs our landlord suffered. However, the decision resulted in the landlord wanting more money than the 9,000,000 yen. So rather than settling our disagreement, the judge's decision gave us a larger problem.</u>

CHAPTER 6

Some Battles worth Fighting, Some Fights you can't Win, Others not Worth Fighting Anyway

I hope we are helping you see that you can do more at your company, or that there are different ways, or more effective ways to do things. That, of course, is the main reason I developed my ABCD approach. And why, should we work together we try so hard to pass our know–how on to you. I needed to be able to offer more and better methods than the usual outside arms-length advice given by most attorneys or consultants. But then again, think twice if something really needs to be done. Also make sure you want to be one of the ones spearheading the effort. We can get ourselves into some unnecessary turmoil and bad situations. Like my whole unpleasant experience with the building I rented for 24 years, and never wanted to leave. I was irrationally committed to staying in that building at any cost. I was upset about all those things that angered me. But in the end I just should have left the building biting the bullet and paying the full rent level. I also should have more quickly reconciled myself not to want to buy that building.

I was against the Vietnam War. I certainly did not want to get drafted. Yet there must have been some otherwise smart people who really believed in that war. There must have been very smart people who believed it was winnable. It was very costly and damaging to human life. It hurt the USA in the eyes of the world, and was definitely a war that the USA lost. There was no Communist-driven domino theory. As soon as the USA left, the Vietnamese faced years of war against another

Communist neighbor—China—their ally against the USA! Similarly, we saw how the wars in Iraq and Afghanistan turned out and are turning out. Maybe quite a lot of wasted effort that was costly, damaging and counterproductive. Something like my love and attachment, and ultimate drama surrounding the building I rented so much of and for so long. I should have faced much sooner how angry I would end up getting. How impossible it would be to have a happy ending to that building saga.

6a. People can get over-committed to the wrong cause, the wrong direction

Sometimes we are so sure we are right. We want justice. But it can just make someone else wrong, and angry. Then an all-powerful judge can enter the situation. He took a look at things in his own way, and for his own reasons, and what he deemed to be "law" delivered his own brand of justice. Sometimes the wrong person is fired, the wrong person hired. Investment is made like crazy into the wrong product line, the wrong company. We hook up with the wrong business or life partner. We are too ambitious. We try and do too much. Instead of closing a plant in Japan, and going to all the effort of starting a plant outside Japan, and learning about running an operation in a foreign country, could it be better to wait until the yen gets weak again, as we have recently scene.

I have often thought that no matter how hard we try, we will never leave a footprint like Soichiro Honda, Konosuke Matsushita, or Akio Morita of Sony. But Steve Jobs, and Softbank's Masayoshi Son, Rakuten's Hiroshi Mikitani, or Uniqlo's Tadashi Yanai, are doing pretty well for themselves. Is Uniqlo over-expanding?

Did Mr. Yanai's trumpeting of Uniqlo's success, ambition, and strategy, bring H & M, or Forever 21 into the Japanese market? Doing nothing and not trying is also not the recipe for a fun life and for fulfillment. How to live our life and the meaning of our lives is the universal question. But rather than struggle with such theoretical nothingness, probably our key to happiness is something to do—now. Action is the key. 'Making a move' is crucial. It also can mean growth. But maybe not too much of that either. No sense in striving without enjoying the sakura, a little sake, and the sunsets.

6b. Is there something in-between "fight or flight"?

Fight or flight is a human and many animals' instinct. Should we fight to keep operations in Japan as much as possible, like Mr. Toyota of Toyota Motors, or fly away from Japan, and the temporary challenges of the strong yen? What is the best course of action that can lie in-between the extremes of fight or flight? One side giving up and surrendering could be one answer. Communicating? Compromising? Innovating? Training? Developing new, high-end technology and products? Create something new, so we don't have to compete on the basis of the old? Worrying alone does us no good. Anticipating problems and working toward solving them is probably the best course. Knowledge is our ally. Wisdom is knowledge tempered by the heat and focus which comes from experience, and living through the events. Experiencing wins and losses and making mistakes. One thing I hope to do for people who read this book is to make sure none of you ever rent for too long a property that you could buy, and that you want to buy! I can also encourage you to check your electric bill that you get from your landlord, as opposed to what the electric utility actually charges your landlord. This should be before you have paid about 63,000,000 yen/$630,000 too much in electricity bills!

And, of course, we can pass on to all of you the wisdom I have learned about managing people, and what can be done in the human resource area, and with personnel policies, regulations, tactics and strategy to keep your companies stronger.

Just studying and learning a foreign language, and that is usually still English, can be something useful. It is not a bad hobby to have, at least on the side. I would say that Japanese staff, managers, and probably people from other less linguistically dominant nationalities, can make at least 3 times as much money during their careers if they know another major language. People can also get new jobs at least 3 times easier just by being fairly competent at English or another major foreign language.

> *6c. Our rewards will be based on what we can do,*
> *how skilled we are, the demand for that job,*
> *and the difficulty of replacing us*

Of course, this is true of any special skill you have—IT, financial/accounting wizardry, software programming, skilled carpenter or craftsmen, people good with design/operation of precision machinery, or high-tech electronics and equipment, or talented artist or writer etc etc. If you can combine such special skills with strong foreign language skills you will have even more of a winning edge. Our rewards will basically be based on the difficulty of the job that we can do, our skill and ability to do that job, the value that this job or service has to others, and the difficulty of replacing us.

Just helping others and trying to do some good in the world, working for a cause that is bigger than ourselves will also give us fulfillment. There is a lot of room to give help to so many people throughout Japan, and especially in tsunami-wrecked Tohoku. Wherever we are, even in small ways each day, we can help others. Just holding the door for someone, just smiling and nodding at someone, or letting a car cross that has been waiting too long at a pedestrian walkway—it makes a little difference to that person. It makes their day just a little easier. Doing something good for other people ends up making us feel good too. If you sow good seeds, a good harvest will come back to you.

People through a sense of justice or grieved by injustice can work together for very big causes leading to dramatic change. The Arab Spring we witnessed in 2011 was a remarkable achievement in many countries. However, there were and are many consequences and prices to pay along with that change. I am sure there are many people in those Middle "East" countries that prefer the stability and predictability that they could largely depend on before the social/political and economic changes that came with the Arab Spring.

6d. An important life lesson is that we cannot control our world, no matter how well-meaning, and how hard we try

We learn that we cannot control our world and all the things that go on around us. This is especially true in this world of global warming with more extreme weather than ever before. We CAN work on us, and on the things that we think about. We become what we think about. These are the only things over which we have complete control. We can try and picture where we want to be in x number of years. We can picture the steps and actions we would have to take to get to that spot. Then we set about doing those things. We can ask and remind ourselves of what we are trying to do, and how we are trying to do it. And then if each action, each day is strong, and we do our best, probably things will fall into place as best they can.

Those key questions from the science/study of time management—"Am I making the best possible use of my time right now?" "Am I doing the things that will get me closest and fastest to my goals?" But let us not forget—merely striving to a place that will not make us happy and content, is also something to watch out for. We achieve the goal. Then we look around and say, "Is this all there is?" We can become disillusioned.

6e. Those who help others, also help themselves

A successful life is a succession of successful single days. A good day is made up of well-used minutes. People are not successful because they have a lot of money; they have some money because they are successful. And the best and fastest way to get some riches, whether they be financial or spiritual, is to enrich others first. Our rewards in life are usually based on our service to others. So those who serve and help others also serve themselves.

Oscar Wilde said something like, 'selfishness is not living as we wish to live, it is expecting others to live as we wish them to live, and unselfishness is leaving others alone, and not interfering with them'. I think compared to people from the USA, and some other countries, the Japanese are pretty good in this area. Sometimes it is important for people not to be too sure of themselves, and not to be too sure they are right. Whenever we have to make ourselves right, we are making someone else wrong. This is probably the source of so much unnecessary conflict and turmoil in our lives and in our world.

These general/universal principles and laws operate everywhere, regardless of which country you work in. Whether we can see this or not, these principles are probably at work—whatever the nationality and culture of the people you work with, or will be working with...

CHAPTER 7

*ABC of Communication between Westerner (and others)
and Japanese—Some Handy Hints on How to Overcome
Frustrating but Not Irresolvable Cultural Differences*

The Japan Times, December 7, 1980

This was written by me, and published in the Japan Times *on
December 7 1980. (This was coincidentally, Pearl Harbor Day
in the USA. People in the States tend to remember that day, just
as the Japanese remember Hiroshima.) I wrote this article during
my 8th year in Japan, when I was 30 years old. It appeared
in my* Japan Times-*published book,* Labor Pains and the
Gaijin Boss, *first printed in 1984. It is interesting to watch how
one develops in a foreign culture. Of my several books, I notice
that I keep discovering new things. I also hate to go back and write
about things I already discovered and was interested in during
earlier years. During the first few years, and even months in a
foreign country our antennas are probably sitting higher, catching
more information, insights and differences than one will catch
later on after many years in the country. You won't forget your
early discoveries. However, the longer you really become a part of a
different country and culture; you come to look at things more like
a native of that country. You probably will not notice differences as
much. This is why sometimes it may be interesting to look back
at your earlier diaries or voice recordings of your experience in the
foreign country. Unfortunately, we are usually too busy to do that.
I can tell you that today I could not write the below* Japan Times
*article as well, or in quite the same way I wrote this one back in
1980. It was written aimed at the Gaijin Boss readers in Japan.
Do you think it is still basically valid?*

I would really like us to place emphasis on similarities, not differences. But, having said that…

Just what are we dealing with? There are indeed some interesting customs or beliefs we can point out—most Japanese, afraid of infection, never wash their ears with soap and water and are shocked when they see foreigners sticking their ears into the shower. Japanese can catch colds through their stomachs, and get a stomach ache because it's cold. Many of them gargle away impurities (even water is OK) when they come into the house after a day "outside" of work or play. Many Japanese open the window (even in winter) in the morning when they make up the bed (or put away the futon) to let the dust out, even though the colder, denser air from the outside is clearly rushing in, etc. , etc.

But we want to learn how to communicate with the Japanese. The Japanese can be the most stubborn people in the world. And worse yet, they have a way of making you think they are with you. In the long run, if a Japanese person isn't convinced, it's virtually impossible to get him to do something he's not excited about. How do you get him excited? You have to bring him into the process, make him a part of it, and let him implement and take action.

A giant step in this direction is to master and utilize skillfully a little theory which I have conceptualized: you must convince the Japanese on their terms, otherwise the difference in terms precludes reaching agreement on issues and substance.

This is really what the art of communicating and convincing is all about. But particularly in the case of the Japanese, this holds true because they are by and large quite convinced that they are basically different from other people in the world, and that their system, sentiments and emotions defy the understanding of non-Japanese.

Here the foreigner is at a tremendous advantage if a truly expert mastering of the Japanese language enables him to discuss all subtleties in flowing and natural Japanese. Then the foreigner enjoys two great advantages: (1) the burden of the communication is fully on his shoulders (he is aware of his own inadequacies and where he must follow up) and (2) if he does in fact come across acceptably close to the Japanese model. He has largely blown away the mist of cultural uniqueness, which the Japanese sometimes feel more comfortable sitting behind, and has precluded the Japanese party from using the "because this is Japan" syndrome. Obviously, Japanese can't use this scapegoat when trying to score points among themselves.

Ambiguity, Flattery

Since most foreigners are not in a position to master Japanese, which in its process is very much the needed cultural and behavior exercise, let us define in English a few characteristics of the Japanese and offer some behavioral guidelines to reinforce communications effectiveness.

Foreigners are often critical of the Japanese for not saying yes or no clearly, and expressing negative feelings and opinions only implicitly. A non-Japanese businessman, for example, should use this to his advantage, realizing that the indirect refusal offers flexibility to both sides when negotiating. It allows time to feel out new ground and allows the other party (or yourself) to temporarily withdraw without losing face, or the business deal.

Non-Japanese are sometimes turned off by the apparently meaningless flattery of the Japanese. Western "tact" does not include saying something that isn't true. Keep in mind that above all, Japanese tact emphasizes making the person feel good over the relative truth of the compliment. The Japanese place more weight on trying to show their willingness to be friendly and trying to please, rather than on the actual words used.

Sometimes foreigners tend to feel that the humbleness that some Japanese seem to project in such a contrived and deliberate fashion is really most hypocritical, especially when we know that a Japanese individual can be as proud and haughty as anyone we have met. The Japanese answer would be that it's a virtue to be humble, and even if one isn't, he makes it all the worse by not trying to act humbly. Thus self-assertion is a respected character attribute in many Western and other societies, while self-depreciation is indeed the time-honored Japanese tradition.

The Japanese identify directness with rudeness. To them it's impossible to be both polite and direct. Maybe that's why there seem to be so many formal and apparently meaningless, fixed greetings of *aisatsu* in so many routine daily encounters. If such *aisatsu* are not given, one will get few positive points for originality and individuality, and rather may be somewhat ostracized as being impolite and strange. Familiar expressions that won't shock or upset are more valued than original expressions.

While Western societies place value on mutual independence, the Japanese like the feeling of mutual dependence. A foreign business manager should be careful in trying to locate the top performer and bestow formal, public credit on him. Japanese often feel more comfortable when their idea becomes a part of the invisible whole. Their feelings of mutual dependence mean that thanks is expressed not only for specific favors, but also throughout the ongoing general relationship. Maybe that's why expressions like *okagesama de* (thanks to you) are so often used even when no specific favors have been given.

Wait for Spokesman

I'm sure there are many foreign businessmen or English teachers who have faced a conference or a class, and asked the group a question. You got no response and were led to believe that the Japanese have no opinions, or must have nothing in their heads at all.

This is very much a problem in cross-cultural communication, for unless there is a most obvious group spokesman (perhaps someone much older or more senior than everyone else), no one individual is permitted to voice a view or even say yes, because to the Japanese this would mean that he is making himself the spokesman for the group. It is also regarded as impolite and poor form to show off ability or seize the spotlight in such a group context.

The foreigner working in any such situation should learn to call on and select the proper, universally recognized spokesman, or should clearly indicate that he is seeking only an individual opinion and should call on specific participants.

Nosy or Just Friendly

Have you ever been annoyed with the string of personal questions that inquisitive Japanese can fire out within 30 seconds? While Westerners have an inherent and underlying respect for the privacy of an individual, personal questions are not at all taboo to the Japanese. In fact, they show friendliness and a willingness to place the other person in the all important "us" category.

While the Westerner can feel cornered or pinned down by a personal question such as, "Do you own or rent your house?" a Japanese finds it difficult to start or continue a conversation without background information such as the group to which a person belongs, or his social, family and economic status. A Japanese apparently feels a compelling need to make some sort of a comparative crossover from the 'them' to 'us' category by way of such exploratory questions, and of course the exchanging of the meishi (calling card). It may also be attempts to determine social status or age and background. More so than with English, and probably most languages, these judgments can affect to what extent 'honorifics'/titles, and what level/type of grammar is used.

While the Japanese are very much open to private questions, they are closed to the ideological prying or the conceptual attacks that so many foreigners relish and engage in with near strangers.

Rather than simply saying that they are closed to someone tapping on or drawing out their philosophies, it might be more accurate to say that they don't particularly identify with the process, nor are they sure of where the foreigner is going, and frequently most unsatisfied when they have arrived, after what seems to the Japanese to be a rather pointless intellectual exercise. Japanese also dislike a game-like approach to arguing. They see it as unnecessarily flippant and insincere.

While Westerners see confrontation as a catalyst, the Japanese revere apology as a lubricant. If everyone is constantly and immediately admitting their fault in any misunderstanding, it has a very defusing and disarming effect. One should always avoid confrontation—it never pays. The Japanese will merely think that you are immature, childish and not capable of controlling your emotions.

You may have noticed that the Japanese don't complain very much. They respect someone who perseveres patiently and works with realities.

In Japanese society it can also be impolite to express one's personal preference. Thus it is not unusual to have a Japanese person somewhat perplexed when the foreign hostess insists that he or she decide between coffee or tea. When Japanese make excuses not to attend a function, etc., they try and avoid expressing personal preference. It is not appropriate to bow out by saying that one would rather play tennis that day than go bowling, nor are family activities a suitable excuse. For this same reason you will rarely catch a Japanese praising his or her own family members, as it comes too close to self-serving and praise of oneself. Instead they tend to fall on the side of degrading family members.

Some Advice

And now for the ABCs of communicating with the Japanese.

a. Attempt to understand, or have some gut perceptions of Japanese behavior and cultural characteristics as exemplified by the above. Don't try and unnaturally fall into and conform to these patterns, but be aware of their existence, be considerate, patient and sensitive.

b. Be a good listener and encourage open and frank communication from the Japanese. Remember that the conversational rhythm in Western conversation is too fast for the Japanese. The pace of give and take in conversational exchange is much slower between two Japanese. They will not as readily interrupt and contradict, so the foreigner should slow down and avoid giving away his views and making conclusions until he has heard from others. Constantly pause and throw out numerous chances for the listener to give his own views and feedback.

c. See ourselves as the Japanese see us. Remember that the Japanese find our unfamiliar foreign communication patterns just as strange and unique as we find theirs. Our directness, confrontation, Western straight-line logic and tendency to demand quick and definite responses, etc., can leave the Japanese feeling embarrassed and frustrated. They can be made to feel that it is hopeless to make themselves understood by foreigners. Keep in mind that the Japanese have their own criticisms of Westerners and many may see us as childish and lacking self-control as well as too simple, immature and insensitive.

CHAPTER 8

Riding Rough Seas—Fighting to Live another Day

(Written mostly to keep and get investment and tourist into Japan.)

*Personal Observations and Personnel/People's Response after
the Big Quake and Tsunami in Japan—Tough Life and Fixing
Mistakes and Tragedies Anywhere, but Charity should Begin
at Home In Japan, the United States, Europe, or Anywhere*

*Tuesday, August 23, 2011—"5.8-Magnitude Jolt Sparks
Terrorism Fears in N.Y." reports 'The Japan Times' in
Tokyo—Less than a Week later Hurricane Irene*

*(This book is available in English. If any of you want a version
of the below to help explain to your foreign friends the Japan
experience on 3/11/11. It can also help reassure foreign friends
about coming to Japan to visit or invest.)*

It is a fraction of what we had on 3/11/11 in Japan, but I'm
sure it was unpleasant enough. If you are one of the many
Japanese staff living in the Big Apple/New York City, you
know what your experience was like. For those of you who
were not living in Japan on 3/11/11, I will tell you a bit about
the big one in Japan as experienced by a *gaijin* in Tokyo. This
is the way we experienced the earthquake and radiation scare
in "the Big Mikan" (tangerine, as we expats call Tokyo). The
next day's news of the 5.8 earthquake in New York reported
that there were few if no deaths, not too much damage,
although the proud Washington DC National Cathedral

and the Washington Monument will need significant repair. There was no mention of tsunami. In the 30 years between 1974 and 2003 just 10 US states led by Alaska, California and Hawaii had 98.2% of USA earthquakes (USGS—United States Geographical Survey statistics). New York City and Washington DC, are normally pretty safe with Virginia ranked a low 26th in terms of the number of quakes, and Maryland even lower ranked 47th. In the northeast, New York State is the leader in earthquakes with 755 reported between 1840 and 2007. Even though New Hampshire's records go back 200 years before that—only 360 earthquakes in New Hampshire. Most of the worst New York State 'quakes have been up along the Saint Lawrence River and the Great Lakes.

8a. Living through the recent big earthquake/tsunami in Japan

According to police reports 26,347 people died in Tohoku/ northeast Japan within an hour or two on March 11th 2011. There have been worse natural disasters, but not too many worse than this. Worse recent earthquake/tsunami disasters were 60,000 to 100,000 killed in Lisbon, Portugal in 1755, 70,000 killed in Arica, Chile in 1868, 70,000 killed in Messina, Italy in 1908, and over 230,000 all over Asia and Africa on the day after Christmas in 2004—that horrible Indian Ocean quake and tsunami. Earthquakes without tsunami and floods have killed even greater numbers of people through the centuries. It is clear that unbelievably large natural disasters and human tragedies are pretty well spread throughout our planet. Since March 11 2011, in Japan, the radiation leaks have taken on a life of their own, and are worrisome, even if they are really not harmful except to those very close to the Fukushima disabled nuclear plants. Such tragedies and challenges to companies and their personnel take place all over the world, just about every day. More recently the government square in Oslo, and the little lake island in Norway, record-breaking downpours and flooding in Australia, South Korea and Seoul; and before that China, India, Brazil, the Mississippi basin in the USA, and many other places; turmoil in Sudan; starvation in Somalia again; a record drought in the USA South, and more recently in California; a speeding bullet train crash in China, and the silent but sinister and unrelenting regional droughts, heat and cold waves just about everywhere... The terrible April and May; 2011 tornados in the USA Midwest, just one of them taking 100 lives, the ongoing horrible aftershocks in Haiti and Christchurch, New Zealand have been dwarfed and almost forgotten with such more recent tragedies. How can we be ready for all kinds of tragedies and calamities—both of Man's and Nature's making? What can be our life, or business continuity plans?

8b. Tragedies within our control, and more slippery ones—
the diapers not the radiation

China's bullet train, the Norwegian police, the Japan TEPCO nuclear plant owners and operators, the pilots and passengers of the 9/11 planes back in 2001, the Army Corps of Engineers and their dykes in New Orleans, were not ready, or were taken by surprise. The only tragedy listed above that will not happen again with sharp implements, and involves exclusively man and his reaction within a predictable/confined location, without the added curse of the sky, sea and earth's crust running amok, were the box cutter boys of 9/11 hitting the World Trade Center Buildings. It will never happen again—at least not for 30 or 40 years. We know now. And nail clippers and nail files also need not be confiscated before boarding an airplane when there is silverware in the airplane—at least in business class! So there are smart responses and actions to take and quite annoying and ludicrous ones as well.

I have been in Japan since graduating from the School of Industrial and Labor Relations at Cornell University in Ithaca, N.Y., so I had better talk about the Japan I know so well. Almost all our buildings and bridges held, even up North closer to the epicenter of the 9.0 'quake. The sea walls were too short, those nuclear power plants could have been located on higher ground, and designed, and maintained better. Electricity pretty much held in Tokyo and most places. Elevators were retested and running within hours, those in the smallest buildings within a day or two. Within hours in the stores there was no bottled water, milk, juices, batteries, cup of noodles, and disposable diapers. One of our consultants went a couple hundred kilometers down to Kyoto, not to escape the radiation, but to buy disposable diapers for his little one.

8c. In time of tragedy, the helpful, and the less helpful

Disneyland, although on land reclaimed from Tokyo Bay, and although it's parking lot was a bit torn up, did an outstanding job of safely getting people off the rides. Those rides must be well engineered and designed. The young Disney staff must be very well-trained, and indeed are very professional. Disney also put up for the night, maybe more than one night, thousands of people, and had bedding, water and food for that. Not a single person was injured. The Imperial Hotel followed its 1923 great Tokyo Earthquake tradition, and many other great hotels like the other top class and huge New Otani

Hotel, the ANA Intercontinental hotel, and many more, did a fantastic job of welcoming the masses who otherwise would have walked home the night of the 'quake until their shoes wore thin. *Kodomo no Shiro*/Children's Castle near our TMT Building, many universities, and concert halls opened their doors and their resources. The trains needed to be tested, and trains and subways were pretty much running by the next day in Tokyo, but on limited schedules to save electricity. But the train operators, especially the JR/Japan Railway closed people out of stations, when those stations had shutters—"for safety reasons"—ugh. Some stations without shutters, such as Shinagawa, let people spend the night there. It was especially cold that night in early March. Other such official places did well, and were more helpful such as opening up Tokyo City Hall for the masses to sleep that night.

What happened at companies? In the greater Tokyo area, most land and cellphone lines were out for perhaps a day. Email from desktop PC's that were not smashed worked. We've learned to immediately open doors that might get stuck, but to be careful running out of your building where there might be glass falling on you. And almost no glass even shattered in Tokyo. Amazing considering cabinets fell and PCs flung off desks. Now we try and teach each other that the 'triangle of life' is actually not under the desk, but the person lying flat to the side of the table or desk. This is because the desk can get largely crushed, but the desk helps build a small life-giving space just to the side of the desk or table, keeping chunks of ceiling slabs off you. Luckily such ceiling chunks did not fall in Tokyo and almost no such damage in buildings closer to the epicenter. Unlike the 1923 Tokyo earthquake where 140,000 died without a tsunami, or the 1995 Kobe 'quake when 6,000 died from the 'quake damage itself, actually, on

March 11 2011, almost no one died from the earthquake in Japan. Japanese building codes and engineering have come a long way. Unlike the earlier faulty construction and fires, it was water this time—the tsunami up on the northeast shores of Japan.

8d. I grew up in New York State. We had earthquakes too!

In the United States it is mostly death by chimney. In South Carolina on September 1 1886 most of the 60 fatalities were crushed by their chimneys. In New York State, since 1737 there have been about 10 strong earthquakes doing considerable damage to nearby towns. The largest one in New York was 5.8 on September 5, 1944. Bridges, roads and buildings have been damaged with most of the bigger earthquakes taking place up along the Saint Lawrence River and over toward the Adirondack Mountains. The States with more earthquake fatalities than the 60 killed in South Carolina are 77 fatalities in Hawaii on April 3, 1868. There were between 100 and 200 killed in Alaskan earthquakes in 1946 and 1964. And then of course there is California with several earthquake fatality numbers similar to the two Alaskan quakes. There were about 3,000 fatalities in the great San Francisco earthquake of 1906. In the United States, and many other countries many more people are killed from floods, blizzards, dams breaking, hurricanes, tornados, heat and cold waves, and fires. And we have to watch out for being on the wrong ship, plane or train on an unlucky day. When we were visiting Seattle, Washington in June 2011, especially in the aftermath of the March 11th Japan earthquake and tsunami, there was much talk about and hope that Seattle would not be next. There are a couple of old nuclear power plants not too far away.

8e. Tokyo electricity stayed on, city water flowed, and within days stores were fully stocked again

Some of our staff were a little afraid to brave going home at first, and many companies did close their operations for a day or two, even if they did not need to. Some firms let staff sleep over. Then I think most firms focused on trying to procure drinking water for their staff however best they could. Tokyo area city tap water continued flowing, except for some reclaimed land particularly over near Disneyland, but people were not sure about the radiation effect on the water supply. For only a couple days after the roof blew off one of the Fukushima reactors, Tokyo water may have been a bit too radiated because there had been a lot of rain, the wind was blowing in the wrong direction, covers were not yet improvised for Tokyo's purification/airing tanks, and extra carbon filters were not yet applied.

Within just a few days, anything needed by consumers was back in the Tokyo area, and most other areas' distribution chains were up. Unfortunately, this did not include needed supply chain parts from factories that had been damaged. This led to at least temporary unemployment at several USA auto manufacturers, and probably other worldwide firms. The remaining concern was the radiation and what it meant. Many of us resident businessmen, especially those without small children, stuck it out. The Italian Ambassador took a very clear position that he would be here and that Tokyo was perfectly normal. This was alas basically true! But a few embassies even set up temporary quarters in the Osaka, Kobe area. Even though Kobe was largely destroyed by an earthquake in 1995! Further from today's radiation, yes. Three days later on March 14ᵗʰ, I had a get-together with about 25 mostly locally based foreign businessmen. I was quiet, and a bit worried. One buddy was boisterously auctioning liquid iodine normally used for cuts, to help with the radiation. A Japanese doctor at the party declared it was not the answer, and would do more harm than good. Still on the way home, unsure of our life's continuity planning, I stopped by a couple Roppongi drugstores to get iodine pills or even iodine drops. Sure enough there was a run on both. And those white masks that Japanese wear, mostly because even then in March it was the hay fever season had also all flown off the shelves. The next morning I was able to buy some white face masks. But by then we realized we didn't need them, and it looked too wimpy. Things in Tokyo normalized very quickly. I remember I was surprised to learn that the next day or two after the big 3/11 'quake that some movie theaters were closed. They may have been more concerned with aftershocks damaging their theater, or trains stopping again? In terms of energy saving, having a lot of people in a dark theater instead of using electricity at home, probably would save energy.

8f. The French Foreign Legion

The French government reaction and that of the French Embassy was extremely protective and generous with French nationals. In just one day, probably the day after the 'quake, either 5 or 7, and probably more, French military and other aircraft were chartered, and made available to fleeing Frenchmen and their families. You were flown all the way to Paris for free, with no need to reimburse anyone, but also no return tickets. Our French consultant and family of 4 were back with us within about 3 weeks, however. Some foreign and Japanese companies decided that at least temporarily it would be smart to diversify operations in terms of location, or suppliers. Then there was a bit of a power shortage, or need to save energy in the Osaka area too, so there was a drift back to the Tokyo area. Also because of the continuing strengthening of the yen, either new, or in any case some Japanese manufacturing operations were moving to foreign countries.

Tourism, especially group tours to Tokyo and the rest of Japan went down for a while. And some foreign entertainers cancelled their gigs. Not Lady Gaga. She sold a ton of earthquake commemorative bracelets and gave the money to the poor Japanese people up north. Those more expert than me said you will get more radiation in the airplane in transit, than you will spending 10 days in Tokyo. And of course places like Kyoto and Kobe are great tourist spots, and are a few hundred kilometers further from the sick nuclear power plant. By June, 3 months after the 'quake and tsunami, luxury spending was back, and this time the growth would be more from local Japanese as there were fewer of what had been mostly Chinese and Korean tourists. At Daimaru Matsuzakaya Department Stores, sales of artwork and precious metals were already up 11.8% in June, following a 15.5% decline in March. At Ikebukuro Sogo and Seibu's flagship store jewelry sales were up 15% and averaged around 150,000 yen (US$1,900) per customer. Isetan Mitsukoshi reported double digit growth in designer goods. Just 3 months later in June expensive imported car sales were up 44% according to the Japan Automobile Importers Association. (These statistics are from July 25 2011, the *Nikkei Weekly*.)

8g. Countermeasures and continuity plans at companies

Within just a few months companies largely found their stride. For example, when the electric bill came, a little Japanese flyer from Tokyo Denryoku/electric utility company (the same guys who fumbled at the Fukushima nuclear plant), enclosed an instructional flyer, with a list of about 10 ways to save electricity, to be sure that no rolling black-outs were necessary. So far, there had mostly been only talk of possible planned rotating black outs. They never were to affect the innermost key central wards out of the 23 Tokyo wards. Not included in their list of 10 items were efforts by some companies to open an hour earlier, go home an hour earlier. Less widespread were companies that allowed staff a 2 or 3-hour siesta during the hottest summer noon and afternoon peak hours when electricity usage is highest. Air conditioners were to be set at 28 degrees centigrade (fahrenheit 82.4). Most companies and staff (except me, when not alone, my client guests and my guys) simply conformed to this, as a responsibility to their greater society. Unnecessary overtime, and hanging around the office in the evening was cut out. Some automobile and other plants were working on weekends rather than during the week when more energy is consumed. "Cool Biz" has really taken root since it was first introduced. Especially the summer after the big 'quake very few people wore their suit jacket or neck tie. This has become more accepted even at more formal meetings with customers. One unnecessary big energy user was keeping shop doors wide open. Funny—it was not just the big department stores and brand stores in Omotesando, Harajuku, and Ginza etc. It was even many little mom-and-pop stores. And this is even though electricity bills were and are getting more expensive. But I suppose it gets overweighed by the desperate hope it is more likely for a customer to enter if the door is open with a smiling sales person visibly looking out on the street.

Good news for foreign capitalized firms already in Japan, or wanting to come here is that even before the earthquake, expat residential and company rents were and are way down. Land prices are down to their 1983 levels, such that even my company TMT bought its own building in Omotesando. Land prices are finally starting to go up but not dramatically. And because building architecture and engineering proved how resilient it is, foreign investment especially from Asia in Japanese real estate and buildings is increasing. Salary levels are no higher than they were 10 to 15 years ago. There have always been some Japanese executives that are attracted to expat life in Asian and other cities. With the complications of children's education, there are others not attracted to assignments abroad. Also, because Japan, especially the Tokyo I know so well, is such an exciting, varied, and safe place to live, some of the Japanese executives of the Japanese companies that are expanding their outside Japan operations would rather not go and live in less safe, less convenient and less pleasant foreign countries. These Japanese executives also figured the greater pollution, for example, in many Asian and other cities had to be as bad for them and their children as the tiny amount of radiation we had in Tokyo. So they are yours to hire. It is a good time to perhaps generously and humanely move some less effective staff out, and go to the next, higher level with some stronger replacements. A strong operation in Japan, for reasons of available technical and managerial experience already gained in Japan and in other Asian and global markets, has always been a reason to use Japan as a stepping stone to developing other nearby markets, or to manufacture in other Asian countries.

Japan may also end up pulling away from nuclear energy, the way Germany so declares. Prime Minister Abe's support of nuclear energy is not popular with many people. Former Prime Minister Koizumi has come to believe that nuclear energy is too unsafe and expensive because of the risks of accidents, and difficulty of storing nuclear waste. The Japanese politicians seem a bit fumbling, bumbling and uncharacteristically slow off the starting blocks in cleaning up and reconstructing the devastated areas up North. But policies and private industry here will move very quickly to improve the power grid, and develop renewable, natural clean energy. The skies over Tokyo and all of Japan will remain bright and blue. With adequate rainfall, fresh water, and topography well suited to build more dams if needed, prolonged drought and out of control flooding is less of a problem in Japan. Extreme weather is less likely, as Japan enjoys the moderating, and more temperate influence of its surrounding seas. The rather narrow width of the land mass limits more extreme continental-type climate within Japan. Japan will be even more ready for her earthquakes, and has been awakened by a tsunami of unimaginable height and force. Japan will not be caught this off guard again. Japan was always one of the safest countries for transport and industrial accidents. And perhaps Japan's biggest advantage will continue to be her hard working, stoic, wise, even-keeled people, not too susceptible to political or religious fervor or frenzy. There is a fortunate lack of religious and other tensions among themselves, while putting the outside world in a healthy perspective. From a foreigner's perspective, the island location, difficulty of assimilation by foreigners, but a foreigner's pride in finally assimilating, and pride in one's newly adopted country, will keep cultural, ethnic, man-made frictions and tragedy in comparative check.

The economy was already improving after the March 11 tragedy. METI data showed the industrial production index, rose in June 2011 by 3.9% to 92.7. During the March, April, and May 2011 quarter, the index had dropped 4.0% to 88.6, even though it had been gradually increasing since the abrupt March drop. METI expected the index to rise by 2.2% in July, and 2.0% in August 2011. Due to recovery in the supply chains since March 11th 2011, Japan's Finance Ministry upgraded its assessment of the state of the economy for the first time in four quarters.

The Chinese know that bases, armies and wars around the world won't be the key to their strength, nor to any country's economic strength, and soft power. But they want us to spend all our money on what they make. The Chinese may kill us with their thirst for the world's technology. They may kill us with their products, but not with their bombs. Japan also learned this after World War II, and will maintain a reasonable balance, realistically adapting to its adjusting position in the world. I think there is still much we can learn from Japan. Many Japanese do not like the more patriotic, somewhat jingoistic messages from Prime Minister Abe, along with his "state secrecy law". Hopefully there will be a roll back in this area. China and Japan should respond with carefully measured steps to each other over their island, fishing rights, sea shelf and other disputes. The consumption tax rise from 5 to 8% has not helped the economy. Many are relieved that the further increase to 10% has been postponed.

8i. Charity begins at home—using scarce money
wisely on ourselves

When World War II broke out, the USA had almost no standing army, and much of the navy was obliterated at Pearl Harbor. The USA had a big part in winning WWII because of our country's skilled workers, natural resources, manufacturing and industrial base, not its military strength. Hitler and Napoleon found that military power has its limitations. All conquests rapidly unravel. Russia's war in Afghanistan contributed to breaking up the Soviet Union. The USA's wars in Iraq and Afghanistan, and the drain of military spending and supporting troops around the world IS big government spending. It can't be helping the USA's government debt/default situation or the USA credit rating. Vietnam War spending largely stopped the USA break-neck-speed space program, increased the debt, and limited infrastructure investment and more worthy programs to spend that money on. At this late date, we have been told it would take years for the USA to be able to again land a man on the moon. What's that?! The Chinese will beat the USA there?

What happened? More recent military spending by the USA has been a trade off for decaying road, bridge, airport and other city and public service infrastructure across America. We seemed to even be risking debt default; the dollar is becoming just another currency, and it costs a small fortune to take our families abroad and stay even in a 4-star hotel. The US of A is looking a bit weak and silly to the world. From 2014 the US dollar has again strengthened. Such cyclical movements never seem to end.

Control over and ability to make key high-tech components, a manufacturing base and high-paying manufacturing jobs is the key to power. Japan was also at another juncture, with the high yen, and the shock to the supply chain from the March, 2011 earthquake/tsunami. There is still movement to get more manufacturing out of Japan, although there is some rethinking on that as the yen weakened in 2014. Let's think twice about the long-term economic interests of our countries, our citizens and our corporations. Pursuit by some corporations of misperceived short term profits is often the flawed long term corporate strategy. In other countries too there are risks of natural and man-made tragedies, and other social and political risks. Inflation and cheaper foreign wages often rapidly rise. Efficient manufacturing operations in Japan, the USA, and Europe ARE economically viable and are needed.

After 9/11/2001 World Trade Center plane attack, when I visited the States, I was surprised to see a flag hanging from most people's houses. If the Japanese did that, it would be a little scary even to the Japanese! That red circle on white still ushers up special images. We were told the USA has a jobless recovery. "Where are the jobs?!" We are told US corporations are sitting on more cash than ever, but they are reluctant to spend it. I hope we can see more concern for our own nations, our own countrymen — patriotism if you will — on the part of US, European and corporations in other developed economies, such that they build factories in their own countries as well, providing employment, and higher paying manufacturing jobs for their own people. A stable and large middle class is always the key to any country's economic, political, social stability, and public safety within that nation. I don't think rich US or other citizens around the world want to have to build walls around them for protection against poor people and crime.

I don't think the more fortunate people want to lose their freedom of movement and community. This gap between rich and poor can be seen in some countries all over the world, but let's have as little of this as possible.

Yes. The yen got strong, but then it got weaker again in 2014. Considering it had been 360 yen to the dollar for decades, and was at that level when I first came to Japan as a student in 1970, the yen has trended up, but it has always been cyclical. It will strengthen and weaken again. Please. No knee-jerk short-term reaction from Japanese companies to rush abroad with their manufacturing jobs. I can't hold a candle to Donald Trump, but as he has expressed, US, Japanese, and European etc. investment and technology has greatly advanced China at an unprecedented and amazing pace. China has been the main foreign country shouldering US debt. Wages have been skyrocketing in China. Most of the struggles for the 20 to 50% annual wage increases, most of the bitter, and sometimes rather violent long strikes in mainland China were directed against the foreign capital invested factories and operations, rather than the indigenous Chinese firms. We don't need to have any enemies. We just need to be a lot smarter about what are the keys to our long-term national and global interests.

8j. For those who value true safety, and freedom of movement and lifestyle over a spoonful of radiation that was soon under control

Yes. With the high yen, and the somewhat warped impression that Japan is an expensive country, initial market entry and investment into Japan seems costly. But as soon as you make money, a lot of profit in your own currency gets sent back home. Whenever the yen rises, a lot of Japan-based, foreign expat CEOs in Japan look like they walk on water. There are so many more dollars or euros to send home. Not a bad step for a Japan *gaijin* expat's next corporate promotion. Now the yen has weakened somewhat, making entry into this market look cheaper. It has also improved profits of big exporters, but increased costs of imported materials, and been tough on some medium and smaller firms. If you keep your manufacturing in the US of A, or in a country like Japan, your technology, patents, brands, and intellectual property remain your own. As for the radiation in Japan, a lot of us got stronger. A healthy glow made bedside night lights unnecessary. A further saving on electricity bills… Seriously, the radiation levels we got in Tokyo were not harmful. Think one extra chest x-ray a year—maybe two? I will opt for that rather than having to worry about locking our office and residential doors during the day. I know there are other cities almost as safe as Tokyo and other Japanese cities, but few people will walk anywhere they want, any place they want to go, anytime night or day, with a wallet full of cash, and not have to worry about how or when they come home at night or in the morning. In other cities as well, the chances of getting physically harmed or killed, a man-made disaster, may not be great. But often to avoid that and make sure we stay safe, most people live with a very different lifestyle than you can live here in Tokyo, and other Japanese cities.

And as for natural disasters, not just extreme weather, but also the tectonic plates are moving so much, even tsunamis can happen anywhere there are unprotected harbors, and a city's shoreline is close to the open sea (unlike Tokyo). On this score, Kobe and Osaka in Japan get some protection from the open sea, but not nearly as much as the narrow gateway to Tokyo Harbor between Miura Peninsula and Chiba Peninsula.

In all but 15 USA states there have been multiple earthquakes of over 5 magnitudes. Europe is not free of this: the Iceland volcano, all too often in Italy, and in May 2011, there was the most deadly earthquake in Spain since 1884. Tokyo and Japan have hopefully had their share. A friend from the Indian Embassy who arrived in Japan recently did not blink, flinch or cower. He told us, "Even in times of such disasters, Tokyo is the best place in the world to be. It is a great place to visit, get to know, live and do business. We arrived just before the March tragedy, but we love it."

8k. Nadeshiko Japan—Ladies Soccer rivals but the best of friends

Yes. Let's take better care of the two countries I know and love—America*, no, the United States of America and Japan. (*A Brazilian friend and many South Americans get pretty upset, as, "We are also Americans!") Maybe Japan really did not deserve to win the FIFA Ladies World Cup in July, 2011. The USA women had many more shots on goal. It was very heartwarming for all of us in Japan to see, that the USA did not seem to very much mind losing to the little-on-average-5' 4" Japanese ladies. The word we get is that of all countries the USA women could lose to, it was easiest, maybe even kind of okay, to lose to Japan—especially in 2011—the year of the big 'quake, the year of the big tsunami—the year over 25,000 lives up in northeast Japan were snuffed out within an hour.

I think the more we look at some of the other countries around us, the more the USA and Japan realize that like with the British, there really is a "special relationship". Even though we are perfectly clueless — in terms of language and culture. That makes it even more special!

The Japanese Self Defense Force (Japan's military), basically threw up their hands thinking that it would take weeks, if not be impossible, to clear all the broken planes, cars, trucks, cargo containers, huge ships and building chunks off the Sendai airport runways (the main city up north where the tsunami hit.) Then the United States Marines and military immediately launched Project *Tomodachi* ("friend" in Japanese). I think it was a US sergeant or max a lieutenant who took charge and had the airport functioning in about a day. The USA military personnel also fixed up and ran the Airport Traffic Control Tower in Sendai at least for quite a few days, because so much of the relief and aid traffic was US-piloted aircraft, and the soldiers have been studying their Japanese. And many Japanese pilots have pretty good English. When we talked about this, I never saw so many tears in the eyes of so many Japanese friends.

The United States and Japan should take even better care of each other. We should take better care of our people. Keeping as much manufacturing, investment, and industry in each other's countries are a good start.

The Japanese people, and all of us living in Japan, welcome all of you to visit. You are needed more than ever. As former longest serving Senate Majority Leader, and Ambassador to Japan, Mr. Mike Mansfield used to say, pointing his index finger toward heaven, "The United States and Japan's bilateral relationship is the most important one in the world—bar none." Let's take even better care of our own citizens and each other.

CHAPTER 9

Some Keys to Better Communications, Smoother Human Relations, Better Team Work and Results

1. Value each other, show respect for each other, and carefully choose your words.

2. Treat and speak to others as you would want to be treated and spoken to.

3. Before you blame or criticize others look inside and see what's wrong with yourself.

4. Don't expect others to change toward you, unless you change toward them.

5. If you want someone to like you, first show that you like them. If you want to influence someone, make sure that person thinks you like that person.

6. Try and understand other people's thinking and position, rather than try and make people understand your position and thinking.

7. Remember that we don't see the world as it is. We see it as we are. Everybody sees it or issues differently. Usually nobody is right, no one is wrong. The trouble with having to be right is we make someone wrong. Change your approach instead.

8. Don't speak at people, speak with people.

9. We have two ears and one mouth because we are supposed to listen at least twice as much as we talk. To us the best conversationalist is the one who lets us do the talking.

10. Our assumptions or preconceived notions are the root cause of most misunderstandings and mistakes. Discover and ask the questions—the questions you never see, and the ones you believe don't need to be asked, are often the most important questions.

11. Anything we say, we already know, so there is little growth or advantage in saying it. If you want to learn and grow, ask questions and listen.

12. When trying to understand someone, repeat back what you think the person said, until the person agrees that is what he or she meant to say.

13. Don't interrupt people. Wait until they are finished.

14. Say about half as much as you want to, and keep in mind that most listeners don't want to, and can't maintain their attention if the speaker talks for more than 30 to 60 seconds.

15. This means when you are speaking, pause every 30 to 60 seconds, to allow the listener to confirm, respond, question or disagree. Or ask the person to rephrase your meaning as in number 12 above.

16. Watch out for your body language and facial expressions especially when listening. Try and maintain an interested, neutral expression, or fall on the side of smiling with your eyes, encouraging the person to continue.

17. If you don't understand ask, "How do you mean?" "Tell me more". "Then what happened?" Ask if you can confirm what has been said.

18. Be sure to give and return cheerful greetings, especially in the morning.

19. When your eyes meet with another staff member, smile with not only your mouth but also your eyes.

20. Smile when you are speaking on the phone. The other party can tell. If you treat your customers better, they will treat you better. Selling is not 'tell and sell' or 'spray and pray'. It is asking questions, understanding the customer's thinking and needs. It is building trust, being liked by the customer, and genuinely caring for the customer's welfare.

21. Remember that your boss is also an important customer. Do immediately and cheerfully anything your boss, or a colleague, or a subordinate ask you to do. Acknowledge their request clearly and cheerfully.

22. Earn a reputation as a person who immediately gets the job done.

23. Pledge to yourself that you will try to never make the same mistake twice.

24. Remember that vacation is only meaningful and fun because we have our jobs. The key to happiness is having something to do. When we have nothing to do, and we don't have to struggle, we turn to depression, alcohol and other strange behaviors (Elvis Presley, Michael Jackson, Obara Joji).

25. Ask your boss, colleague, or subordinate how you are doing, and what they like about what you're doing, and what they don't like about what you're doing.

26. Ask colleagues if there is anyway you could better serve them, or help them succeed.

27. Try and match and mirror the speaking style of the person you are dealing with. If they speak slowly and quietly, you will get along better and they will have less resistance to you if you go slower and softer. Likewise if someone is loud and fast, they will feel resistance to you if you are too slow and soft. Remember that people who are like each other, tend to like each other.

28. If you're a disorganized person with poor memory (sometimes/selectively), develop filing, and other systematic mechanisms to compensate for your weakness.

29. Learn how to prioritize. Do first things first. Work on the important things that are not always the most urgent things. But do the necessary urgent things immediately. Prioritize into A, B, C categories. A–1 activities are the most urgent and important things. Gain a reputation as the person who responds immediately.

30. Although it isn't easy, try and keep in mind that we become what we think about. We can work toward controlling our moods and physical and mental well–being with our thoughts. Happy people see happy pictures. Gloomy people see sad, gloomy pictures. We will be as happy as we make up our mind to be.

31. As long as we have to go to work with our colleagues why not enjoy our jobs and them as much as possible. Be cheerful and upbeat. Upbeat people are fun to be around. They are the ones who get better pay. There is no perfect job or colleague out there for us. When we don't understand this, and we don't change ourselves and the way we think, we probably just pack up all our defects, grumblings, blaming, and dissatisfactions into our old baggage, and bring it to the next company.

32. We need to keep studying, learning, and growing from books, seminars and the people we encounter in our lives. Specific tools and knowledge can help. Become the person who has the helpful answer. When getting things done through others tell colleagues not just what to do, but why it needs to be done. Or when delegating work, find out in what area a subordinate is confident and wants to be left alone, and what areas a subordinate

wants and needs coaching, guidance, or even specific instructions.

The above list will only be helpful if it is reviewed and reflected on once a week for the next two or three years. After that, maybe once a month will do.

CHAPTER 10

A Few Words about Having Fun and Fitting into any
Foreign Country You may be Sent to, or Decide Yourself to
Go and Live—Mostly for You Less Traveled Guys

If you use the above common sense guideline list and
reminders you can be happy and succeed anywhere and with
anyone. When I wrote the preceding chapter's list in 2001 to
give out at my personal growth and development seminars,
I certainly did not have "Japanese people" or fellow "USA-
ers★" in mind. At that point, I had lived in Japan 29 years.
Fundamentally, I knew that in matters that counted in human
relations, communications, and work activity, there was really
no difference between Japanese people and other people
around the world.

Yes, the Japanese may not sell themselves too aggressively. But
really, I don't think any of us in any countries greatly like and
respect people who brag, are self-centered, too loud, or sell
themselves, or their products too directly or aggressively.
Whether you are selling your idea, your product, or yourself,
a consultative approach where you ask questions, and learn of
other people's position, thinking, and needs, will always get
you the furthest.

10a. Among "Americans" and fellow native speakers of
English, there are things even we should watch out for

Japanese are a bit unique in some ways. Maybe you are not
as open, and do not fully express ideas as completely as some

Westerners, other Asians, or South Americans. This may be particularly true of the men. By the way, the reason I called myself a "USA-er" above in this chapter, is that Brazilians, Argentineans and most people from Central and South America, also naturally consider themselves Americans. Some of them have told me that they don't like the USA folks who have seized the name "American". Just as the USA basically seized the Southwest, Texas and California from Mexico/Spanish influences only about 160 years ago! Interesting—I never heard a Canadian make this complaint. I suppose it is mostly because, for many years now, we are more used to meeting each other, and they are probably very proud of Canada. For years we had and still have a lot of migration between our countries.

These days if I meet someone who sounds like he is from the USA, I often first ask if the person is from Canada, or the States just in case the person is from Canada. It seems like the wise thing to do. If I meet a British/UK/Australian/New Zealand-sounding person, I have learned to ask them if they are from the UK, even if there accent is far off from traditional upper-class Queen's English. I think even USA-ers, let alone Australians and New Zealanders have a bit of a "mother country" complex. I know many British-born USA-ers who have lived in the States for 10s of years, say they deliberately keep their British accent, because they feel USA people like the sound of it. They say they can get further and have certain advantages with their British accent. Probably Australians do not mind if they are mistaken for someone from the UK/Britain. However, a British person not speaking the Queen's English might not want to be mistaken for an Australian. These are subtle areas, and you need not worry too much about it. There must be similar things going on between regions and dialects of many big countries such as China, India, Russia, and Indonesia.

10b. *From noodle slurping to handshakes*

One thing that is less subtle, and Japanese people need to watch out for is slurping up your ramen or soba, or other soup like dishes. I can tell you that most foreign people around the world would be surprised at a loud noodle-sucking sound. Japanese women tend not to slurp and suck. But the Japanese guys out there reading this should be careful about this one. It is probably about as shocking as some Chinese people throwing those bones and such out on the tablecloth. And then there are the Spanish/ Portuguese at tapas bars, where it is okay to throw things such as shrimp skins down on the bar floor. Probably it is best to avoid all such unique or extreme behaviors even if you are in that country. Maybe it is unnatural and not becoming to assimilate that much? Maybe it would be a bit like me doing a repeated 90-degree or even 70-degree bow when in Japan and when speaking Japanese.

Handshakes vary with country and cultures. It is typically said that a man does not begin a handshake with a woman in the USA, Europe, and probably most other regions. If the woman extends her had, the light grasp that she gets must be very different than the handshake you offer or engage in with a man. When shaking a man's hand, make sure your index finger and thumb are wide open so you can lock in deep, otherwise you can get your fingers a bit crushed. Also be ready to apply quite a bit of power, if you are getting a power handshake. A weak handshake among guys gives a bad impression.

You need to keep your hands washed pretty often so they are not clammy and sticky. At the ever-present cocktail parties, and mixers, you should keep your cold drink in your left hand. This way you won't have a cold, wet hand when that handshake comes at you. Have plenty of *meishi*/business cards. Don't expect to automatically get one back. It is okay to ask if the person has a *meishi*. They very likely may not, but why not give out yours anyway. That is as Japanese as taking pictures — or as, American as apple pie. (Now we have learned that some South Americans don't like that USA use of 'American'. But on CNN, BBC etc. that is still the word used referring to 'USA-ers'.)

10c. Convenience store training manuals can affect cultural habits—at least until the manual gets changed

If anything, in Japan, especially after the SARS, and Bird Flu-type scares, I have fallen on the side of not shaking hands as much with Japanese people. I don't know if that increases our chances of staying healthy, but I guess all of us think about it. The last few years in Japan, from about 2004, I noticed that a part of some convenience store training apparently was to lightly touch the customers hand when you give him/her? the change and the receipt. In my case, I rather liked it if it was an attractive lady. I didn't get too excited when it was a guy. Excited? More like '*muka, muka*'/'nauseating' feeling! There was probably also less touching between a male sales clerk and a male customer. Was that also in the training manual? I've noticed that since around 2010 there is less of this touching. Maybe training manuals changed, with concern about spreading the flu and other viruses? Things like this are small things, but are surprising things you will discover in your new country. Some things you notice may be very recent customs that will soon die out.

10d. Two very different uses for handkerchiefs—more on customs you don't need to copy

One thing that I am really ashamed of and is part of some cultures in the USA and Europe, and probably many other cultures, is one disgusting habit of men, even very educated and wealthy men. They often carry a handkerchief, which they blow their nose into. And then they put that handkerchief back into their pocket, and shake your hand before you can run out of the room. It is gross and I am sure a real shocker to Japanese, or other people that don't have this custom. Just be ready for it, and try not to eat your *ningyoyaki* (fish-shaped crepe filled with sweet bean paste) just after that! I feel sorry for these guys' suit/pants pockets, and for all of us not use to this. I think most of us in Japan have a handkerchief or two to dry our hands. We also have a little packet of Kleenex tissues just in case we have to blow our nose. This is probably true of guys as well as the ladies.

In Europe, with the lady executives or wives of my friends and business contacts, I finally got a little more used to the European double-sided kiss/cheek to cheek thing that men and women do. They do this even if they hardly know each other! But, if the European, South American-type woman does not start that for a Japanese person or someone else from a different culture, it is nothing personal. She may really like you, but as with me, especially at the first few meetings, she knows that it will freak you out. I think they can feel us cringing and wishing we were back in Tokyo. Also make sure you don't get excited and plant a kiss smack dead center on their lips! Even if the lady wishes you would.

10e. Cultural reactions and treatment between men and women will naturally vary

Japanese guys in foreign countries might feel they have a disadvantage over Japanese women in meeting and getting close to foreign guys. Sorry. But I guess that would be the case. That is the way nature made about 90% or more of us. Japanese ladies can help us *gaijin* guys a lot more, in so many ways—reading and paying bills, handling paper work, getting things done in general etc. There are many foreign women wanting to get really close to Japanese guys in Japan, and all over the world. Probably "Cool Japan", and more and more Asian models, and movie stars are helping pick up any gap there was. There are baseball stars like Ichiro Suzuki, Big Matsui, Little Matsui, Daisuke Matsuzaka, golf greats like Ryo Ishikawa, a tennis star like Kei Nishikori. There are Nadeshiko Japan, and the incredible gymnasts. Hiroyuki Sanada from *The Last Samurai* is a lot cooler than Tom Cruise.

Japanese guys can have a tremendous advantage over other foreigners when they are in some foreign countries. I remember an experience when I visited the Philippines in maybe 1979 and met President Marcos along with a delegation of fellow USA types from the American Chamber of Commerce in Japan. That meant nothing to the Philippine ladies who were working at a Makati, Manila department store I visited. But as soon as I switched from speaking English to speaking Japanese, everything changed. All of a sudden a few of them all wanted to be my friend. I was a rock star. They would have followed me everywhere and anywhere. You Japanese guys were/are lucky!

10f. There are different advantages, but good possibilities in just about any country you go to live

So this does bring up the topic of which countries you really want to work in and why. Yes. If you are a single Asian guy, I suppose you could have a lot more Asian ladies following you if you were working in the Asian region. I suppose another reason is Japan is closer, and it is seen as a good and easier place to live for many of these ladies. It would not matter much which other Asian country, just a matter of degree. Nowadays they say Chinese girls want to marry a Chinese guy, or be our buddies only if we have a nice house etc. But if your company is sending you abroad, you will probably have pretty nice living quarters! If you are going abroad on your own, you can probably more easily get a good job in a foreign country than you can in Japan! This is especially true if you traveled off, or fell off the traditional "elite" course or ladder that we have in Japan. In other countries they don't know or care as much about what that course or ladder is. Often the most successful people in the world are those who built their own ladder.

Europe, and surprisingly old South American, Europeanized cites such as Buenos Aires, and Lima are great if you like old buildings and culture. No thanks, I'll take the ladies, you say? It is probably more important to speak the local language well, or at least English well in Europe, and the West. This might be less important if you were living and trying to have fun in southeast Asia, where more local people probably know Japanese. There are also chances that you will find people even in Europe, South American and other places studying and speaking Japanese. Although nowadays more people around the world may be studying Chinese. It really is amazing how quickly things change, isn't it?

10g. 'Ladies first' is still there, but is getting more complex

I remember many years ago when I visited Hawaii, there were some typical USA ladies waiting with me for quite a while in front of the hotel elevator. A tour group of Japanese came through the lobby door. They were mostly men. They followed the tour leader flag rushing right into the elevator, basically pushing aside the three USA ladies. The USA ladies were pretty surprised and upset. If looks could kill, at least several of those Japanese tour members would have been buried in Hawaii, never making it back to Japan.

So you Japanese guys should be sure and do the ladies first thing. I suppose even if you are in a Muslim country or Africa it is probably the safest way to go… at least until you learn otherwise. Holding the door for a lady and letting her go in first is a good idea. Also standing up when a woman comes to, or leaves the dining table, whether at a restaurant or at someone's home will win you some points. The exception to this would be if the woman is more senior than you at your company, or perhaps if it is in a work setting. Watch the cues from the local men around you. Also look at the ladies body language and response when you do these things for the ladies. With women's lib and equality between the sexes there is a movement in the direction of moving away from these niceties that I grew up with. My mother and father made me do these things.

10h. Is giving everyone's age in brackets on Japanese television unique to Japan?

Asking age, especially women's age, is, of course, taboo. Japan has an amazing custom, which I suppose is unique to Japan. But if you find this in other countries please drop me an email. As a Japanese you may not even notice how strange non-Japanese think it is that on all kinds of news, wide-shows, and some variety entertainment shows, a man and woman's age routinely appears in brackets after their name. This is whenever someone's name appears on the screen, as the one making the comment, being interviewed, or reported on etc. To us it seems like a lot of work, and there is this necessity to research the people's ages. The closest thing I have seen to this is that on Wikipedia, birthdays and ages of people around the world are routinely given. But I think some people ask to have it deleted, and anyway have it deleted on Wikipedia.

It is pretty easy for Japanese girls to make friends with guys just about anywhere on this planet we call our earth. For Japanese guys to make friends with guys I have just a few tips. Actually, for guys to make and keep friends with guys, is a very different skill set, and is not always so easy. I can't write too much here because I want you to be able to read this book on a train or in the *furo*/bathtub, without hurting another passenger, or without the book dropping and getting wet. Knowing something about sports can help—playing it, having played it, or following it on the internet or TV. Other ice breakers could be talking about movies like *Black Rain*, or the *The Last Samurai*. Guys don't remember Sayuri/Memoirs of a Geisha. But you can ask guys you get to know how long it took them to fall asleep when they saw that Memoirs 'chick flick'. Maybe burn and give some guys a CD, DVD, or YouTube reference to Morning Musume, AKB48, Speed, Perfume, or some other Japanese female pop groups. It should be good fun. You could compare J-pop with K-pop girl groups such as Girls Generation, Kara, Wonder Girls, or 2NE1. Remember, in general, Japanese guys may like younger women more than a lot of guys in foreign countries. But I'm not so sure about this…

10i. Other ways for you to make friends when living abroad—guys with guys is especially difficult

Introducing some websites with info about Japan, manga, and other aspects of Cool Japan could be interesting. How about giving friends a copy of this book?! It will start to give you things to talk about. Knowing about and following some local TV dramas, and going to, and knowing about popular local movies can also help. And then there are things that my old JETRO friend, Shinsaku Sogo did. When he was in New York, and other cities, he joined and became active in local clubs like the Chamber of Commerce, and Rotary Club. I know more about the USA, but I think many such social clubs have international memberships. Maybe even clubs like the Lions, Elk, Moose, Kiwanis, 4H, and other such clubs? Yes. Why not become the only Japanese Free Mason in your town or village?

Probably the most important thing is being cheerful, and walking around with a smile. Maybe not so much with your mouth, as you may look a little crazy—just as you would in Japan. Instead a twinkle in the eye will do. A willingness and readiness to laugh always helps—even if you are clueless. If everyone else is laughing, it must be funny. If they ask you if you got it, and understood it, just answer quickly, "No. Of course not!" I guarantee another laugh from all. I would not recommend telling jokes, but saying stupid things, and giving wacko/*kankei nai* answers can be very funny. It does not really matter if people are laughing with you, or at you. Either way, you become a guy who is fun to be with. You will get included in stuff.

10j. Being a little foolish, and fun to be with helps

One thing that I have been doing with my bilingual Japanese wife, whatever language we are speaking (and there are only two possibilities!), is to repeat back the way we heard it, even though we know it makes no sense. Try it. You will like it. Don't clear your throat, seriously admitting that you did not catch what someone said. Don't bother to ask them to repeat it. Instead, just immediately repeat what you heard. It will be gibberish nonsense, but it will also make people laugh. In a funny way it will sound similar, but will make no sense. Once you learn how to make people laugh, you will want to bestow this gift more and more. But like everything else in life, don't overdue that either. You don't want to become the "too much" over-dominating Japanese guy, either.

10k. Insight from a reunion meeting with Professor Haruo Shimada

I mentioned earlier in the book that I first met Professor Shimada when he was studying at the School of Industrial and Labor Relations at Cornell University in Ithaca, New York. Since then Shimada Sensei has gone on and become a famous professor at Keio University, written tens of books, advised, taught and done research throughout the world, is currently president of Chiba University of Commerce, and has been a special advisor for Economic and Fiscal Policy to the Cabinet Office and Prime Minister—one of the main "Koizumi Brains". When my staff wanted us/TMT to visit the section in charge of bringing international and other business and investment into Tokyo, the Tokyo Metropolitan officials we met told us that Shimada, Haruo Sensei was their top advisor in charge of that effort.

After Golden Week, 2012, I went to see Professor Shimada at his office near Keio University. As expected he had back-to-back meetings that day. I was able to briefly join in a meeting with several officials from Kawasaki City who are in charge of international and other business development and investment for the city of Kawasaki.

In just a few minutes I got a few, "ah hahs!" or insights from Shimada-Sensei, which I thought I should add to this book. Shimada-Sensei pointed out that more so than in the time of Japan's rapid economic growth, when Japan's technology and ability to manufacturer was singularly strong, there is more competition now from places like Korea, Taiwan, India, Singapore and of course mainland China. Many things have changed. For example, fifteen years ago the English level of Korean businessmen was not high. But their level of English has greatly improved, while the Japanese seem to have even less interest in learning English or living abroad.

During these 15 years and from before that, many foreigners have gotten better at the Japanese language. I learned another interesting point from Shimada-Sensei. He pointed out that the Japanese have to improve their communications, image and build better relationships with foreigners and the outside world by having much stronger ties to foreigners, even if this means speaking Japanese with the foreigners. Shimada-Sensei said, "We have to learn more about their hearts and minds, and the way they tick. This can be done in the Japanese language if necessary." So maybe the ideal thing is to alternate and 'double communicate'. It is best if a Japanese person first tries to say something in English or in the foreign language. And then better explains it and repeats it in Japanese for the foreigner who is struggling to learn Japanese. This will also make the struggling non-Japanese foreigner feel good, because the Japanese person was humble enough to offer the explanation in Japanese, after the Japanese speaker tried to make his point/ communicate in English.

Likewise the non-Japanese speaker could first try and use his/ her Japanese. Then after that, immediately repeat it in English or the foreign language the Japanese person is struggling to learn. This would make the Japanese participant feel good, as it is a way for the non-Japanese person to pay respect to the ability of the Japanese person to speak and understand the foreign language. This would build better bonds and better communications. It would also lead to the bonds of helping each other learn each other's language.

This method might avoid a lot of misunderstandings, save a lot of communications, get better, faster results, and maybe even save lives in emergency situations. CPR (Cardio-Pulmonary Resuscitation) can prevent fatal heart attacks and save lives. Maybe we can call this technique of repeat communications in both languages, CPR—Communication Process Repeat!!

So in just a brief meeting, I learned many things from my Cornell University *senpai* (more senior or experienced person). Actually we ran our own meeting in a somewhat similar way. At first we spoke in Japanese even after the *Kawasaki* officials left us. Then I switched to English, which is after all easier! Shimada-Sensei always has another new book in Japanese coming out. I will struggle to learn from them too!

If you come across strange things that are characteristic of Japan, and/or surprise you when you discover them in the countries you are living, drop me an email, okay? In Japanese is also okay. As much *kanji* as possible is easier for me to read. *Kana* is a nuisance. (Afraid of wasting time and my focus, I've been avoiding social networking sites. But we are pretty good at answering email—nevins@tmt-aba.com)

Have fun, work hard, stay physically fit and strong, and enjoy your life and the new world each day that surrounds you!

Footnotes

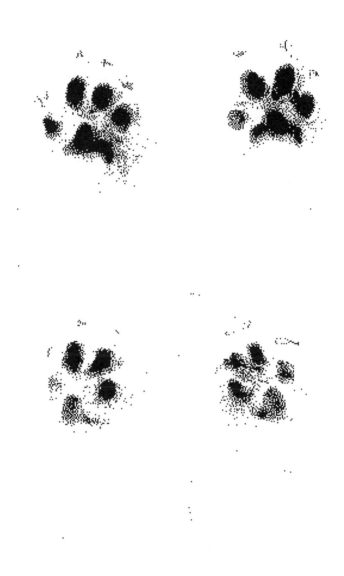

Conclusion

Staying Put or Moving Forward

Along with the main body of the book, I've including an introduction and insight into the potential of my own original secrets to more effectively managing restructuring, and improving individual and company performance problems. This results in building stronger companies, better use of our own individual talents, greater flexibility in the labor market, and more effective utilization of man and womanpower. Governments are proving they can't do this for us. Each of us has to do it, along with a new synergistic coalition of leading global private sector firms involved in investing, M & A, outplacement, recruiting, training, and providing corporate in-house child care/day care facilities. This will bring more parents into the aging and shrinking working populations of so many countries much sooner. The fast and surprisingly simple ABCD method invented and developed by me, hand in hand with my clients, works in Japan, and will work in any country. ★The masterless ronin Samurai is finally joining up with a much more powerful clan.

If you are approached by a party, or see an advertisement claiming to be a TMT-trained and authorized party, before entering into a consulting or business relationship, please confirm that they are officially authorized representatives of our group. Please drop me an email at nevins@tmt-aba.com.

There are 87 testimonial and case study letters appearing on the traditional TMT Inc. website at www.tmt-aba.com These tend to be more detailed in the more recent *Japan True or False* publication. These letters from our clients appear with the client's full name and signature in those various hard copy books and publications.

Before you get started on this book, please be sure and read the 'Dedication and Acknowledgements: *Lucky Settings, Unlucky Settings: People, Places, and Events that are the Atoms of Our Lives and Our World*', 'Introduction to the Unholy Bible and its Unusual Format', and 'Who Will Find Something of Interest in this Unholy Bible?' entries at the beginning of this book.

Other Books by the Author

Tom is author of *The Complete Handbook of U.S. Personnel,* and *Labor Relations Practices for Japanese Corporations*, 1980 JETRO (former MITI-Japanese government), two books published by the *Japan Times* – Japan's leading English daily—*Labor Pains and the Gaijin Boss* (1984) and *Taking Charge in Japan* (1990), *Japan True or False* (2004), *Know Your Own Bone* (2004), and *Gaijin Boss's Power Pill* (2011). Tom graduated from the Cornell University School of Industrial & Labor Relations (ILR, B.S. 1972).

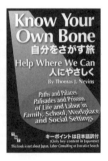